W9-AFQ-355

PRAISE FOR *HOW THE NATIONS RAGE*

"This is a book worth reading. Leeman is clearheaded, tenderhearted, and extremely thoughtful about an enormously critical topic. While I may not agree with every jot and tittle of Leeman's analysis, I was helped, stirred, and provoked by what I read. We need more books like this."

—KEVIN DEYOUNG, SENIOR PASTOR, CHRIST COVENANT
CHURCH, MATTHEWS, NORTH CAROLINA; ASSISTANT
PROFESSOR OF SYSTEMATIC THEOLOGY, RTS CHARLOTTE

"Jonathan Leeman's *How the Nations Rage* contains truths that will make any Christian—Republican, Democrat, Independent, or otherwise—squirm, and that's what makes it worthwhile. In this time of political polarization, Leeman offers an opportunity for people to step back from the headlines and the harangues to reevaluate what it means to represent Christ in the public square and one's local community. If read carefully, *How the Nations Rage* can smooth some of the sharp edges of our current political discourse and move people of faith toward being truth tellers and peacemakers instead of mere partisans."

—JEMAR TISBY, PRESIDENT, THE WITNESS, A BLACK CHRISTIAN
COLLECTIVE; COHOST, *PASS THE MIC* PODCAST

"Few waters are more difficult for Christians to navigate than political ones. This book helpfully steers us between the opposite errors of worrying too much about politics or investing too much hope in them. One of my biggest challenges as a pastor has been how to shepherd my people on this issue, and Jonathan has given us an invaluable resource to that end—whatever political persuasion they bring to the discussion. In his characteristically amenable but candid manner, he opens the Bible and shows us the way forward."

—J. D. GREEAR, PH.D., PASTOR, THE SUMMIT CHURCH,
RALEIGH-DURHAM, NORTH CAROLINA

"These are fraught political times, both inside and outside the church. The 'culture wars' model of the previous century has proven inadequate in addressing the polarization of our current social climate. *How the Nations Rage* provides a more mature, deeply biblical, and much needed pastoral understanding of the relationship between the church and the public square. In these pages, Leeman balances correction and encouragement, as well as principle and wisdom."

—KAREN SWALLOW PRIOR, AUTHOR OF *BOOKED: LITERATURE IN THE SOUL OF ME* AND *FIERCE CONVICTIONS: THE EXTRAORDINARY LIFE OF HANNAH MORE*

"Most thoughtful Christians know in their hearts that while government is necessary, the solution for the difficulties of life and the social order will never arise in the nation's capital. Jonathan Leeman has written *How the Nations Rage* in part to show the futility of the political solution. His determination is not to have Christians avoid political agendas but rather to face honestly the insufferable difficulties in the machinations of men regarding political order. Eventually, Leeman recognizes the the church is subject to being pummeled by just about everybody in the political order, and yet, the church and its message of love in a hate-filled world is the only thing that offers any real solution. Any Christian concerned with political affairs should read this book."

—PAIGE PATTERSON, PRESIDENT OF THE SOUTWESTERN BAPTIST THEOLOGICAL SEMINARY

"Do our political convictions flow from Scripture or from American traditionalism? Do our political hopes find their roots in earthly governments or the heavenly government to which we have been called? Leeman calls Christians to reevaluate and 'rethink faith and politics from a biblical perspective,' reminding us that we are to represent King Jesus as faithful ambassadors working out of the heavenly embassies that local churches are meant to be. So, whether you're on the Evangelical Left or Right, in the majority or minority culture, or from the Greatest Generation or Generation X, Y, or Z, pick up this book and start anew, making certain that our politics flows from Scripture so that we may faithfully represent our heavenly government well, as we sojourn on this earth."

—JUAN R. SÁNCHEZ, SENIOR PASTOR, HIGH POINTE BAPTIST CHURCH

"To what extent should Christians be involved in the political process? In *How the Nations Rage*, Jonathan Leeman provides a careful and theologically compelling treatment of the relationship between faith and politics. This book is an urgently needed resource for Christians seeking to faithfully integrate their Christian commitments with their political engagement. Leeman is careful, cogent, and unflinchingly biblical in his presentation. This book deserves careful consideration by any Christian who seeks to walk faithfully in the public square."

—R. ALBERT MOHLER JR., PRESIDENT, SOUTHERN
BAPTIST THEOLOGICAL SEMINARY

"Jonathan Leeman has written not simply a good book, but an important book. Using the ever-deepening political divide in the United States as a starting point, *How the Nations Rage* exhorts Christians not to allow politics to rule our lives, but to allow God to do so. Leeman challenges readers to jettison the petty gods we often serve, and, rather, choose submission to Christ in all corners of the public square. This volume challenges our presuppositions about earthly power, informs our hopes for the heavenly kingdom, and repositions the center of our political lives inside the church of Jesus Christ."

—THOM S. RAINER, PRESIDENT AND CEO, LIFEWAY CHRISTIAN RESOURCES

"What has the church to do with politics? Is there a proper, biblically informed relationship between church and state? In *How the Nations Rage*, Leeman exhorts the church neither to withdraw from nor to dominate the political sphere, but to represent heaven to a world in turmoil. What timely counsel, especially to the American church! This work is highly accessible and deserving of praise."

—JOHN MACARTHUR, PASTOR, GRACE COMMUNITY CHURCH,
SUN VALLEY, CALIFORNIA

"As the son of Korean immigrants, I grew up wishing I was an Irish American Catholic, like all my friends at St. Mary's grammar school. Identity inspired a good amount of confusion and angst in my life. Even earlier in life, as a five-year-old in the year of our nation's bicentennial, I distinctly recall my father insisting to my mother and all his friends in the immigrant Korean church we were part of, that Christians had an obligation to vote for a faithful, Southern Baptist peanut farmer from Georgia named Jimmy Carter—my first run-in with identity politics. Thank you, Dr. Leeman, for spurring me to deeper rethinking and reflection on the issues involved through this title. When Christians overcomplicate their identity in Christ (we are simply ambassadors of his kingdom rule and reign), we tend to settle on oversimplifying our politics to partisan and identity. This must change."

—WON KWAK, LEAD PASTOR OF MARANATHA GRACE CHURCH IN
ENGLEWOOD CLIFFS, NEW JERSEY (WWW.MARANATHAGRACE.ORG)

"As a pastor on Capitol Hill, I'm often asked what book I would recommend on politics for the Christian. Jonathan Leeman has produced a new standard. Well illustrated and engaging, this carefully reasoned book should be read in our churches before we come to an election year contest again."

—MARK DEVER, PASTOR, THE CAPITOL HILL BAPTIST CHURCH,
WASHINGTON, DC; PRESIDENT, 9MARKS

HOW THE NATIONS
— RAGE —

JONATHAN LEEMAN

HOW THE NATIONS RAGE ——

Rethinking Faith and Politics in
A DIVIDED AGE

NELSON
BOOKS

An Imprint of Thomas Nelson

© 2018 Jonathan Leeman

All rights reserved. No portion of this book may be reproduced, stored in a retrieval system, or transmitted in any form or by any means—electronic, mechanical, photocopy, recording, scanning, or other—except for brief quotations in critical reviews or articles, without the prior written permission of the publisher.

Published in Nashville, Tennessee, by Nelson Books, an imprint of Thomas Nelson. Nelson Books and Thomas Nelson are registered trademarks of HarperCollins Christian Publishing, Inc.

Published in association with the literary agency of Wolgemuth & Associates, Inc.

Thomas Nelson titles may be purchased in bulk for educational, business, fund-raising, or sales promotional use. For information, please e-mail SpecialMarkets@ThomasNelson.com.

Unless otherwise noted, Scripture quotations are taken from the ESV® Bible (The Holy Bible, English Standard Version®). Copyright © 2001 by Crossway, a publishing ministry of Good News Publishers. Used by permission. All rights reserved.

Scripture quotations marked NIV are taken from the Holy Bible, New International Version®, NIV®. Copyright © 1973, 1978, 1984, 2011 by Biblica, Inc.® Used by permission of Zondervan. All rights reserved worldwide. www.zondervan.com. The "NIV" and "New International Version" are trademarks registered in the United States Patent and Trademark Office by Biblica, Inc.®

The stories in this book reflect the author's recollection of events. Some names, locations, and identifying characteristics have been changed to protect the privacy of those depicted.

Any Internet addresses, phone numbers, or company or product information printed in this book are offered as a resource and are not intended in any way to be or to imply an endorsement by Thomas Nelson, nor does Thomas Nelson vouch for the existence, content, or services of these sites, phone numbers, companies, or products beyond the life of this book.

ISBN 978–1–4002–0765–7 (e-book)
ISBN 978–1–4002–0767–1 (audio)
ISBN 978–0–1–4002–0764–0 (HC)

Library of Congress Control Number: 2017956957

Printed in the United States of America

18 19 20 21 22 LSC 10 9 8 7 6 5 4 3 2 1

To my daughters, Emma, Hannah, Madeline, and Sophie,
for the sake of the world you will inherit

CONTENTS

Contents

A NATION RAGING, A CHURCH UNCHANGING

I am writing this late in the evening on July 4. My daughters are in bed. The sizzle and crackle of fireworks are over. But the music from PBS's coverage of the concert outside the US Capitol building still rings in my ears. The show combined patriotic music, words from well-known American heroes, and photos of iconic American images—the Statue of Liberty, the Lincoln Monument, the Grand Canyon, the Golden Gate Bridge, and so on.

O beautiful for spacious skies, for amber waves of grain.

I feel a swell of emotion. Independence Day, for me, brings with it a sense of nostalgia, almost like a birthday does. A birthday evokes memories of childhood. July Fourth evokes memories of, well, how do you describe it? Memories of America? What it is, what it represents, what we want it to be.

I don't recall when I first became conscious of my affection for the United States. Maybe it was amid the glint of sparklers on the

Fourth of July as a child, or during an elementary school lesson on Abraham Lincoln, or into my third helping of sweet-potato casserole at Thanksgiving, or while watching a Cubs game at Wrigley Field in high school.

I do remember discovering Walt Whitman's poem "I Hear America Singing" in college and being enlivened by it.

> I hear America singing, the varied carols I hear . . .
> Each singing what belongs to him or her and to none else . . .
> Singing with open mouths their strong melodious songs.[1]

I also remember discovering the American composer Aaron Copland in college. His ballets and orchestral suites inspired thoughts of Appalachian songs, prairie nights, and Western hoedowns. To this day when I hear his music, I can feel a deep yearning for decades I've only read about and places I've only seen in black-and-white photographs—all deeply American.

These snapshots are some of the symbols of my own love of country. What has been difficult for me over the last decade or two, however, has been to watch a growing divide between America and my Christianity. I might even say the relationship is becoming downright contentious.

CONTENTION AND DIVISION

I was in Southeast Asia several weeks ago spending time with a friend, Michael. Michael is an American missionary, and his family has been absent from the United States for more than a decade. Over dinner one evening we strayed into politics.

"I keep up on the news," he said. "But what's it really like?"

Missionaries are kind of like cultural time capsules. They leave the homeland, and their sense of the homeland's trends and styles gets frozen in time. "Why are you wearing baggy pleated pants, brother? It's not the 1990s." Keeping up on the news, of course, doesn't give someone a *feel* for what it's like living in the States.

"Honestly, it's really intense," I said in answer to his question. "There's a lot of division and contention." I then spent several minutes trying to give Michael a feel for that division.

For instance, the political Left and Right used to talk and reason with each other. Now they just shout. When a liberal guest lecturer at the University of Notre Dame was asked if she could find common ground with conservatives on race and gender, she answered, "You cannot bring these two worlds together. You must be oppositional. You must fight. For me, it's a line in the sand."[2]

Then there was the man who spent $422 million bankrolling the campaign to make same-sex marriage legal in all fifty states. When asked about his plans, he replied, "We're going to punish the wicked."[3]

And there was the Harvard law professor who described his posture toward conservatives: "The culture wars are over; they lost, we won. . . . My own judgment is that taking a hard line ('You lost, live with it') is better than trying to accommodate the losers."[4]

"It's a nasty time. It's a nasty time,"[5] concluded the late Supreme Court Justice Antonin Scalia as he thought about the modern climate and recalled how Republican and Democrat powerbrokers fraternized and clinked glasses at Washington, DC, dinner parties in the 1970s and '80s. This "doesn't happen anymore." Scalia was elected to the Supreme Court in 1986 by the US Senate in a 98–0 vote. Today's Supreme Court nominee battles, however, are nearly straight party-line votes.

Scalia made these comments in 2013. Think of what's transpired since: the Supreme Court's legalization of same-sex marriage in the *Obergefell* case, the legal showdowns between LGBT rights and religious liberty, the explosion of police-brutality videos and the emergence of Black Lives Matter, the sudden prominence of the transgender movement, the rise of the alt-right, the growing divide between globalists and nationalists, and the still-bewildering 2016 elections.

Meanwhile, a conservative lobbying organization in Washington sent out a fundraising e-mail shortly after Donald Trump's election. With all caps and bold-faced warnings, it promised the "radical Left *won't accept*" the election's results but "*will subvert* the future." The Left has "already violently protested the election" with "money from Hollywood-Washington elitists." Everyone who loves "faith, family, and freedom" should therefore watch out for "the Left's massive attempt to DECEIVE, INTIMIDATE, AND SIDETRACK lawmakers." It would "try EVERY POLITICAL TRICK IN THE BOOK." But you can "fight back" and help win "the 2017 policy war." So "donate now."

Whether or not you agree with this release, consider its language: *radical, subvert, violently, deceive, intimidate, fight, war.* I asked a friend who works at a similar religious-right organization whether such strident language was typical.

"It's the standard vernacular," he said. "It's us versus them. Either we'll take our country back (for God) or they (the progressive liberals) will take over." He also explained, "By and large politics is no longer about people participating in a shared project of societal order. There is very little desire to actually persuade. The strategy nowadays is to acquire enough political power to have your way. There may be more groups that are more nuanced and charitable in their language, but groups on the Far Right and Left set the tone on the ground."

In fact, Pew Research shows that Democrats are more left-leaning and Republicans more right-leaning than they were two decades ago. And both increasingly see each other as an existential threat to the nation.[6]

The contentiousness is hardly limited to DC interest groups. Ask Jordanna. She's twelve. Her parents are Christians, and her father worked for a previous Republican administration. Those two facts alone have made her the butt of jokes and ridicule in her public school. Meanwhile, the teachers and administration increasingly advocate for Gay Pride and other such causes. Shortly after the 2016 elections, Jordanna's school (teachers and students) participated in an anti-Trump march. Jordanna's parents were not Trump supporters, but they asked if their daughter could be exempted from the march. Permission was granted, but Jordanna became the lone standout. Students bullied. Old friends stopped speaking to her. "Why do we have to be so different?" she pleaded with her father through tears.

I didn't give Michael all these examples as I laid out how things have grown increasingly divided, but a number of them were fresh in my mind. "It's as if we are in a contest between two warring planets—the Left versus the Right," I said. "Or perhaps it's more like one planet that has broken into multiple pieces, with guns shooting every which way as the pieces drift apart. Remember that game Asteroids on the old Atari systems from when we were kids? That's what it's like."

One thing is certainly true: America is in the middle of an identity crisis. Ask those wearing the red "Make America Great Again" ball caps and those holding "Black Lives Matter" picket signs what unites us, and you'll hear pretty different answers.

INSIDE THE CHURCH TOO

"What's even sadder," I went on to explain to Michael, "is how much these battles have shown up among Christians and in our churches."

Consider the 2016 presidential election. Among evangelicals it felt like someone dropped a lit match into a box of firecrackers. Tweets whistled like bottle rockets, and Facebook posts popped like cherry bombs. Pastors who had never in their careers endorsed a political candidate from the pulpit suddenly felt conscience-bound to speak. Christian leaders with a national stage did the same thing.

Michael had picked up this much just from watching the Web. His local friends often queried him about the elections. But what Michael couldn't know firsthand was the quibbling and tension building inside of churches too. One friend in another part of the country shared in an e-mail, "We were having dinner with some friends from our church the other night. I offered a few of my thoughts on Trump. People got pretty mad. All this is crazy! I have to quit talking about the elections. They're really putting a damper on our friendships. Too dangerous."

The media, popcorn in hand, noticed all this bickering. Headlines buzzed: "Donald Trump Reveals Evangelical Rifts That Could Shape Politics for Years" (*New York Times*, 10/17/16) and "Evangelical Christians Are Intensely Split over Trump and Clinton" (*Faithwire*, 10/17/16).

The elections especially divided Christians by ethnicity. Whites leaned hard toward Trump, nonwhites marginally toward Clinton. After the election, African American friends of mine wanted to be "done" with evangelicalism.

"All these tensions showed up in my own Sunday school class-room," I told Michael. That fall I taught a class on Christians and government in my church, which gathers six blocks away from the US Capitol building. The Sunday after the election I opened the class with a few comments on our need for unity in the gospel. An older black woman raised her hand and lamented that she had felt no empathy from the white majority. A middle-aged white woman responded by declaring all Democrats "evil."

Wait, why did I choose to teach this class?

"My concern with all this was not that Christians might disagree on which candidate was best," I explained. "It was the emotional temperature of the disagreements. Trust began breaking down. Relationships were jeopardized. Christian liberty was threatened."

What I didn't get into with Michael was something I thought about later. If we truly stop and consider where all this strife came from, we'd see that the confusion and conflict American evangelicals experienced during the 2016 elections cannot be isolated to that relatively short moment in time. They were symptoms of larger confusions, larger troubles.

Pan the camera back and consider the perspective of the last few decades. Christians feel that they have been losing the culture wars on front after front. Born in 1973, I don't remember the sexual revolution of the 1960s or the nationwide legalization of abortion the year of my birth. Yet I remember firsthand the successive waves of moral changes throughout my childhood, college years, and beyond: the positive portrayal of a cohabitating couple on television in 1984, a children's book about two lesbian mothers in 1989, school board debates over the distribution of condoms in the early Clinton years, and the growing number of gay characters on television shows and movies in the '90s and '00s. Add the judicial doubling-down on abortion in 1992's *Planned Parenthood v. Casey*. Add the state-by-state advance of same-sex marriage laws starting in Massachusetts in 2004, culminating in a nationwide decision with *Obergefell v. Hodges* in 2015. Add the battles over religious liberty this created, such as when corporate America threatened commerce in Indiana due to Governor Mike Pence's proposed Religious Freedom Restoration Act. Also throw in the political controversies that quickly followed in 2016 over transgender bathrooms, as well as the workplace controversy over gendered pronouns shortly thereafter.

And there you have my generation's cultural autobiography.

Little by little Christians have felt pushed to the outskirts of whatever America is becoming. We still light the sparklers, enjoy the sweet-potato casserole, and root for our ball teams. But something is changing—has changed. It's beginning to feel like a different America. Like the media is sneering, the universities are stigmatizing, the government is sidelining, and Hollywood is scoffing. Religious liberty, which is explicitly written down in the Constitution, seems to be losing in court to erotic liberty, which is nowhere near the Constitution.

Amid our cultural war losses and dropping church attendance numbers, Christians have bickered about how to best engage the culture. Some want to strengthen the evangelical voting bloc. Others want to pursue social-justice causes. Still others would leave the public square to the pagans and get on with the so-called spiritual work of the church.

Now zoom the camera back in on the 2016 elections, where disagreements like these finally boiled over. After several decades of losses, evangelicals felt a growing sense of desperation. It was like watching the fourth quarter of a game where a team that fully expected to win suddenly realized how far behind it was. Players began to take higher risks. The risks didn't pay off. The team became more anxious. Tempers flared. More fouls, more whistles. Players and coaches started blaming one another. Team unity broke down.

Perhaps the saddest example of this inside American churches remains the ethnic divide. Black churches exist in America in large part because whites pushed them out in centuries past. Since the 1980s, many whites have tried to welcome blacks, but it's back into *their* white churches. The message people of color often hear remains, "Give up your cultural preferences so that I can keep mine."

It's like the explanation I gave of my enjoyment of Independence Day. I can talk to you about what *I* think it means to be "American." But I speak as a European American. Ask an African, Asian, Latino, or Native American what the noun *American* means. Certainly people within each of these groups will not share uniform perspectives. Still, you may hear certain family resemblances inside each group as they tell their versions of the story. In chapter 3, for instance, I'll point to one African American pastor who feels internal conflict over the Fourth of July holiday. His regard for America is less nostalgic, more painful than mine.

We all bring different perspectives, and frankly the majority and the minority have a hard time hearing each other. We use terms like *guilt* and *privilege* and *justice*, but we mean different things by them.

It's my sense that one of Satan's greatest victories in contemporary America has been to divide majority and minority Christians along partisan lines. White Christians lean heavily right. Black Christians lean heavily left. (Honestly, I'm unsure about Latino, Asian, and Native American evangelicals.) And this partisan divide hurts trust and breaks down Christian unity even further.

Perhaps it's time for Christians to rethink faith and politics?

Goal 1: Rethinking Faith and Politics

This is one of the first goals of this book: to rethink faith and politics from a biblical perspective. At one point the working title for this book was *Political Restart*.

There are a number of books on faith and politics being published at the moment, some advocating for a kind of withdrawal, others for a more active engagement. Such books have their place, and I've benefited from them. Yet many of them depend on the author's ability to read the moment and offer his or her best advice about responding to it. I, too, am looking at the present divided and contentious moment in American life. But that's not my primary interest. Instead, I want to help us build on something more solid and certain. That's not my wisdom. It's God's, as revealed in his Word.

Let me characterize my first goal this way. Once a year, my friend Patrick and his wife rethink their financial priorities through what he calls "zero-based budgeting." With zero-based budgeting, everything in the family budget is *out* until they can justify putting it back *in*. Does their family need that size of a house? Should they give more money to the church? They don't take anything for granted. The alternative is "incremental budgeting," where you accept everything from last year's budget but then add or subtract items in bits and pieces.

There is wisdom in both approaches, but it serves a family to occasionally rethink their priorities from scratch. One year Patrick and his wife decided they had "too much" house. So they did a radically un-American thing: they downsized!

I want to take a zero-based budgeting approach to Christianity and politics in this book. Assuming we take nothing for granted, what might a biblically driven vision of politics look like? What are the biblical principles that we must hold with a firm grip? What are the matters of wisdom and judgment to hold with a loose grip? And what should we discard altogether? Too often, we cling to our political judgments with as much certainty and zeal as we maintain God's.

I once asked a friend who takes his political opinions very seriously whether he assumed Jesus would agree with his positions on health care and tax policy. I asked almost as a joke, but he said yes! I would say, in response, that confusing our judgments with God's turns our judgments into idols, which in turn divides the church and leads to injustices inside and outside the church.

It's easy for Christians (as with all people) to approach the topic of politics like incremental budgeting. We take the views, assumptions, and practices into which we were born for granted. Then we look for ways to make marginal improvements. And, frankly, much of the time, that is the better approach, especially if you believe there is wisdom in the past and you don't assume that you or your generation knows better than everyone who came before. I'm not a political radical. I'm not calling for a revolution. I don't want to unlearn all the good things we have learned in the last several thousand years of human history about freedom and justice, democracy and rights.

Still, as Christians who prize God's wisdom above that of men and women, we should strive to stop from time to time and say, "Wait a second. Is this biblical?" and be willing to throw anything and everything off the boat if necessary. And we should do this even with the things that our nation, our tribe, and our people regard as most precious. An unwillingness to try may indicate a political idol, even if it's not as visible as the statue built by Nebuchadnezzar.

More foundationally, I am concerned that sometimes we let principles of Americanism determine the way we read Scripture, rather than letting Scripture determine how we evaluate principles of Americanism. It's like we have a big pot of stew that has been simmering for centuries and contains all our favorite phrases, like so many potatoes, carrots, and chunks of meat:

- "render to Caesar"
- "be subject to the governing authorities"
- "life, liberty, and the pursuit of happiness"
- "no law respecting an establishment of religion"
- "wall of separation between church and state"
- "of the people, by the people, for the people"
- "I pledge allegiance to the flag"
- "in God we trust"

The political lines of Scripture cook together with the sacred lines of American history, each flavoring the other.

For instance, think of that favorite biblical phrase for many American Christians: "render to Caesar the things that are Caesar's, and to God the things that are God's" (Matt. 22:21). My sense is that most American Christians interpret that phrase like this: you have the domain of government and politics in one circle and the domain of God and church and religion in another circle.

CAESAR'S THINGS
(POLITICS,
GOVN'T, ETC.)

GOD'S THINGS
(WORSHIP, FAITH,
CHURCH, ETC.)

Hold on. Is that what Jesus was saying? Might we be letting certain American ideals overdetermine our understanding of Scripture?

On the one hand, Jesus was surely telling these Jews under Roman rule to respect their Roman ruler. Many in Jesus' day were saying that a non-Jewish government was illegitimate and that they needed a Jewish king again. Jesus was saying otherwise. The Old Testament's church and state arrangement—to risk an anachronism—was coming to an end. Americans rightly get this, and we rightly separate church and state.

On the other hand, consider the verse in context. Jesus looked at a coin and asked whose image was on it. Answer: Caesar's. Okay, but in whose image was Caesar? Answer: God's. Which would mean: giving to God what is God's includes Caesar! Jesus was not pushing God into the private domain, concluded New Testament scholar Don Carson. Rather, "Jesus' famous utterance means that God always trumps Caesar."[7] The real picture is like this:

GOD'S THINGS

Caesar's things

Fast-forward to Matthew 28, where Jesus said he possesses all authority in heaven and on earth. Jesus will judge the nations and their governments. They exist by his permission, not the other way around, even if states don't acknowledge this fact (John 19:11; Rev. 1:5; 6:15–17).

The separation of church and state is not the same thing as the separation of religion and politics. But it's not until we dump the pot of stew onto the counter and examine each chunk a little more carefully that we'll see this.

That's why this book's subtitle mentions "rethinking" faith and politics. We are dumping the stew onto the countertop and starting over. Mixing metaphors, we are adopting a zero-based budgeting strategy for thinking about politics. The goal is not to discard everything we've learned, but it is to make sure we are thinking rightly, acting rightly, loving rightly, even worshipping rightly in our political lives.

When you're done with the book, you won't have gained much if you are relying on my wisdom. You want to rely on God's. It's a much steadier place to stand.

In that sense, I hope the book proves helpful not just for early twenty-first-century Americans, even though that's the context for the conversation. I hope it will prove useful for Christians in every nation.

Goal 2: Investing Our Political Hopes Firstly in the Church

If the first goal of the book is to help us rethink religion and politics, the second goal is to encourage us all to invest our political hopes first and foremost in our local churches. That's why another working title I discussed with the publisher was *Church Before State*.

Perhaps this goal surprises you. The church isn't political, is it? Make no mistake, rethinking things means blowing up a few of our present paradigms. And this is one of the first things I want to blow up. Church and state are distinct God-given institutions, and they must remain separate. But every church is political all the way down and all the way through. And every government is a deeply religious battleground of gods. No one separates their politics and religion—not the Christian, not the agnostic, not the secular progressive. It's impossible.

Let me give you a taste of what I mean about the political nature of the church with a true story about one of my fellow church members, Charles. Charles is a Washington, DC, speechwriter. He has written speeches for cabinet members, party chairmen, and other

DC insiders. Charles's work, to be sure, puts him at the center of American politics.

Charles also spends time with Freddie. Freddie, who was homeless, became a Christian and joined our church. After several good years, the church discovered Freddie was stealing money from members to support a drug addiction, so they removed him from membership. That's when Charles entered the picture. He began reading the Bible with Freddie, and little by little, Freddie began to repent. Eventually Charles helped Freddie stand before the entire church, confess his lying and stealing, and ask for forgiveness. The church clapped, cheered, and embraced Freddie. Charles and Freddie cried for joy.

Here's the GDP-sized question: Which Charles is the "political" Charles? The speechwriter or the disciple-maker? To ask it another way, which Charles deals with welfare policy, housing policy, criminal reform, and education? Answer: both. In fact, Charles will tell you that the political life of the disciple-maker fashions and gives integrity to the political life of the speechwriter. It's the same man working, the same King ruling, the same principles of justice and righteousness applying, the same politics in play.

This speechwriter has many political hopes for better laws and fairer practices. But the greatest of his political hopes comes to life in the congregation. The local church should be a model political community for the world. It's the most political of assemblies since it represents the One with final judgment over presidents and prime ministers. Together we confront, condemn, and call nations with the light of our King's words and the saltiness of our lives.

Unlike Charles, however, many Christians in America continue to invest their greatest political hopes in the nation. Since colonial times, we have called the nation "a city on the hill." Since Abraham Lincoln's day, we have asked our leaders to provide "a just and lasting peace among ourselves and with all nations." Yet is it possible that all the contention and division Christians presently face is the catalyst

God means to force some of us to rethink where our political hopes really lie?

Just think: Where do we *first* beat swords into plowshares and spears into pruning hooks? Where should love of enemy *first* dissolve a nation's tribalism? Where should Lincoln's just and lasting peace *first* take root and grow?

Answer: in our local churches.

Conversion makes us citizens of Christ's kingdom, places us inside embassies of that kingdom, and puts us to work as ambassadors of heaven's righteousness and justice. Churches are the cities on hills, said Jesus. Not America.

Goal 3: Learning to *Be* Before We *Do*

This brings us to the third goal of this book. If our political hopes should rest first in our churches, we must learn to *be* before we *do*.

My church gathers six blocks from the US Capitol. It is filled with young people like Charles who moved to DC wanting to make a difference by working in various spheres of government. And their work matters. After all, good governments are prerequisites to the rest of life, including the life of the church.

But as one of the elders, or pastors, of the church, I often remind our Hill staffers, K Street lobbyists, and military officers that real political action starts in the teaching ministry of our church and then flows outward from there—from our relationships with other members, to our families, our workplaces, and beyond. First be, then do. Don't tell me you're interested in politics if you are not pursuing a just, righteous, peace-producing life with everyone in your immediate circles.

Paul asked the Jews of his day, "You who preach against stealing, do you steal?" (Rom. 2:21).

I've got a few questions of my own.

You who call for immigration reform, do you practice hospitality with visitors to your church who are ethnically or nationally different from you?

You who vote for family values, do you honor your parents and love your spouse self-sacrificially?

You who speak against abortion, do you also embrace and assist the single mothers in your church? Do you encourage adoption? Do you prioritize your own children over financial comfort?

You who talk about welfare reform, do you give to the needy in your congregation?

You who proclaim that all lives matter, do all your friends look like you?

You who lament structural injustices, do you work against them in your own congregation? Do you rejoice with those who rejoice and weep with those who weep?

You who fight for traditional marriage, do you love your wife, cherishing her as you would your own body and washing her with the water of the Word?

You who are concerned about the economy and the job market, do you obey your boss with a sincere heart, not as a people-pleaser but as you would obey Christ?

You who care about corporate tax rates, do you treat your employees fairly? Do you threaten them, forgetting that he who is both their Master and yours is in heaven and that there is no partiality with him?

Finally, as you share your opinions about all these issues on social media, do you gladly share the Lord's Supper with the church member who disagrees? Do you pray for his or her spiritual good?

"All politics is local," said former Speaker of the US House of Representatives Tip O'Neill. He spoke better than he knew.[8]

Politics should begin with our putting away the verbal swords we might be tempted to wield against church members who vote differently than we do. Any political impact our fellow members make in and through the church will last forever. I love how my church's senior pastor Mark put it: "Before and after America, there was and will be the church. The nation is an experiment. The church is a certainty."

When I say we must *be* before we *do*, I mean the local church should strive first to live out justice, righteousness, and love in its life together. Then it can commend its understanding of justice, righteousness, and love to the nation.

With these last two goals I want to shift our focus from redeeming the nation to living as a redeemed nation, like Charles and Freddie together. Our congregational lives should tutor us in the justice and love that God desires for all humanity. And then the lessons we learn inside the church should inform our public engagement outside of it.

God establishes governments to build the platforms of peace and basic justice on which we can live our lives. Christians, as they have opportunity in government, should therefore work for principles of justice. Yet God establishes churches, among other reasons, to mark off the people who will present a fuller picture of justice. The work of Christians in Washington, your state capitol, your town hall, or your school board means little without the radiating glow of kingdom embassies behind them and the ambassadorial witness of every Christian.

Goal 4: Preparing for Battle and for Rage

As the church moves outward and into the public square, we must be prepared for battle. That's the fourth goal of this book, and the source of the title the publisher and I finally settled on: *How the Nations Rage*.

Did you pick up on the reference to Psalm 2?

> Why do the nations rage
>   and the peoples plot in vain?
> The kings of the earth set themselves,

> and the rulers take counsel together,
>
> against the LORD and against his Anointed, saying,
>
> "Let us burst their bonds apart
>
> and cast away their cords from us." (vv. 1–3)

The division and contention of our present cultural moment is just one more illustration of the nations' rage against the Lord. Division inside the church roots in such rage. The disdain you feel in the media, academy, or courtroom roots in such rage. The arguments on social media depict this rage. Ironically, news sites even know that rage leads to more "clicks." Rage means advertising dollars.

If the public square is a battleground of gods, the saints should expect the rage of the nations to burn hot in the square. Political philosophers often claim that we can greet one another in the square on religiously neutral terms through what they call a social contract. I will argue in chapter 2 that this is a Trojan horse for idolatry. In fact, every combatant will fight for his or her god's brand of justice. Every time. All the time. They will even send lions to devour the saints wherever we oppose their gods and their version of justice.

But amid the heat and the lions, every Christian, for love of neighbor, must use whatever political stewardship God has given, even if that stewardship doesn't include the insider's access of a Washington, DC, speechwriter like Charles. We should enter the public square as what I will call principled pragmatists.

Here's an awkward question that the reality of the battle raises: how often do you think Americans think of Psalm 2 when asked about verses on politics in the Bible? More uncomfortably, how often do we locate America in Psalm 2: Yes, one of those raging nations and peoples plotting against the Lord and his Messiah is America.

Or did you think America was exempt from Psalm 2's indictment?

I'll confess, it's an idea that makes me uncomfortable. It almost feels like criticizing your home.

Goal 5: Becoming Less American and More Patriotic

I want to help us be *less* American so that we might be *more* patriotic. To put it another way, I want to help you and me identify with Christ more so that we might love our fellow citizens more, no matter the name of our nation.

When you become a Christian, your identity dramatically changes, and you gain a new citizenship. Suddenly, the most important thing about you is not your gender, who your parents are, where you are from, how much money you have, what color your skin is, your nationality, your intelligence or beauty, whether you are married, or anything else that humans ordinarily use to identify one another. The most important thing about you is that you are united to Christ through the new covenant and made a citizen of his kingdom.

Who are you, Christian? You are: A new creation. Born again. An adopted heir. A member of Christ's body. A citizen of the kingdom. A son or daughter of the divine King.

When all this happens, then you find yourself having to renegotiate how you relate to all those old categories. How do you relate to your parents, your colleagues, your friends, your ethnic group, your government, the public at large, even what society says it means to be a "man" or a "woman"?

The Bible calls Christians "aliens" and "strangers" and "sojourners" and "exiles," depending on your translation. Each of these labels reminds us that this world is not our final home, and that we await another city whose architect and builder is God. The labels resonate with Jesus' instruction to live *in* but not *of* the world. And knowing how to strike both sides of the in-not-of balance is challenging in every area of life, perhaps especially in our relationship to the public square. How do we live as citizens of a nation while being a citizen of the kingdom of Christ?

Step one is letting go of America and our American identity long enough to give it to the Lord and let him fashion it as he pleases. We become better friends to America by loving Christ first. This frees us to be honest and not blind to our national failings. "Faithful are the wounds of a friend; profuse are the kisses of an enemy" (Prov. 27:6).

Step two is remembering that Psalm 2 is not about the *power* of the nations' rage, but its *futility*.

> He who sits in the heavens laughs;
>> the Lord holds them in derision. (v. 4)

The psalm promises the victory and rule of Christ over every nation, military, and government:

> Ask of me, and I will make the nations your heritage,
>> and the ends of the earth your possession.
> You shall break them with a rod of iron
>> and dash them in pieces like a potter's vessel." (vv. 8–9)

We come therefore with the word of the King of kings and Judge of judges, and his word goes out to every nation, including ours:

> Now therefore, O kings, be wise;
>> be warned, O rulers of the earth.
> Serve the LORD with fear,
>> and rejoice with trembling.
> Kiss the Son,
>> lest he be angry, and you perish in the way,
>> for his wrath is quickly kindled.
> Blessed are all who take refuge in him. (vv. 10–12)

As I mentioned earlier in this chapter, a losing team becomes desperate and takes desperate measures. But what might it look like for the church's politics if we became convinced—really convinced—both that we will have trouble in this world and that Jesus has overcome this world, as he promised? Might we present a strange and winsome confidence that is not desperate to win the culture wars but is also tenderly and courageously committed to the good of others?

The primary goal of this book is not to help Christians make an impact in the public square. It is not to help the world be something. It is to help Christians and churches be something.

My posture in this book is a pastor's. I want Christ's people to follow Christ in every area of life, including in their capacity as voters, officeholders, lobbyists, editorial writers, jurists, and citizens.

So this is a book for Christians.

Now, I hope that what follows does equip some readers to make an impact in the public square, and that all readers might know what it means to live peaceful and quiet lives (1 Tim. 2:2). But we need to start with knowing who we are and being true to that identity.

So remember your baptism. Your baptism argues that you have been buried and raised with Christ, and that you should represent his righteousness, justice, and love everywhere you go.

A Christian's political posture, in a word, must never be *withdraw*. Nor should it be *dominate*. It must always be *present*, and we must do this when the world loves us and when it despises us. Anyone who tells you, "Withdraw, we're losing!" or, "Push forward, we're winning!" may have succumbed to a kind of utopianism, as if we could build heaven on earth. Instead, heaven starts in our assemblies, even if only as in a mirror dimly. Christians are heaven's ambassadors, and our churches are its embassies. Neither panic nor triumphalism become us. A cheerful confidence does. We represent this heavenly and future kingdom *now*, whether the skies are cloudy or clear.

CONCLUSION

Indeed, here is the irony we will discover at the end of all our rethinking: the church's political task is unchanging. Until Christ returns, the nations will rage and plot in vain. We, meanwhile, point to the Lord and to his Anointed, both in word and deed. We're on the right side of history so long as we stand with the Lord of history. His vindication will be our vindication.

Honestly, you may or may not make a public impact in this life. You may or may not make a difference "out there." Society may get better; it may get worse, regardless of the activities of faithful Christians. That is outside of your control and mine. What is within our control is whether we seek justice, love our neighbor, and do both these things wisely, not foolishly.

On the Last Day, God will not ask you, "Did you produce change?" but, "Did you faithfully pursue change in those places where I gave you opportunity and authority?"

PUBLIC SQUARE: NOT NEUTRAL, BUT A BATTLEGROUND OF GODS

Governments serve gods. This is true of every government in every place ever since God gave governments to the world. The judge judging, the voter voting, the president presiding, all of them work for their gods. No citizen or officeholder is religiously indifferent or neutral.

Let me explain in two steps. Step one: our religion or worship is bigger than what happens at church. It involves everything we do. To see that, just ask why, why, why.

I'm having oatmeal for breakfast.

Why are you having oatmeal?

To be healthy.

Why do you want to be healthy?

So that I can work hard.

Why do you want to work hard?

So that I can get what I want.

Why do you want to get what you want?

So that I can be happy.

Why do you think that will make you happy?

If you keep asking a person "why," eventually you will reach a backstop—something with nothing behind it and that doesn't move. Here you find that person's gods. Our gods are the backstop or foundation for all our thinking, longing, and acting. Our gods are

whatever we cannot imagine living without,

whatever we most love,

whatever we most trust, rely on, and believe in, and

whatever is our final refuge.

Our gods motivate our big and small decisions alike. This is why the apostle Paul told us to "glorify God in your body" and to do so "whether you eat or drink" (1 Cor. 6:20; 10:31), be it oatmeal or Frosted Mini-Wheats, which I prefer.

One of the top legal philosophers of the latter half of the twentieth century, Ronald Dworkin, made just this point. "Religion," Dworkin said, "is a deep, distinct, and comprehensive worldview" and "a belief in a [supernatural] god is only one manifestation or consequence of that deeper worldview." Religion is whatever gives a person's universe purpose and order. So Dworkin described himself as a religious atheist.[1]

Non-Christian novelist David Foster Wallace drew out the lesson: everyone worships. He wrote, "In the day-to-day trenches of adult life, there is actually no such thing as atheism. There is no such thing as not worshipping. Everybody worships. The only choice we get is what to worship."[2]

You probably noticed that I'm saying gods—plural—not god or

God, because our hearts usually contain multitudes. One moment it's the God of the Bible that we worship. The next moment it's the god of our parent's approval. Then the god of fleshly desire. Then the god of cultural acceptance. Then the god of cool. Then the god of our skin color. Then the god of a Super Bowl hero. Then the god of personal ambition. You get the point.

Our hearts are battlegrounds of gods.

So step one for understanding my claim that governments serve gods is seeing that our religion is bigger than what happens at church. Step two is seeing that our politics are bigger than what happens in the public square. In fact, our politics involve everything we do.

Typically, we think of politics as the stuff of congressmen and councilmen, school boards and voting booths. That's part of politics. But there's a bigger story. The story of politics is the story of how you and I arrange our days, arrange our relationships, and arrange our neighborhoods and nations to get what we most want—to get what we worship. Every one of us employs whatever power we possess, including the mechanisms of the state, to gain whatever we find most *worthy* of worship—what we *worth*-scipe, as the Old English had it.

Just as our natures are religious, being designed to worship, so our natures are political, being designed to establish a social order.

You see this when children play house and offer each other various roles. "You be the kid. I'll be the mommy." You hear it in their disputes over whether the ball rolled out of bounds.

Or, had you been present, you would have heard it from the four-year-old son of a lawyer friend of mine. One day at preschool the boy's teacher asked him to come inside after playtime. The four-year-old, son of a lawyer, replied sincerely, "I will take it under advisement."

In a fallen world, all of us game the rules and play the people over us in order to slant life's benefits to our advantage. That's why, even if you don't think you are interested in politics, you are deeply interested in politics.

As children, we trade obedience for cookies. As adults, we leverage job choices, marital fights, clothing styles, artistic pursuits, body type, skin color, national identity, gender stereotypes, insider social cues, rolling eyes and sighs, church attendance, automobile brand names, friendships, and more all to shape our little plots of dirt according to our hearts' desires. Whenever we can grab onto the levers of state power, we do the same. The sword of state is just one more tool for this larger political project of rule and acquisition.

No king or queen rules for rule's own sake. Every king and queen—insert your name and mine here—rules for a reason. And that reason is our religion, our worship.

Politics serves worship. Governments serve gods.

WARS OF RELIGION

Americans today talk about the culture wars. It might be slightly more accurate to call them wars of religion, because religion is at the root. None of us steps into the public square leaving our objects of worship behind. We take our gods with us. It's impossible to do otherwise.

Last week I was teaching a class of Christian college students doing internships in Washington, DC. One student asked whether we had the right to impose our morality through law. I said, "Name one law for me that doesn't impose someone's morality."

The class paused. Thought. Then chuckled. "Right, there is no such thing."

Similarly, a US senator on the Senate Judiciary Committee recently expressed her concern about a Roman Catholic law professor who had been nominated for a circuit court judgeship. The senator explained, "I think whatever a religion is, it has its own dogma . . . And I think in your case, professor, when you read your speeches, the conclusion one draws is that the *dogma lives loudly within you*, and that's of concern when you come to big issues that large numbers of people have fought for years in this country" (emphasis added).[3] If I could, I would pose the same challenge to the senator that I posed to the college class: Senator, please name one big issue that doesn't depend on every side's dogmas. Or one small issue? Senator, do you assume your own dogmas don't motivate your positions and decisions?

More to the point, behind every Senate Judiciary Committee vote, Supreme Court decision, protestors' picket line, editorial board meeting, social media campaign, interest group press conference, political action committee e-mail, campaign television advertisement, and presidential veto is someone's basic worldview of *how things ought to be*. And behind that worldview is *a god*. This is true whether the matter up for debate is abortion, same-sex marriage, tax policy, immigration law, or funding for national parks.

Likewise, a nation's constitution and laws are those places where a consensus exists between our many gods or where one god has defeated the others. They are the terms of victory, the peace treaties, the détentes from decades and centuries of battles. No one god wins all the wars. Rather, a nation's laws are a collection of competing values and commitments, cobbled together over time by compromise and negotiation.

We can't help but bring our gods into the public square. Harvard political philosopher Michael Sandel did not use the language of different gods—that's a biblical way of putting it—but he agreed with the basic point. The pro-choice position, he said, "is not really neutral on the underlying moral and theological question." Instead, it "rests on the assumption" that Christian teaching on this topic "is false." Both the case for banning abortion and the case for permitting it presuppose "some answer to the underlying moral and religious controversy." He proceeded to say the same thing about same-sex marriage: "the underlying moral question is unavoidable."[4] Sandel then pointed back to the Lincoln-Douglass debates to make his point. In the 1858 Illinois senate race, Stephen Douglass said he was neutral on slavery. Abraham Lincoln replied that only someone who accepted slavery could say that. Douglass, like everyone else, had a moral position on slavery, and behind that a religious position.

Just as our hearts are battlegrounds of gods, so the public square is a battleground of gods, the turf of our religious wars.

Either we ask the state to play savior, or, to say the same thing a different way, we demand it plays servant to our gods. Sometimes our gods agree with one another; sometimes they don't. And that's when the fighting starts in the public square.

What is the public square? It's all those places where the nation goes to talk, debate, and make decisions that bind the whole public. It's the letter to the editor, the Parent Teacher Association, the hallways of Congress. A nation's public square is where a citizenry wages war on behalf of their gods.

There the ambassadors of Jesus and Allah, the representatives of the Christian's big-G God and the Darwinist's little-g god, the agents of this party's idols and that party's idols, come together to hustle and grapple, joust and cross swords, for the purpose of winning the day and pulling the levers of state power.

So it was in ancient Greece. Think of Socrates, that stout old figure of philosophical lore. He was executed, Plato told us, for "believing in deities of his own invention instead of the gods recognized by the state."[5]

So it was in ancient Rome. Caesars and senators like Tacitus accused Christians of atheism and hatred for the human race because they would not pay tribute to Rome's gods. And the Romans believed the gods' favor sustained the prosperity of the empire.[6]

So it was in ancient Israel, who, one prophet would say, had as many gods as it had cities (Jer. 2:28; 11:13).

So it was in the communist revolutions in China and Russia, when Mao and Lenin both thought they could exterminate that worst of political rivals, God.

So it can be among those who adhere to conservativism, liberalism, and nationalism. Conservativism can idolize tradition; liberalism, freedom; nationalism, the nation.

Our gods, whatever they may be, are always present in the struggle for who gets to rule.

The holy battle rages on, even if we deny it. Our gods determine our morality, and they determine our politics—unavoidably. They are not always consistent with one another. They are not always apparent to us. But they are always there, determining our political postures and positions. There is no such thing as a spiritually neutral politics.

Just as China's Communist Party tried to dispose of God, so did those who protested the Communist Party. "We want neither gods nor emperors," sang the students as they gathered in Beijing's Tiananmen Square in the spring of 1989. They wanted to be their own gods and emperors, of course. In our sin, my children and I sympathize. So do you and your children, if you know your own hearts.

BUT SHOULDN'T WE KEEP POLITICS AND RELIGION SEPARATE?

Of course, talking this way goes against the way Christian and non-Christian Americans alike have been trained to talk and to think.

We learn in school how carefully the Founding Fathers sought to separate government and religion. President and so-called father of the Constitution James Madison said, "An alliance or coalition between Government and religion cannot be too carefully guarded against."[7]

While you may hear politicians peppering references to the Almighty into their speeches and even the president closing every State of the Union with "And may God bless America," the legislatures that make the laws and the judges who review them wouldn't dare invoke a divine authority. So said Supreme Court Justice Oliver Wendell Holmes: "The common law is not a brooding omnipresence in the sky."[8] The Constitution is "the supreme Law of the Land"; it testifies to itself in article 6.2.

We strive to keep politics and religion separate in our churches too. I walk into Sunday school. The teacher explains that the gospel of Jesus Christ is the good word of salvation, not the promise of political change. Later, I open my study Bible and read the study notes on Matthew 5:3, which say that Jesus "is a spiritual deliverer rather than a political one."[9]

This is how we talk and think. Some people say that politics and religion must be entirely separate. Call them the hard separationists. They would say the institution of the state deals with political stuff, while the institution of the church deals with religious stuff. Like this:

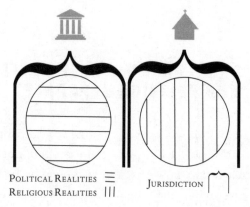

POLITICAL REALITIES ≡
RELIGIOUS REALITIES ⦀   JURISDICTION ⌐¬

Most Christians think of themselves not as hard separationists, but as soft separationists. They believe that politics and religion should overlap in a few places but mostly remain separate. Like this:

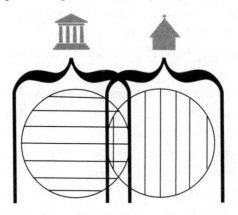

You wouldn't talk about practicing your religion in the voting booth or the jury's box. Nor would you say that church services are for engaging in politics. Right?

There are sensible historical and theological reasons behind the impulse to separate politics and religion. The emperor and pope once ruled "Christian" Europe together. Like this:

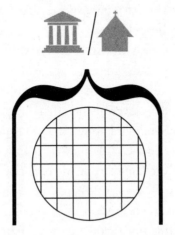

This shared rule of church and state, particularly when combined with a view of church membership that ignored the need for regeneration, helped to create whole nations called Christian that were filled with people who weren't actually born-of-the-Spirit Christians. The shared rule forced false faith. It killed and tortured people in Jesus' name. It distracted churches from preaching the gospel.

The Protestant Reformation didn't immediately solve this problem. In some respects, it temporarily made the arrangement worse. The princes of Germany and kings of England became supreme over everything, including the church. They offered the previous graphic, only they put the state on top. And so Protestant and Catholic sovereigns went to war with each other. Across the Atlantic in the American colonies, one Protestant denomination would suppress another.

Yet something else was unleashed in the Reformation: Martin Luther's emphasis on the individual conscience, which would eventually yield a doctrine of religious tolerance. By the early 1600s Baptist theologians like John Smyth and Thomas Helwys argued that God does not permit governments to meddle with religion or matters of conscience. By the late 1600s philosophers like John Locke made this point in a more philosophical way. Locke argued that governments should concern themselves with "outward things" such as life, liberty, health, money, lands, houses, and the like. Churches, however, should concern themselves with "inward things" like the care of souls and the mind.[10] Governments, therefore, should make room for Protestants and Catholics, Anglicans and Baptists.

A century later, in the 1770s and '80s, Thomas Jefferson, a fan of John Locke, made the same distinction between the inner and outer person. He then drew the conclusion, "It does me no injury for my neighbor to say that there are twenty Gods, or no God."[11]

Around the same time Baptist minister John Leland said something very similar: "Let every man . . . worship according to his own faith, either one God, three Gods, no God, or twenty Gods; and let government protect him in so doing."[12]

THE AMERICAN EXPERIMENT

So think about what's happening here. Enlightenment folk like Jefferson and Protestant folk like Leland might have had slightly different reasons for wanting to separate government and religion— one claiming to rely on reason, the other on revelation—but both parties agreed they should be kept separate. So, at the risk of over-simplifying, they shook hands and made a deal. Today we call that deal the American Experiment.

The American Experiment is the idea that people of many religions can join together and establish a government based on certain shared universal principles. Think of it as a contract with at least five principles. Principle one of this contract is that governments derive "their just powers from the consent of the governed," says the Declaration of Independence. Principle two is religious freedom. Three is other forms of freedom and equality. Four is the idea of justice as rights. And five is the separation of church and state.

Now, the founders lived in a formally religious society. In many of their writings they appealed to natural law to justify these various principles: God exists, and everyone has a primary responsibility to God for his or her conduct and behavior, and then to the state. The Constitution never invokes these justifications, but those who signed it arguably intended for it to give Christians a favored place in the public square, even while protecting churches from governmental incursions.

Yet here is what's crucial. Just because two religious people make a contract doesn't make the contract *itself* religious. And the founders' idea of government by consent doesn't include God in the contract. In fact, the legal terms they set forth in article 6 of the Constitution, forbidding any religious test, made belief in God like a sunroof on a car: an optional extra. A citizen might believe in him or not, but the contract establishing a government is still a contract, just like a car is a car with or without a sunroof.

Likewise, the argument for religious freedom does not depend on believing in a big-G God. After all, how can you require people to believe in God in order to accept the argument that says they are free not to believe in God? From the beginning, therefore, the argument for religious freedom was built on the right to a free conscience. Everyone, whether they believe in a big-G God or not, wants a free conscience.

The same is true for the affirmations of general freedom, equality, and rights. One *can* offer a theological defense for each of these principles, as the founders and generations of Americans did. But the principles are freestanding, and one need not provide such a defense.

Back to the car analogy: It's as if the founders designed a car with good drivers in mind, but nothing in the design of the car prevented bad drivers from getting behind the wheel and crashing it. They wanted to keep faith and politics, religion and government, separate. Yet the ironic truth is, we can't help but drive the car on behalf of our God or gods.

We would be fools to think otherwise.

IDEOLOGICALLY RIGGED METAL DETECTORS AND TROJAN HORSES

What happens when people fool themselves into believing that it's possible to separate our politics from our religion?

For starters, you create the illusion of a public square that's religiously neutral, or at least partially neutral. But what you really have is a square rigged against *organized* religion. Organized religions are kept out. Unnamed idols are let in.

Imagine an airport security metal detector that doesn't screen for metal but for religion standing at the entrance of the public square. The machine beeps anytime someone walks through it with a supernatural big-G God hiding inside one of their convictions, but it fails to pick up self-manufactured or socially constructed little-g gods. Into this public square the secularist, the materialist, the Darwinist, the consumerist, the elitist, the chauvinist, and, frankly, the fascist can all enter carrying their gods with them like whittled wooden figures in their pockets. Not so for the Christians or Jews or Muslims. Should they enter and make a claim on behalf of their big-G God, the siren will sound like a firetruck. What this means is that the public square is inevitably slanted toward the secularist and materialist. Public conversation is ideologically rigged.

Here's another illustration. The illusion of separation is like a Trojan horse for idols and nameless gods. Do you remember how the Greek soldiers hid inside a massive wooden horse and left it outside the gates of Troy? The people of Troy pulled the horse inside the city gates. Then, while the city slept, the soldiers snuck out and destroyed the city. In the same way, claiming to separate politics and religion keeps organized religion outside the city gates while hiding idols and unnamed gods inside this very claim.

When we're not paying attention, even those three hallmark American principles of rights, equality, and freedom become Trojan horses. After all, who gets to decide which rights are right, or how to define equality, or which freedoms are just? Shall we affirm the *right* to an abortion, marriage *equality*, and the *freedom* to define one's own gender? Well, the answer depends on what your God or gods say. Christians, therefore, find themselves in the peculiar position of wanting to say that rights, equality, and freedom are good God-given gifts, but looking around and seeing people treat those gifts *as* gods, or at least as Trojan horses that hide their real gods.

For instance, a recent survey of 1,500 undergraduate college students suggested that free speech is "deeply imperiled" on US campuses.[13] Is it the case that free speech is imperiled, or is it the case that our society's sense of what's morally acceptable speech is quickly shifting between one generation and another? The college students and administrations of, say, 1790, 1840, or 1950 would not have tolerated every conceivable form of speech. Imagine how campus administrators and students would have responded to the prospect of a pro-abortion or pro-gay marriage speaker in 1840. I don't deny that some nations have broader and some have narrower boundaries for what's morally permissible speech. But every nation has some boundaries, and those boundaries depend on its prevailing gods. The concept of free speech is a Trojan horse. It's hiding someone's gods.

Might we even say the same about religious freedom? Amid America's quickly shifting moral consensus, it's tempting for Christians to fall back on religious liberty as a stop-gap measure, at least to protect themselves. But hold on. We've defined religious freedom as freedom of conscience, remember? And what if my conscience demands things that your conscience finds abhorrent? Whose conscience wins in court? The very idea of a free conscience begins to look like an empty Trojan horse. People can pack the soldiers of any god they want inside of it.

For example, the 1992 Supreme Court case *Planned Parenthood v. Casey* said that "men and women of good conscience can disagree" on abortion. Therefore, we should protect a woman's right to choose an abortion as a way of respecting *her* conscience. That is, we should protect abortion as a religious freedom. After all, isn't sexual freedom a religious freedom in a pagan culture? Isn't it an altar of worship? It was in the ancient world. And pro-choicers do fight for their cause with religious zeal.

In other words, when you define religious freedom apart from the God of Scripture, eventually those terms will be used against the people of that God. Yes, that's the paradox of religious freedom.

Don't misunderstand: I will present very *Christian* reasons to affirm religious tolerance, along with rights, freedom, and equality generally—those American ideals—later in the book. Still we find ourselves in this strange moment of American history where the *American* arguments for religious freedom just might be destroying religious freedom, and the *American* arguments for rights and equality just might be destroying rights and equality.

CHRISTIAN LANGUAGE BECOMES IRRATIONAL

So the first result of pretending we can separate politics and religion is that we ideologically tilt the public square floor against our Christian moral heritage and organized religion generally. The second result is that it makes some elements of Christian speech—especially related to the family, sexuality, and religion—sound irrational and therefore unjust.

Think about it like this. You're sitting at lunch with a non-Christian friend. The question of same-sex marriage or transgender bathrooms comes up. You try to think of some way to say that same-sex marriage is wrong, or that God created people male and female. But you know that stating the matter this plainly will get no traction. In fact, such words might not even make sense to your non-Christian friend. "It's wrong? What do you mean by 'wrong'?"

I remember sharing a lively political conversation one afternoon in graduate school with nine of my political science classmates. The year was 1996, and I was the only professing Christian. The first topic of debate was abortion. I alone defended the life of the child.

The other nine pushed for a woman's right to abort her child. Yet the conversation was respectful and courteous because I was able to use language that my classmates recognized and understood: "The baby has its own DNA," "Biology textbooks will tell you it's a human life," "The baby has rights too!" and so forth. They disagreed with me, even strongly. But they respected me because they understood my logic.

Then the conversation switched to the topic of the morality of homosexuality. Once again, I stood alone in making a case against it. But this time the tone of the conversation changed. It was no longer courteous and respectful. My classmates were shocked and offended that anyone would hold such an intolerant view. (And this was 1996!) I remember thinking afterward that the topic of homosexuality was going to prove more divisive and difficult in the so-called culture wars than even abortion had. My views didn't make sense to their version of rationality or their version of justice.

In the public square, people fear the irrational and become angry toward injustice. Irrationality and injustice are linked because the first often leads to the second. And such fear and anger make sense. You're wise to fear a powerful force that's irrational, and you're morally right to be angry toward injustice. It's easy, therefore, to size up a nation's gods by asking where that nation gives moral approval to fear and to anger—even to rage.

My classmates were angry at my views on homosexuality in 1996. They found them both irrational and unjust. And that same fear and anger toward Christian views of the family and sexuality increasingly permeate America's public square today. To employ such language today sounds irrational and unjust. It evokes rage.

The only moral vocabulary that is permitted in the public square today is the language of rights, equality, and freedom. That language works fine for Christians when everyone shares a basic Christian-*ish* morality. But it effectively leads to a dishonest conversation when our moralities and religions radically diverge. It hides what's really at stake, like the senator telling a judicial nominee that her dogma lives loudly within her, as if it doesn't live loudly within the senator.

In a way, I think the American founders understood all this. George Washington said in his Farewell Address that "true religion and good morals are the only solid foundations of public liberty and happiness." John Adams similarly observed, "Our Constitution was made only for a moral and religious people. It is wholly inadequate to the government of any other."[14] These two founders, in other words, would have given at least some credit to our nation's success and durability not to democracy or liberal values (liberty, rights, equality), but to "true religion and good morals." They seemed to understand that the American Experiment is like a gun: how it will be used depends on the morality of the person holding it. Or like a car: much depends on the driver. Or like a Trojan horse: Whose soldiers are hiding inside?

Writers and pastors sometimes say the solution to today's culture wars is to get back to the American founders. I don't think we have ever left them. What's changed is the source of our morality. Whether Christians or not, the generation of the founders shared a Christian-*ish* morality (apart from the topic of slavery and the inequality of blacks and whites, and the treatment of women). That's no longer the case.

Our rights might have come from God, but we've made them god. We are like rich and spoiled children who have forgotten that all the wealth we possess comes from our parents. And so we squander our wealth foolishly.

SEPARATION OF CHURCH AND STATE

I was speaking on the phone with a friend several weeks ago who was complaining about American evangelicals. Thinking of himself as a separationist, he critically called them "soft theonomists." Theonomists believe in some combination of church and state, often along the lines of what God ordained in ancient Israel. *Theos* is the Greek word for God and *nomos* the word for law. Put them together and you get God-law, which practically becomes church-state, or something like that.

Is that what I'm endorsing? Well, if, by theonomist, you mean I'm going to take some of my religion into the public square, then, yes, because *everyone* is a theonomist in this fashion, including my friend. No, I won't take all my religion into the public square. But what I enter the public square with represents my religion. The same is true for everyone. There's no such thing as separationism in this sense. It's all a bluff. But if, by theonomist, you mean I'm going to blend church and state, then, *no*, I'm not advocating theonomy because I'm a staunch supporter of separating these two God-ordained institutions. As I said in chapter 1, we *can't* separate religion and politics, but we *must* separate church and state. The perspective of this book, therefore, is this:

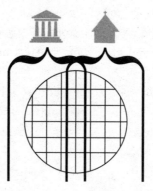

All of life is both political and religious, because we are political and religious creatures. But church and state possess distinct, God-given authorities with distinct jurisdictions. We'll explore this further in later chapters.

That brings us to a second paradox for this chapter. The first, you may recall, is that the logic of "religious freedom," if not the language itself, will be used against God's people in an unvirtuous society. The second is this: nearly every American today affirms the separation of church and state, but that institutional distinction is a Christian one, and it applies uniquely to Christians (and perhaps to members of other organized religions, but I'm going to focus only on churches for now).

Therefore, the separation works splendidly between Christians in churches of different denominations. Don't make me pay taxes to support your Anglican church, and I'll respect your freedom to baptize your infants.

Yet the conversation changes when you apply it to a Christian and a non-Christian. The non-Christian, after all, doesn't have a church. When the non-Christian affirms his belief in the separation of church and state, he means separation of government from *my* church, not his own. He effectively says, "You can't impose *any* of your beliefs and morals on me because they come from your church." Okay, but does that mean he cannot impose his idolatrous and non-Christian views on me? Ah, there's the catch. He has no official church and no god with a name. And there's no such thing as the separation of idolatry and state. Too bad for me. Lucky for him. Do you see what I mean when I say it applies uniquely to the Christian?

Biblically understood, the separation of church and state isn't about who gets to decide what morals will bind a nation. It's about the fact that God has given the state one kind of authority and churches another kind. Yet how many non-Christians do you think can define what church authority is, much less care to? How many Christians, in fact, do you think know what church authority is? Yet unless you can explain what the authority of a church is, you cannot explain the separation of church and state. The separation, after all, means the state must not do what God authorized the church to do, and vice-versa. Do you know what he has authorized churches to do? We'll unpack it later.

For now, we can say that the Christian belief in the church *sidetracks* us politically. It keeps us from imposing not all but a host of our beliefs on unbelievers—like the belief that Jesus got up from the dead and is the King of kings. Our doctrine of the church says, "Hey, Christian, apply your belief that Jesus is king over *there*, among your fellow church members."

Unbelievers don't have a doctrine of the church that sidetracks them. They impose whatever beliefs and morality they want. People often criticize John Calvin for his argument that the state should enforce the first two commandments (no other gods, no idols), and I would agree with those critiques. Yet it occurs to me that more and more secular progressivists do what Calvin did—they publicly promote their gods and prosecute forms of worship that offend them. My friend Andrew T. Walker recently tweeted:

> Don't be fooled: Secularism is a form of theocracy. It's very jealous for its own glory, commands our worship, & demands a set of ethics.

How do secular progressives do this? Certainly through the ordinary legislation and judicial processes. Yet it's also worth highlighting the work that public schools and education policy do in making disciples. Education is a society's "paramount moral duty," said political philosopher John Dewey, since it is "the fundamental method of social progress and reform." Through the public schools the children of a nation come to "share in the social consciousness" of that nation.[15]

To put it another way, public schools, as agents of the state, participate in the religious indoctrination of their students. Before the Civil War, schools reinforced a Protestant orientation. In the late nineteenth and early twentieth centuries, school lessons began to move in a naturalistic direction. After World War II, secular progressivism became increasingly predominant. Schools today especially work to cultivate students who are conscientious in matters of social justice.[16]

A member of my church whose children attend a Washington, DC, public school recently received an e-mail announcement from the school notifying parents of the school's participation in a Gay Pride parade. I appreciate the fact that the school sent an e-mail. That doesn't always happen now. The letter explained that the school "values diversity" and "strives to create a safe and inclusive environment." The administration believed that participating in the parade would be "a great way to proactively engage your child(ren) in a conversation about LGBTQ people in a way that focuses on acceptance, respect and understanding, promoting the spread of correct and positive information."

I, too, hope that schools will foster "acceptance, respect and understanding" for all people, no matter how they identify themselves. Yet my Christian faith does *not* treat every conceivable identity-construct as morally legitimate. Should we foster "acceptance, respect and understanding" for those who identify themselves as thieves, adulterers, or (as I saw on one courtroom television show) vampires? For the people themselves, yes. For their identities as thieves, adulterers, or vampires? Not according to my faith.

What this school e-mail represents, then, is the state's concerted effort to religiously indoctrinate my friend's ten-, eight-, and five-year-olds in a different faith. A faith that worships the gods of self-definition and self-expression.

Through the classroom, the legislator, and the courtroom, today's secular progressive is only too happy to use the state to enforce his moral and religious codes. Why wouldn't he? There is no big-G God telling him to do otherwise. So his little-g gods and priests walk unnoticed into the legislative chamber, courtroom, and classroom. My doctrine of the church, however, keeps me from trying to impose everything the Bible says about sexuality on every American through the public-school system.

Again, in today's thinking, the separation of the church applies only to those who believe in an organized church. Hence, the separation of church and state politically rigs the system against Christians, at least in a certain kind of society.

AMERICANS AS RELIGIOUS AS EVER

There is no doubt about it: Americans today remain as religious as ever. I don't mean they identify as Methodists, Mormons, or Muslims. I mean they worship *something*. And that worship shows up in their politics.

Mary Eberstadt, in her book *It's Dangerous to Believe*, said that "a new body of belief" and "orthodoxy" has replaced the Judeo-Christianity of yesteryear. "Its fundamental faith is that of the sexual revolution," she said. The starting point of this new secular faith is that "freedom may be defined as self-will." The second principle is that "pleasure is the greatest good." According to this new religion, the sexual morality of biblical Christianity represents "unjust repression." Yesterday's sinners have become today's saints, she observed, and yesterday's sins have become today's "virtues" and "positive expressions of freedom."

The first commandment of this faith is that "no sexual act between consenting adults is wrong—possibly except in cases of adultery." Therefore "whatever contributes to consenting sexual acts is an absolute good, and that anything interfering, or threatening to interfere, with them is ipso facto wrong." She also asked the reader to observe the absolutist character of this new religion. Contraception and abortion are treated as "sacrosanct and nonnegotiable." It won't even draw the line at the horrifying procedure of partial-birth abortion. Instead, she said, "abortion within this new faith has the status of religious ritual. It is sacrosanct. It is a communal rite."

It's not the heresies of the past like Pelagianism and Arianism that are a threat to Christianity, she observed. The single biggest religious challenger to Christianity in the contemporary West is "sex." In a chapter entitled "Anatomy of a Secularist Witch Hunt," she explained:

> After all, Christians and other dissidents aren't threatened with job loss because of writing in self-published books [as the Atlanta fire chief was] about the biblical teaching against stealing, say. Military chaplains are not being removed from office and sidelined for quoting from the book of Ruth. No, every act committed in the name of this new intolerance has a single, common denominator, which is the protection of the . . . sexual revolution at all costs.

She then concluded the point: "Secularist progressivism today is less a political movement than a church." And the so-called culture war does not pit people with religious faith on one side and people of no faith on the other side. "It is instead a contest of *competing faiths*."[17]

The only qualification I would add to Eberstadt's remarks is this: the heartbeat of this faith is not finally sex, it is self. The Enlightenment philosophies of Locke and Jefferson began with the self. The American Experiment, wonderful in so many ways, particularly among a virtuous people, ultimately exalts the self. The sexual revolution may have been the inevitable outgrowth of the Enlightenment's exaltation of self all along. God gave us sex to give us the faintest whiff of what our union with him will be. Whenever humanity replaces God with itself, therefore, we often create houses of worship around that very gift. So it was among shrine prostitutes of the ancient world and among goddesses like Aphrodite. So it is today among a nation that worships its Hollywood heroines and Internet pornography.

CONCLUSION

Later in the book we'll return to most of the themes raised here and try to get more practical. My purpose for now is to help you see the landscape a little differently—to give you a slightly different map than the one many Americans use.

So let's return to where we began the chapter: governments serve their gods. It will be one god or another. Our politics and our worship are not as divided as we think. Both involve bowing. Both involve saying who is worthy to rule and to judge.

The citizens of the ancient world commonly regarded a king as either a god (as in Egypt) or a unique representative of a god (as in Babylon). Again and again God therefore tells his people not to put their trust in their own king or in foreign kings. And he tells foreign kings not to put their trust in their gods. Our trust always shows who our gods are.

Which is to say, our politics reveals our worship. It did then. It does now.

Our entire lives are fundamentally political because our entire lives are measured in relation to King Jesus and his claim on our whole person. This is true for Christians and non-Christians. We live in either submission or rebellion. The mechanisms of the state are merely one tool we use in this larger political contest.

The non-Christian nations do not trust God. Therefore, they rage against him and his Son. That is why the public square is a battleground of gods. It may be the case that this battlefield hosts multiple gods pitted against multiple gods. Yet the fundamental battle pits all the gods against the God. They rage against him.

Becoming a Christian, however, means we change our worship and our politics. We submit to King Jesus in all things. We acknowledge that he is praiseworthy and worthy to rule all things. Our politics and worship unite around him.

He creates a whole new politics for us, a political rebirth, a political new creation. We turn to this next.

HEART: NOT SELF-EXALTING, BUT BORN AGAIN AND JUSTIFIED

It was July 5. Work had not yet begun. I was quickly glancing at my regular Internet haunts to see what I had missed over the Independence Day holiday. Two posts caught my attention. Both authors were thinking about July 4 in light of America's many failures. I'll tell you about one now and save the other for the end of the chapter.

The first, published in the *New York Times*, was entitled, "The Making of a Non-Patriot." The author, an atheistic professor of philosophy at the prestigious Duke University, described how Americans should remove the rose-colored glasses and take a long, hard look at the nation's many historical sins: the herding and killing of Native Americans, the centuries of slavery, the Jim Crow "separate but equal" laws, the World War II Japanese internment camps, the denial of citizenship to the Chinese "coolies" who built the transcontinental railroad, the democracy-impeding elements of our Constitution such as the electoral college, and more. Such an honest look, the author thought, should kill our patriotism. His concluding sentence: "Once the process of disillusionment is completed, so is the making of the non-patriot."[1]

The problem, said the professor, is that we romanticize American history, particularly through our movies. Pick any historical sin from the list you want, and you can find a movie that rewrites and glamorizes the affair. The slaughter of Native Americans? Check out this fun cowboys-and-Indians flick starring John Wayne! Unequal representation in the US Senate? Never mind all that. Did you see Jimmy Stewart's courageous Senate filibuster in *Mr. Smith Goes to Washington*?

I admit I was annoyed by the article. Part of what annoyed me was the author's elitist tone. His subtext seemed to be, "If you believe in America, you're naïve at best, hypocritical and complicit in the nation's sin at worst. I, on the other hand, am progressive, honest, and thoughtful."

Yet the main impulse to annoyance was rooted in his criticism of something I love: America (and those movies). I know the facts he mentioned are true. Yet that does not require us to despise America, does it? It's never easy to hear criticisms of groups you love. My instinct was to downplay the significance of those facts and judge the messenger. If he was going to snub patriotic people like me, then in my heart I was going to snub him. "Well, Mr. Professor, you're just an insecure, self-loathing, America-hating academic. So there!"

Politics usually involves feeling defensive about the groups to which we belong, whether a family, nation, political party, economic class, ethnicity, team, gang, even workplace. Why? Because our groups give us a sense of identity. "I am American." "I am Chinese." "I am a Republican." "I am a police officer."

Some group memberships mean more to us than others. In

Anthony Doerr's novel *All the Light We Cannot See*, for instance, the narrator gave voice to the inhabitants of Saint-Malo, France, this way: "We are Malouins first . . . Bretons next. French if there's anything left over."[2] Their first loyalty was to their city (Saint-Malo), then their ethnicity (Breton), and last their nation (France).

We can equally imagine someone prioritizing his nation, his ethnicity, or something else entirely. However the loyalty list is prioritized, we all identify ourselves through the groups we occupy. They provide us with a sense of belonging, purpose, value. "Wait, you grew up in Oregon? So did I!"

Implicit in these group loyalties are political rivalries. Rivalries—individual and group—drive politics. Part of what made President Franklin Roosevelt so effective was his ability to employ the power of individual rivalry to his advantage. The president would assign a staff member to a job. Then he would quietly and separately assign a second staffer the same job. When the first staffer reported back, the president could question the first with information he had already received from the second. His staff quickly learned the game. They had to outdo one another to keep the president's favor.

Let me risk a little conjecture. My guess is that, despite this pitting of individuals against each other, those staffers still felt like a team whenever identifying as Democrats with their boss against his Republican challengers, or as Americans against Germans during World War II. Individual rivalries give way to group rivalries with a change of battlefields.

That's how it works for most of us. I might harass my younger brother at home, but if you pick on him at the playground I will treat you as picking on me. Politics is both an individual and a team sport, and we continually slide back and forth between one competition and the other.

This is how it works among the nations and their rulers, according to Psalm 2. Nations make war against one another incessantly.

We know that. But the psalmist observes that they "take counsel together" against the Lord and against his Anointed" (v. 2). Interesting. History's greatest political rivalry, it would seem, is between the nations of the earth and the Messiah.

Behind all the competition—among presidential staffers, brothers, the nations, and so forth—are the desires of the human heart. The nations rage because the hearts of humanity oppose the rule of the divine Father and Son: "Let us burst their bonds apart and cast away their cords from us," (v. 3) said the kings of the earth on behalf of their people.

James offered a similar indictment: "What causes quarrels and what causes fights among you? Is it not this, that your passions are at war within you? You desire and do not have, so you murder. You covet and cannot obtain, so you fight and quarrel" (James 4:1–2).

Individual and group rivalries are made of the same stuff. Our hearts want. They want to be exalted. They want to be worshipped. They want to rule. They want what they want. We employ our group identities for good God-designed reasons, yes. But we also employ them in the grand enterprise of self-exaltation and rule. And this enterprise is another name for politics in a fallen world.

The politics of creation began with hearts seeking the glory and fame of God. God created us in his image to reflect *him* through our dominion (Gen. 1:26–28).

The politics of the fall, however, began with hearts seeking their own fame and glory. Adam and Eve felt enticed when the serpent told them they could "be like God" (3:5). That didn't work out, of course, so Adam used a press conference to blame both God and Eve: "The woman whom you gave to be with me, she gave me fruit of the tree, and I ate" (v. 12). His son Cain would later repeat his father's exercise in self-worship and self-protection, yet now the means of self-exaltation became murder.

Notice then how worship and rule belong together. The one

who is most worthy of worship possesses the right to rule. That's God. Sin begins with a desire to be worshipped (to "be like God") and leads us to grab hold of the reins ("and I ate").

It's hardly surprising that so many people say they hate politics. Politics in the public square puts all those fallen hearts on display, like malformed mannequins in a department store. Newscasters jockey for ratings. Politicians play for elections. Press secretaries spin. We sit at our breakfast tables and complain about the folk in Washington. But what they do *out there* we all do *in here* at home: promoting ourselves and our agendas. The politicians and pundits just have bigger platforms. Adam's bite and Pharaoh's bloodshed are the same thing. Pharaoh simply swung a bigger hammer.

One of my friends and fellow church members, Kyle, encountered the self-promoting nature of politics while sitting in front of the eight-person Animal Control Commission for our Maryland county. Kyle's next-door neighbor claimed that his dog, Bo, barked too much during the daytime. The neighbor was a stay-at-home lawyer who resolved her life problems through litigation (she had sued both our town and county multiple times). Kyle, whose wife and children were home all day, denied the barking. But there he was in "dog court"—his term. Apparently, the chairman of the commission had let the power of dog court get to his head. He began, emotionally and in a high-pitch, "People think they can ignore us and get away with it. They can't!" A four-minute harangue followed. Kyle, who formerly worked in government intelligence and at the time advised a US senator, replied that he would not be "interrogated." The now red-faced chairman replied that that's exactly what he would do. A policeman on the commission, rolling his eyes, pulled the chairman into the hallway and explained—apparently—that, no, they were not allowed to interrogate people in dog court. The chairman returned to his chair and calmly asked for Kyle's side of the story.

Ah, politics in a fallen world.

In the last chapter, I offered a map of the political landscape by characterizing politics as a battleground of gods. That battleground exists in each of our hearts as well as in the public square at large, to say nothing of the rivalry among nations.

So let's turn to what motivates every individual actor on that landscape: the heart. We have to start with the heart if there is to be hope of true political change. It's the wellspring of life, says Proverbs (4:23). Jesus said something similar: It's not what goes into a person that counts. It's what comes from within, from the heart (Mark 7:18–23).

The trouble is that governments cannot change the heart, which is precisely why God has authorized them to use force. They might incentivize fallen hearts here and there, like Roosevelt playing his staffers' self-interest against one another for the greater good. But a government can no sooner change the nature of a heart than a zookeeper can change a leopard's spots (Jer. 13:23). It cannot make people want genuinely righteous things.

As Christians, however, we must start with the heart if we're to make our own new political beginning. What the Bible offers, you might say, is a new-creation or a new-heart politics.

If the goal of the last chapter was to consider what Adam and Eve's fall handed us politically, the goal of this chapter is to consider what Christ's redemption offers us politically. Think of this as our erasing the whiteboard and starting over, or hitting the political reset button.

SELF-RULE DEPENDS ON SELF-JUSTIFICATION

If the fallen heart's grand purpose is self-worship and rule, it strives continually to grab hold of this trophy through self-justification.

I'll explain. A justification is an argument. So self-justification is an argument for why you deserve to get what you want.

"But, Dad, she got to sit in front last time. It's my turn."
"Put me in the game, coach. I'm faster."
"They should promote me. I have the highest sales."
"He might have won in the electoral college, but I won the popular vote. We need to change the Constitution."

Notice what's happening in all these statements. A person is making an argument for him or her to be exalted. And he or she is trying *to justify* that desire. Self-justification is the throne on which self-rule and worship sit. They *sit on* or *rely on* that argument. Make sense?

Now here is one of the most crucial points of the chapter: all rivalry, all strife, all factions, all discrimination, all oppression, and all war in the history of human politics depend on this type of self-justifying argument.

"I'm wiser than you. Therefore, I deserve to rule over you."
"I'm wealthier than you. Therefore, I deserve to exploit you."
"I'm whiter than you. Therefore, I deserve to enslave you."

With each example, there is a self-justifying argument, and upon the throne of this argument sits rule, exploitation, or enslavement. Even a cartoonish supervillain like Lex Luthor has convinced himself by some self-justifying argument that he has a right to kill Superman and rule the world, whatever cockamamie argument that might be.

Let's back up in the timeline for a moment. When God created Adam and Eve, he justified them. He told them and all the universe that their existence was good and worthwhile because *he* had created them. They were valued and precious in his sight. "And God saw everything that he had made, and behold, it was very good" (Gen. 1:31). Adam and Eve's justification depended on him. He called them "good." It was his word, therefore, that gave them the right to rule: "And God said to them, 'Be fruitful and multiply and fill the earth and subdue it, and have dominion over the fish of the sea and over the birds of the heavens and over every living thing that moves on the earth'" (v. 28).

Then the fall happened. Adam and Eve cast off God's rule, and in so doing they also cast off his word of justification. They wanted to rule on their own terms, not his, and so they had to find a new argument. For the first time, they needed to justify themselves. Hence, Adam blamed God and Eve, as we have already seen. And Cain pointed to his sacrifice of fruits and vegetables. "Look at my works, God."

So the raging and plotting of Psalm 2 began.

All human history, at this point, became a quest for justification. Every morning every one of us began waking up and planning our days in order to affirm our existence. Every room we walk into we go looking for such an affirmation: "my life matters, my presence counts, I am good." The fallen self feels intrinsically compelled *to do* something—*to work*—for its own justification.

Laws of one kind or another are the things we employ to justify ourselves and our existence, like this: "I kept God's law. I'm good enough. He must accept me." Or this:

"I respected the *law of fairness*, Dad. Put me in the front seat."
"My speed will allow us to win according to the *rules of the game*. Put me in."
"My success in sales means I have met the *expectations for a promotion*. Promote me."
"The *rules of democracy*, properly speaking, mean that I should take office. I have the most votes, after all."

In other words, laws became the hooks on which we hang what the Bible refers to as our "works." This is what the biblical authors meant when they talked about trying to justify ourselves by our works. It's another way of saying we try to justify ourselves by the law.

When we're denied what we want, we rage. We feel rage when something flies in the face of our justifications, our arguments. The daughter sulks because she doesn't get the front seat. The player bad-mouths the coach. And so forth.

Yet it's not only individuals who spend their lives justifying themselves. It's teams, businesses, ethnicities, schools, churches, armies, and nations. It's all our groups. Every one of them feels compelled at the very core to fight for the right to exist, to make decisions, even to rule whatever battlefield they are placed on. The team that never wins will lose its fan base and eventually be sold. The business that cannot make enough sales will die. The nation that cannot convince its people that it deserves to exist—that something worthwhile unites them—will be conquered. Indeed, what is the history of civil rights in America? It's a decades-old argument that African Americans *matter*, that they deserve to be treated as equals relative to lighter-skinned European Americans. It is an argument for justification.

To be sure, the justifying arguments of some are righteous and just, particularly when they depend on the law of God. Such is the case with the civil rights movement. In its best forms, it insists that all people have been created in God's image and are therefore worthy of equal dignity and respect.

Too often, however, our self-justifying arguments serve the purposes of self-worship, which results in the belief that we can rule *over* others, that we can exploit them, that we can even dominate and destroy them. Hence, Cain killed Abel. Jacob swindled Esau. Pharaoh slaughtered the infants. David murdered Bathsheba's husband. Absalom overthrew David. Assyria conquered Israel. Herod and Pontius Pilate conspired against the Anointed One, nailed him to a cross, and so fulfilled the rage of the nations (Acts 4:25–28).

The takeaway is that self-rule depends on self-justification. Self-justification is the "deserve" in the statement, "I deserve to rule." And self-justification leads to oppression, discrimination, violence, and rage.

So what can we do to walk away from self-justification and toward a new-creation or new-heart kind of politics? Jesus' Beatitudes provide the answer.

Step 1: Accept Our Condemnation

Whether or not Israel aimed to justify itself by keeping God's law, it couldn't do it. The law only condemned the nation and its citizens. Likewise, God's law condemns all of us.

This brings us to the first step toward a new-heart politics: we must accept our condemnation before God's law.

Perhaps you have been in an argument with a spouse, colleague, or member of another political party. Then, seemingly out of nowhere, the person admits he or she is wrong. When this happens, it can feel like the tension in the room evaporates. The bomb is defused. Your heart even warms to the person. His or her confession, ironically, creates a sense of unity, even if only temporarily.

The first step toward a new-heart politics begins when the self-justifying arguments end, when we say from the heart, "Yes, I am wrong." It begins when we acknowledge our sin and that we have forfeited the right to rule, because we have not proven worthy. We acknowledge that the throne we are sitting on is a sham, cardboard throne. Our arguments are stupid. Our rage is foolish and misplaced. And so we vacate the throne. We give up the rule.

"Blessed are the poor in spirit," said Jesus in the Sermon on

Mount. That is, blessed are the ones who have stopped trying to promote themselves and their rule. Instead, they have reached the end of their arguments. They have closed their mouths. They have stopped defending and admitted that they are weak.

"Blessed also are those who mourn," Jesus continued with the next beatitude. They mourn their sin and culpability. They mourn the hurt they have caused others by trying to rule. They see the folly of their self-worship and the damage done by pretending to be the god of the universe.

Strange, isn't it? The existence of hell is one of the most difficult things in the Bible to believe. Yet the path to political peace, harmony, and wholeness begins with the acknowledgement that we deserve hell. Until we do, we will continue to assert our right to rule. And as you assert your right and I assert mine, we cannot help but clash. "Give me the steering wheel." "No, give me the steering wheel."

Step 2: Seek God's Forgiveness and Righteousness

The second step toward a new-heart politics is part and parcel of the first: when we accept our inadequacy before God's law, we then must seek God's forgiveness and the righteousness only God can give.

"Blessed are the meek" (Matt. 5:5). It is only when our self-justifying arguments come to an end and we rely instead on God's justification that we climb off God's throne and rightly ask him to rule. "Oh, God, my rule has made a mess of things. I deserve punishment. Will you please forgive me and be the king in my life?"

When we don't seek God's forgiveness and instead hold stubbornly to our own rule and justification through works, we continually try to prove ourselves by some earthly measurement: race ("I'm Aryan"), ethnicity ("I'm Hutu"), gender ("I'm male"), class ("I'm aristocracy"), nationality ("I'm Serbian"), wisdom ("I'm a Marxist" or "libertarian"), religion ("I have kept God's law"). And what sometimes comes out of this mind-set is the use of such measurements to oppress and make war. So it was with the Aryan Nazis over the Jews, the Hutus over the Tutsis, men over women, aristocrats over peasants, the Serbians over the Croatians, the Marxists over the royalists, and Pharisees over sinners.

However, when we recognize that we are justified by faith alone, we know we have no right to rule over others or to oppress them. We know we have gained acceptance purely as a gift of God's mercy. The political standing we have in God's throne room and the worth we possess before all creation is not of us. It's a gift.

Once we have humbled ourselves and asked God for forgiveness, God declares us to be "righteous." "Blessed are those who hunger and thirst for righteousness" (v. 6). This passage in Matthew may not refer specically to Paul's doctrine of imputation, but the larger theological reality is that, along with forgiveness, God gives Christ's own righteousness to those who hunger for it. It's like the mutual exchange of assets and debts that occurs when two people covenantally unite to each other in marriage. When my wife and I got married, for instance, she took ownership of my student loan debt. And I took ownership of her Honda Civic. This is what Martin Luther would have called a "great exchange." Indeed, it was! Of course, Luther was talking about the transfer of our sin to Christ, and Christ's righteousness to us. Or, in Paul's words, "For our sake he made him to be sin who knew no sin, so that in him we might become the righteousness of God" (2 Cor. 5:21).

Christ did not say "I do" to us and grant us all his righteousness in that great exchange because of anything we have done. He did it, again, as a gift. Which means we have nothing to boast about. We no longer lord it over others. We no longer say, "I'm wiser" or "I'm whiter" or "I'm wealthier." We only say, "I'm a beggar who has been given bread!"

The most politically significant verse in the Bible for fallen humans just might be, "Then what becomes of our boasting?" (Rom. 3:27).

It's a rhetorical question. Boasting is another word for self-justification. Paul had been meditating on the fact that we cannot be justified by works, but only by faith. And being justified by faith means we are done making arguments, we are done boasting, and we are done putting ourselves above others.

Step 3: Show Mercy and Seek Peace

When a heart stops arguing for its own righteousness and right to rule but relies on God's righteousness instead, it takes another step: it shows mercy and seeks peace.

Listen to Jesus again: "Blessed are the merciful" and "blessed are the peacemakers" (Matt. 5:7, 9).

The self-righteous religious leaders of Jesus' day didn't show mercy or make peace. Instead, they condemned and lorded it over others. Think of Jesus' parable of the unforgiving servant (18:21–35). He described a servant who was forgiven millions of dollars by his master, but could not forgive the few hundred that someone owed him. So the master threw him into prison. Here was a man who did not understand that his life and liberty depended entirely on forgiveness.

I'm often struck by how unmerciful and pharisaical so much political talk in America today is. The rich scorn the poor, and the poor scorn them right back. The racist belittles the minority, and the minority and her defenders return the favor. Progressives bash conservatives, and conservatives do the same. One side calls the other side bigoted, who in turn accuses the first side of being blindly partisan, which is another way of saying bigoted. Do you see the impulse to rivalry and one-upmanship and boasting?

The president of one think tank in Washington, DC, observed,

"We don't have an anger problem in American politics. We have a contempt problem in American politics." Contempt he defined as the "utter conviction of the worthlessness of another human being." Sadly, he noticed, "if you listen to people talk to each other in political life today, they talk to each other with pure contempt."[3]

His solution? "Practice warm-heartedness."

It's not bad advice, so far as it goes—not too different from showing mercy and seeking peace. The trouble, of course, is that human hearts are what they are. The only true, long-term solution to our political contempt, rivalry, and rage is a born-again heart. You can't really get to step three without steps one and two.

A new-heart politics begins by laying down the weapons of war. It recognizes that it has received mercy, and so it extends mercy.

This is exactly what happened after twenty-one-year-old Dylann Roof shot and killed nine members of the Emanuel African Methodist Episcopal Church in Charleston, South Carolina. When Roof appeared in court, so did members of the church, and one by one they forgave him. In so doing they collectively laid down what would have been justifiable weapons of war and testified to their shared hope in a man who died for his enemies and overcame the rage of the nations.

INTERLUDE: A POLITICS OF NEW CREATION

Before turning to step four, I wonder if a sense of tension is building inside of you with steps one through three. Could Jesus actually be calling Christians to enter the public square confessing sin, declaring justification by faith alone, and showing mercy? If so, how do we stand up for justice, or prosecute injustice?

The tension, if that's what you're feeling, is the tension between a politics of the fall and a politics of new creation. Both create and shape a people. Both give order to their lives. Both require submission and obedience. Both seek justice. Both look toward a final judgment by the sword. Yet the first governs its citizens by the sword right now, while the second governs its citizens by the Word and Spirit right now. The first works by force, the second by changing hearts and natures. The first emphasizes principles of fairness, the second principles of mercy and grace. The first depends on the seen, the second on the unseen.

But make no mistake: We are not talking about politics versus religion. We are talking about two different politics based on two different religions. The politics of the fall is a necessary response to the religion of self-worship; the politics of new creation is nothing other than God worship.

This is why Jesus' Beatitudes are so striking, profound, and otherworldly. They are like an alien ship that lands on Earth. They bring the politics of new creation into a world governed by the politics of the fall.

Centuries before Jesus, God had promised a politics of new creation through the prophet Jeremiah. The backdrop to this prophecy was wayward Israel in exile:

> Behold, the days are coming, declares the LORD, when I will make
> a new covenant with the house of Israel and the house of Judah. . . .
> I will put my law within them, and I will write it on their hearts.
> And I will be their God, and they shall be my people. And no
> longer shall each one teach his neighbor and each his brother, say
> ing, "Know the LORD," for they shall all know me, from the least
> of them to the greatest, declares the LORD. For I will forgive their
> iniquity, and I will remember their sin no more. (31:31, 33–34)

Notice the ingredients of this new kind of politics. First, there is a righteous ruler, God, and there is a people: "I will be their God, and they shall be my people." So this new kind of politics isn't just an individual thing. It actually unites you and me to a new people, all of whom are united to this God. It creates new loyalties and a new sense of identity.

Second, there is a realignment of the people's desires with the rule of the ruler: "I will put my law within them, and I will write it on their hearts." The participants in this political society want what God wants because God makes it so. Through the prophet Ezekiel, God makes this same point like this: "I will give you a new heart, and a new spirit I will put within you. And I will remove the heart of stone from your flesh and give you a heart of flesh. And I will put my Spirit within you, and cause you to walk in my statutes and be careful to obey my rules" (36:26–28). This is why we must speak about a new-heart politics. God gives us a new heart by his Spirit, and we begin to obey.

A third ingredient: there is a lack of rivalries inside of this group, because all possess equal opportunity and political access to God's throne room: "And no longer shall each one teach his neighbor and each his brother, saying, 'Know the LORD,' for they shall all know me, from the least of them to the greatest." No political insiders and outsiders here. We're all insiders. We're all princes and princesses with access to the throne room whenever we want.

Fourth and finally is the foundation of mercy undergirding this redeemed political community. They don't belong to this society by birth or by merit, but by mercy: "For I will forgive their iniquity, and I will remember their sin no more." They have nothing to boast about in themselves.

Here we have all the ingredients for an ideal political community. They are the people of a righteous ruler whose desires align with his, who all have equal access and therefore have no rivalries, and whose group foundation is one of mercy. They have taken the three steps described earlier—accepting their condemnation, seeking God's forgiveness and righteousness, and showing mercy and seeking peace, and now together they show the world something totally different.

Of course, I am talking about the church, the people of Christ's kingdom.

INTERLUDE CONTINUED: A CHURCH

As Christians who are part of this ideal political community, some might think we would only take part in the politics of new creation, but, in fact, we must participate in both the politics of new creation and the politics of the fall. No, I am not saying there are "two kingdoms," as some writers have described it. There is one kingdom, and Christ rules over all. To speak separately of a politics of the fall and of new creation means we must live in light of the fall and in light of new creation—at the same time. We don't live in two kingdoms; we simultaneously live in two ages, the age of the fall and the age of new creation.[4]

God gave the sword of government to all creation because of the fall. Christians, like all humanity, must wield the sword as occasions require. Yet God also gave the Word of the gospel and his Spirit for the sake of a new creation. Christians must also preach the Word. Because of the fall, Christians must sometimes emphasize principles of fairness, retribution, and prevention. They must act as police officers, judges, and congressmen. For the sake of redemption, Christians must sometimes emphasize the principles of contrition, mercy, forgiveness. Different contexts call for different emphases, but the principles of fairness and redemption continually remain in motion for the saint.

Even so, here's the key, in some ways, to this entire book: *For a Christian, the political life must begin inside the church—in our new-creation life together as local congregations.*

Heart: Not Self-Exalting, but Born Again and Justified

The local church is where we practice the beginning three steps to this new-creation or new-heart politics we've been discussing. In the Lord's Supper, prayers of confession, and songs of lament, we express our poverty of spirit, mourning for sin, and hunger for righteousness. Through the preaching we hear the King's commands and learn what true righteousness and justice looks like. In our fellowship, we practice living it out. A gospel culture develops as we make ourselves vulnerable and transparent, trusting the righteousness of another. The local church is where we structure and organize our lives as a model for all humanity. It's where the rage stops and we acknowledge King Jesus' good and rightful claim on our lives.

Simultaneously, as we've mentioned before, our membership in this new political society changes our relationship with every other group we belong to. Our new heart politics doesn't remain quarantined inside our churches. As non-Christians, we use our group identities ("I'm American," "I'm Republican," "I'm a businessman," "I'm Asian American") to fortify our personal identities in the grand project of self-justification. When God justifies us and gives us a new heart, we don't stop belonging to our different groups—I'm still an American, for instance—but we no longer *need* them to feel justified. I don't need them to make me feel worthy, or good, or better than other people. What's more, I no longer need to bend over backward to keep the rules of the group and prove to everyone in the group, "I really am one of you guys!" And that changes how I relate to my groups.

Keeping the rules of the group is crucial where I live—in Washington. If you're a Democrat, be sure not to talk *too* much about your opposition to abortion. If you're a Republican, don't say *too* much about your concern with mass incarceration. Speaking either way might cause party insiders to question your credentials.

Of course, it's not just Washington. Families do this. Ethnicities do this. Sports teams do this. Video gamers do this. Environmentalists do this. Armies and law-enforcement officers do this. And what's behind it all is self-justification.

Joining the new-covenant community means we can be done using our various groups in the grand project of self-justification. We no longer need to prove we're insiders to anyone, least of all to ourselves. It allows us to hold all those memberships with a loose grip. We can use them for good where we can, but let them go where we cannot. We are no longer slaves to any of our groups.

Remarkably, the doctrine of justification by faith alone is history's grand source of political unity. It robs political actors of the incentives to warfare and domination by giving them what all people, nations, and armies seek: justification, standing, the affirmation of existence. The Holy Spirit then gives born-again hearts that desire for true righteousness and justice. And it creates a peaceful, life-giving, and just political community.

The rest of Matthew 5 describes this harmonious political community as filled with people who do not hate, discriminate, or murder, but seek reconciliation (5:21–25). They do not exploit or use others (vv. 27–30). They honor God's common covenant ordinances (vv. 31–32). They speak truthfully on all occasions (vv. 33–37). They employ their property to protect and equip others (vv. 38–42). They even love their enemies—"so that you may be sons of your Father who is in heaven" (vv. 44–45).

Mark Zuckerberg, founder and CEO of Facebook, wants to turn the world into just such a peaceful, life-giving, and just political community. He even called Facebook a church! Two billion people belong to Facebook, but only 100 million, he said, belong to "meaningful communities." That's not enough, said Zuckerberg. We should aspire for more, for better. "This is our challenge," he said: "we have to build a world where every single person has a sense of purpose and community. That's how we're gonna bring the world closer together. We need to build a world where we care just as much about anyone—a person in India or China or Mexico or Nigeria—just as much as we care about a person here." He's confident that, with the right "product roadmap," he can do this. "I know we can do this. We can reverse this decline."[5]

The ambition is admirable, if foolhardy and proud. Can Zuckerberg recreate the human heart? Can he grant an alien righteousness, justifying people so that they no longer have anything to prove and go to war no more?

That is what's necessary for a just political community. What Zuckerberg needs is not a product line, but a church.

Step 4: Expect Persecution and Praise

A politics of new creation, as I said, must not remain contained entirely inside of the local church, like a jar with a lid screwed on tightly. The lid must be removed and the contents spilled out.

A fellow elder of mine, before he came to our church, worked as the commanding officer of a military base. If you will permit me to be vague, I'll simply say that one of the soldiers on his base made a huge mistake, one which cost people's lives. The media covered the affair. My friend, the commanding officer, accepted all responsibility: "It was our fault." The media, in response, was amazed. Nobody takes public responsibility! Well, my fellow elder did. Promotions eventually followed. And rightly so.

Or remember my fellow church member Kyle who went to dog court? He stood up for himself in court, as he should have. He defended himself according to the principles of fairness through the institution of government as God provided it for the sake of the fall. But after the fact Kyle and his wife invited their litigious neighbor to dinner. They looked after her daughter. They worked even harder at keeping their dog quiet. And little by little they "won" the woman's friendship. None of this would have happened if my friend had been a proud man unaware of his own sin. He worked within the confines of the politics of the fall, or dog court, but then went beyond that and exercised the politics of new creation by offering peace and mercy.

Others' responses to the church's politics, mind you, will not always end up like this. More often it will be complicated and confusing: sometimes the church will encounter rage, and occasionally it will enjoy admiration.

The rage is not hard to understand. People spend a lifetime trying to make a case for themselves. Then comes the gospel, which says that all their arguments, all their hard work, all their justifications, are not good enough. Instead, Christ had to die for their sin, and they must surrender. Rage ensues because the logic of God's condemnation of them combined with his promised mercy contradicts their own logic of merit and self-justification. "Don't you see how hard I've worked?!"

When the world's response is one of admiration, it isn't hard to grasp either. God has given every person a conscience, and our consciences, like hardwired programming, recognize the rightness of contrition, humility, and mercy. Somehow, these things make sense to us, even in the hardness of our hearts. Somehow, we find ourselves rooting for the humble and opposing the proud in stories like *Beauty and the Beast*, where a proud man is cursed but eventually surrenders to meekness, mercy, and love. The rightness of these things seems to be programmed deeply in the hard drives of our hearts.

This brings us to the fourth step for our new-heart politics: expect persecution and sometimes praise. Jesus tells us to expect both opposition and admiration in his final beatitudes and in the words immediately following: "Blessed are those who are persecuted for righteousness' sake" and "Blessed are you when others revile you and persecute you and utter all kinds of evil against you falsely on my account" (Matt. 5:10–11). When our self-justifying arguments end, a new righteousness begins, and that righteousness the world too often hates. Moments later, however, Jesus described his people as the light to the world. People will see that light through our good works and "give glory to your Father who is in heaven" (v. 16).

The passage puts more emphasis on persecution, if measured by word count. Yet clearly the world's response to our new-creation, new-heart politics is divided. They will like it and they won't like it. And different times and places may lean more in one direction or the other. Ask Christians in fourteenth-century Mongolia, seventeenth-century Japan, or parts of the Middle East today. Christians are hunted down. Twenty-first-century America seems to be shifting toward disfavor, but even then it remains comparatively mixed. This mixture, in fact, is the challenge of Christianity and politics. It's why the public square can feel so hot and cold, so contentious and divided, today.

Sometimes the world hates us for doing right; sometimes they love it.

OUR POLITICAL CHALLENGE

The challenge for Christians is to approach politics always considering both the fall and redemption. The first means prosecuting injustice and standing up for truth. We call the slaughter of unborn children horrific. We argue same-sex marriage is a fiction. We point to the dehumanizing effects and evil of white supremacy. We advocate for the poor. We say the earth should not be trashed. We acknowledge that God gave government to humanity for the purposes of peace and flourishing. For love's sake, we get to work for these ends.

Yet, when approaching politics *only* in light of the fall, we go with only half the solution to unrighteousness and injustice, like a doctor who can tell you what not to do, but not what to do. Like ancient Israel, we forsake our own hearts and approach politics merely as an external matter, something to be treated only with laws and courts. We become like the unpatriotic philosophy professor who identifies and litigates the crimes of others and condemns them without offering something redemptive on the other end. We become like Inspector Javert in the musical version of *Les Miserables*: "I am the law, and the law is not mocked."[6]

Non-Christians respond by calling us self-righteous, hypocritical, and arrogant, just as Jesus characterized the Pharisees. And they are right. Like the children of a self-righteous pastor, our non-Christian neighbors know all too well that we are not as good as our moralistic sermons.

Might this be a fair indictment of so much Christian activity in the public square today? How easy it is to enter the public square neglecting the plank in our own eyes!

A better path does not forsake the politics of the fall. Yet it begins with the recognition that politics always starts in the heart. It possesses a fuller doctrine of humanity. It therefore enters into the public square with a fuller sense of the self's own sins: "I may not have murdered, but I have hated. I may not have committed adultery, but I have lusted." The better path prosecutes injustice and stands for truth, but it does so meekly, full of mercy and compassion. I cannot dictate how to strike the balance between standing up for God's righteousness in the public square while also adopting a posture of poverty of spirit in every situation you might face. It will depend on the circumstances. But that's the balance you and I have to strike.

Let's return to the book of James. Remember, it diagnosed the source of all our political rivalries: "You desire and do not have, so you murder. You covet and cannot obtain, so you fight and quarrel"

(James 4:2). Notice now where James went for the solution. He reminded us that "God opposes the proud but gives grace to the humble" (v. 6). Then he exhorted, "Submit yourselves therefore to God" (v. 7). It's a politics of new creation in action. He continued, "Be wretched and mourn and weep. Let your laughter be turned to mourning and your joy to gloom. Humble yourselves before the Lord, and he will exalt you" (vv. 9–10).

The outward political ramifications followed: "Do not speak evil against one another" (v. 11). He expressly told the wealthy, "Come now, you rich, weep and howl for the miseries that are coming upon you. Your riches have rotted and your garments are moth-eaten" (5:1–2). Weep why? "Behold, the wages of the laborers who mowed your fields, which you kept back by fraud, are crying out against you, and the cries of the harvesters have reached the ears of the Lord of hosts" (v. 4).

Here's one of the greater political ironies of life: People will commit themselves to fighting fervently according to the politics of the fall. The young idealist moves to Washington, DC, with the best of ambitions. He debates truth and fights injustice. He even makes great sacrifices for the cause. Yet along the way he becomes like the wealthy people James spoke to, giving into the desire to rule and losing sight of God's call to humility, peace-seeking, and service. Instead, he turns into a holier-than-thou, self-righteous Pharisee and therefore an illustration of injustice—the very thing he claims to fight against. Hence, the charge of hypocrisy follows. This is the story of ancient Israel, and it's the story today too often of Christians and non-Christians alike.

How does this happen? Remember, a new-creation or new-heart politics begins only when the self-justifying arguments end. And until they end, a man remains his own god. That means that he will eventually begin to measure and judge the whole universe by his own law, even if he began with God's.

CONCLUSION

As I said, I read two articles the morning of July 5, both trying to negotiate America's imperfections. The first, by a white professor of philosophy, indicted America for its injustices and condemned it.

The second was by an African American pastor. His experience of America's sins was a bit more personal. He meditated on what to tell his children about the Independence Day holiday. Their African American forefathers fought for independence from Great Britain, and he wanted his children to thank God for the freedoms and blessings America gives. At the same time, he could not overlook the fact that America asked these soldiers to fight for their freedom and then enslaved them when the fighting was done. And this mix of blessing and curse has characterized the African American experience ever since. It would characterize his children's experience.

This pastor, who lived and ministered in a neighborhood that was left behind by "white flight" in the 1960s, would not have his children idolize their nation. But neither would he have them scorn it. He did not intend to train up "unpatriots," like the comparatively privileged Duke University professor. Instead, he meant to direct their hope in a better direction—toward a kingdom that promises an inheritance that will never perish, spoil, or fade.

What's the point here? A few nations are truly awful. Most are mixed. And the heart of a citizen of heaven should reflect that fact. We thank God for the good. We acknowledge and work against the bad. We keep our hope fixed on a heavenly city throughout it all.

Those false religions who believe that this earth is all we have— communism, secular progressivism, evolutionary materialism, fascism—will justify coercion, even violence, in order to create what they believe will be a better world. But those like this pastor, who put their hope in the eternal, bring a completely different way of living. Contrary to what people might think, it's the most heavenly minded people who are free to do the most earthly good. They are free to pour themselves out, or give themselves away, because they are not trying to store up their treasure on earth.

Let me put it like this. Was there ever a time in your life when you *really* wanted something, but circumstances kept that thing just out of reach? Maybe it was being admitted to a certain college, or getting a particular job offer, or hearing someone you loved say yes. You felt like you *had* to have it, or you would be miserable. But then, an older, wiser Christian pulled you aside. He or she suggested that you needed to let it go and give it back to God. The thing you wanted might be a good thing. But the point, said your older Christian friend, is that God wanted your heart to want *him* more than you wanted that thing—be it a college, a job, or a spouse.

Are you with me? Have you had that conversation?

That's the conversation I want to have with you about America, or any group that you might love. Good governments and righteous civil societies are good things, just like marriages and jobs are good things. Still, at the risk of sounding clichéd, you have to let America go. Give it back to God. He might take it away. He might give it back. You will be okay either way if you have him. That doesn't mean you stop working for the nation's good. With or without the world's favor, we can practice true righteousness and justice and glory and joy now. With or without the world's favor, we can have assurance that—precisely at his chosen time—the kingdom of the world will become the kingdom of our Lord and he will reign forever and ever (Rev. 11:15).

BIBLE: NOT CASE LAW, BUT A CONSTITUTION

Zach worked as an elected political official during the years preceding the US Supreme Court's *Obergefell* ruling. The high court had not yet made up the nation's mind for us on same-sex marriage.

Zach is a friend and fellow church member. I was excited when he won office. Yet I didn't envy him when, a couple months into his first term, he encountered a same-sex marriage bill. Zach found himself swarmed by media, interest groups, and powerful political figures all pushing him to vote yes.

I remember sitting outside of our church building one afternoon on a metal park bench with Zach discussing the issue. A significant part of the conversation revolved around the question of how Christians should view the Bible in relation to people who don't believe the Bible.

Zach and I agreed the Bible teaches that God created marriage for one man and one woman. Yet we also agreed that America is a pluralistic nation filled with people from many different faiths who disagree on what the Bible is and what it teaches about marriage. And his job was to serve and represent all these people, regardless of their beliefs.

Do you see Zach's dilemma? As Christians, we know we must live our lives according to God's book, the Bible. This is something we do in all of life, not just in private. Yet we also know that we must not impose our faith on other people. Doing so is futile. People must be "born again" by God's Spirit. And imposing the Christian faith creates hypocrites at best and makes people despise Christianity at worst.

So how was Zach supposed to vote?

In the end, the legislators pushing the bill tabled it because they didn't have enough votes. Zach could keep his powder dry for another day. But the conversations got me thinking about the Bible and politics. How do we think about its political relevance for a nation filled with people who don't believe in the Bible?

THE BIBLE, POLITICS, AND THE CHURCH

Zach's story forces us to think not only about the outward challenge of how the Bible applies to outsiders or non-Christians, it also points to an inward challenge for the church: How do we maintain unity with one another inside the church when we disagree on what the Bible teaches on important political matters? Furthermore, what role do pastors play in addressing such matters from Scripture?

Zach and I agreed on what the Bible teaches about marriage, but we had to think through what that teaching means for public policy on marriage. The Bible does not explicitly say how to view same-sex marriage laws. Then again, you might disagree. You might think the Bible is very explicit. And that's just the thing: Christians often disagree on what the Bible does or does not "say" on different political issues.

Here's another example: Christians agree that the Bible condemns racism. But does it address what people today call "structural racism"? Some say yes, others no. (We will think more deeply about structural racism in chapter 8.) Churches then divide as some members feel like the pastors *must* address perceived instances of structural racism, while others insist, "There is no problem!"

Speaking of pastors, they play a crucial role here. Let's think for a moment about a pastor's biblical job description, whether a staff pastor who is paid for the work of pastoring or a nonstaff pastor (like me) whom the congregation has ordained but earns an income elsewhere. A pastor's job is to teach a church what to believe about the Bible. He lays out the path of biblical obedience, even binding consciences with it: "The Bible says you must walk this way, not that way." Which means, a pastor without a Bible is a man with no authority and no message. The Bible doesn't give him authority to bind the congregation's consciences on the best dental practices, the most effective accounting methods, or the advantages of drywall over plaster. He only has authority to unite the church around God's Word, not around his personal opinions.

Sometimes a pastor's teaching will be a condition of church membership, as with what he teaches on Christ's resurrection. Sometimes it leaves room for disagreement among members, as with one's view on spiritual gifts. "Christian freedom" is what we call those places where pastors and Christians might have biblically informed convictions, but where they agree they can disagree and still be members of the same church. In places of freedom, a good pastor takes care not to lean into the consciences of his members. He does not try to convince them that his own view of such-and-such is necessarily the biblical one. He leaves each person's conscience free or unpressured.

So think about all this in relation to political issues: Should a pastor endorse or denounce a political candidate? Should he share his position on various policy matters like immigration or health care? Tax policy or global warming? Same-sex marriage or abortion? My guess is, your instincts tell you the answer is, "It depends." If so, I'd say your instincts are right, though it's going to take me a little while to explain why.

In the scenario at the beginning of the chapter, politician Zach and pastor Jonathan had a conversation about the Bible and its possible implication for Zach's decision. That fact alone might have unnerved some readers. There is strong tradition in America, especially in my own Baptist tradition, that says pastors should never advise politicians.

Here's a story about another pastor from my church on Capitol Hill. K. Owen White pastored my church from 1945 to 1950. He left and eventually became the pastor of First Baptist Houston. When the 1960 presidential election rolled around, White and a number of other Protestant ministers began to worry that the Roman Catholic candidate John F. Kennedy might "take orders from the pope." Hoping to address the fear, candidate Kennedy attended a meeting of the Houston Ministers' Association on September 12, 1960. One of the sharpest interrogators in the room, said the *New York Times* report, was K. Owen White. Would the Roman Catholic Church shape his presidency? White and others wanted to know.

Kennedy attended the event precisely to answer this challenge, and he offered one of the more important speeches on the topic of church and state of his campaign. "I believe in an America where the separation of church and state is absolute," Kennedy said, "where no Catholic prelate should tell the President (should he be a Catholic) how to act and no Protestant minister would tell his parishioners for whom to vote." He wanted an America "where no public official either requests or accepts instruction on public policy from the

Pope, the National Council of Churches, or any other ecclesiastical source."[1]

After the speech, White said of Kennedy, "I have nothing against him. I think he's a fine man. But my questions remain about the policies of the church. There's no question in my mind that they [the Roman Catholic Church] require members to take certain positions on public matters."[2]

Both men made pretty strong statements. Kennedy didn't think any politician should accept or request counsel on public policy from a pastor, as if religious convictions could be entirely separated from public policy. And though White denied it, he basically agreed with Kennedy. A church must never tell one of its members how he or she must vote on a public matter.

My park bench conversation with Zach on same-sex marriage flew in the face of both Kennedy's and White's comments. I walked Zach through a biblical framework of what this issue entailed and was clear about policy implications. I assume this former pastor of my church would have agreed with me on the nature of marriage, but would he have disagreed with my counsel to Zach, I wonder.

In most instances, I would agree with White. A pastor should *not* offer policy or election advice. A member of my church once pulled me aside after a class I taught on Christians and government. She wanted to know how she should vote in the upcoming DC mayoral elections. She didn't want to vote for a pro-choice candidate, but all three candidates were pro-choice. And based on other issues she definitely favored one candidate over the others. My judgment in that moment was to leave her conscience free or unbound. So I offered her some criteria for thinking through the decision, but I did not tell her how to vote.

I suspect you're beginning to feel how jumbled and complicated this topic is. It's like a busy traffic intersection where a number of roads all collide and there are no traffic lights! The first question is how to interpret the Bible politically. The second is whether we should work to "impose" biblical teaching on non-Christians through our political activity. The third is how much room we should leave for Christians in a church to disagree. The fourth is the pastor's role in all this. And on and on the questions collide.

It's easy to err in at least one of two directions. Either we can assume that the Bible says *nothing* on matters of public policy. This is the side that Kennedy and maybe White claimed to represent. Or we can treat the Bible like a book of case law. We approach it looking to find the right answers on immigration policy, health-care policy, tax rates, and more.

You see this latter tendency among people across the political spectrum. Politically conservative pastors and theologians point to the Bible's teaching on stealing to argue for private property and flat tax rates. Politically liberal pastors and theologians point to the Bible's teaching on creation or caring for the poor to argue for environmental and welfare policies.

WHAT IS THE BIBLE?

Here's what I want to help you see: when it comes to thinking about politics, the Bible is less like a book of case law and more like a constitution. A constitution does not provide a country with the rules of daily life. It provides the rules for making the rules. It establishes who the rule makers are and what the purpose of rule is.

The first sentence of the US Constitution, for instance, reads,

We the People of the United States, in Order to form a more perfect Union, establish Justice, insure domestic Tranquility, provide for the common defense, promote the general Welfare, and secure the Blessings of Liberty to ourselves and our Posterity,

79

do ordain and establish this Constitution for the United States of America.

This long and elegant sentence explains the source of authority: we the people. It explains the purpose of the constitution: to form a union, establish justice, insure tranquility, provide defense, promote citizens' welfare, and secure freedom. And it declares the people's act of ordaining the constitution and therefore the government of the United States.

Then, as you read through the constitution, you won't find anything about speed limits, housing construction codes, or tax rates. Instead you find who will make those kinds of decisions and how. It says there will be three branches of government, a bicameral legislature, popular elections, judicial review, and more. Again, it establishes who the rule makers are and the rules for making rules.

When it comes to the work of civil governments, we might think of the Bible as similar to a constitution. Let's think about how theologians describe the Bible for a moment. Were you to join my church, you would have to affirm this statement about the Bible (slightly modernized here):

We believe that the Holy Bible was written by men who were divinely inspired. It is a perfect treasure of heavenly instruction. God is its author, salvation is its purpose, and truth without any mixture of error is its content. It reveals the principles by which God will judge us. Therefore, the Holy Bible is now and will be to the end of the world the true center of Christian union and the supreme standard for evaluating all human conduct, creeds, and opinions.

Think of this statement as a human preamble to sacred Scripture. I want us to draw two lessons from it.

First, the Bible is the book by which all our political activity will be judged. This is true for Christians and non-Christians. As my church's statement puts it, the Bible is the supreme standard for all human conduct, creeds, and opinions. It reveals the principles by which God will judge us. You might call it God's grand judicial review.

In other words, the Bible does not tell us what to do on trade policy, carbon dioxide emissions, and public education. But it does tell us that whatever we do in these domains will be measured by the principles of righteousness and justice explicitly established in the Bible.

In my conversations with Zach, it was God's promised judicial review that I highlighted most prominently. Sitting on that bench, I pulled out these verses and read them:

> Then the kings of the earth and the great ones and the generals and the rich and the powerful, and everyone, slave and free, hid themselves in the caves and among the rocks of the mountains, calling to the mountains and rocks, "Fall on us and hide us from the face of him who is seated on the throne, and from the wrath of the Lamb, for the great day of their wrath has come, and who can stand?" (Rev. 6:15–17)

Why will the kings and generals and every political class—slave and free—fear the coming of Christ's wrath? Because they did not use their political opportunities, whether high or low, to live and rule perfectly according to God's Word.

It doesn't matter if a majority of the American public, the justices of the Supreme Court, and the US Congress do not acknowledge God or God's Word. He is their God, and he will judge them by his standards, not theirs.

It doesn't matter whether people acknowledge the Bible as their book. The relevance of the Bible to politics depends entirely on the reality of God and the judgment of God. If either God or his judgment is not real, the Bible has no relevance whatsoever. But if God and his judgment are real, the Bible is eternally relevant.

Does that mean Christians should *impose* the whole Bible on fellow Christians and non-Christians alike? Well, we don't have the right to impose anything on anyone. But God does. The better question is, *what* commands does God impose on *which* people and *how* and *when*? Yes, he means to impose *some* things on everyone right now through governments. That's why he gives authority to governments in the first place. Other things he imposes right now on children through parents. And still other things he imposes right now only on members of churches. In short, God assigns different jurisdictions to different institutions. Our task, then, is to pay close attention to what jurisdictions God has established for governments, for parents, and for churches, and only recommend those commands that he has authorized for each. And he will ultimately judge everyone accordingly.

For instance, has God authorized governments to prosecute all forms of sexual sin? It's not clear to me that he has. He has authorized churches, however, to speak out against such sin and particularly to correct it among its members.

Yet marriage laws are different from laws that criminalize something. Marriage laws support, sponsor, and subsidize certain activities. So the question for Zach was this: has God authorized governments to support, sponsor, and subsidize homosexual activity? The easy answer is no. Zach's refusal to support same-sex marriage would not be about imposing a Christian sexual ethic on others. It was about refusing to let the world impose its sexual ethic on him, which it was doing by asking him to endorse something God has not authorized government to endorse. It was about refusing to put his hand to anything that will provoke the judgment of God at the end of history.

Now, let's return to my church's statement of faith and consider a second point: it says the Bible has salvation for its end and is the center of Christian union. It doesn't say that the Bible is a political strategy book, a legislative manual, or a book of case law. Instead it says its primary purpose is pointing people to redemption and what the redeemed life looks life, which is our Christian union. Our lives together within each of our churches should then illustrate or model how the nations should live. Our words and deeds in churches reveal the principles by which the nations will one day be judged. But that's not the same thing as saying that all these principles should be legislated right now. Again, church and state possess different jurisdictions in the here and now. Most of the Bible's emphasis, in other words, is on the people of God, not on principles for good government.

In fact, as we will see in the next chapter, even what the Bible says about good government it says in service to God's people, the purposes of salvation, and the goal of Christian union.

What the Bible does say about good government itself is fairly meager. It's not a long constitution, you might say, but a short one.

WE NEED TO DISTINGUISH BETWEEN LAW AND WISDOM

The two truths affirmed of Scripture by my church's statement of faith puts us in the position of needing both law and wisdom. On the one hand, the Bible is the supreme standard, and where it does speak in binding ways, both we and all humanity are bound. That's law. On the other hand, the Bible's purpose is not to build up an empire or a nation-state, though it provides principles for understanding human life in all its domains. That's why we need wisdom.

Distinguishing between law and wisdom is absolutely critical for knowing how to read the Bible politically.

Law is absolute and unchanging. I don't care what nation or century you live in, you shall not murder. You shall not steal. All people are made in God's image and are worthy of dignity and respect. And a government should reward the good and punish the bad. Think of these kinds of biblical laws as your constitutional basics. They should apply in all times and all places, whether you are the king over a kingdom or one of two hundred million voters. Christians will disagree over what counts as our laws or constitutional basics. Fine. But let's at least acknowledge that the category exists.

The domain of wisdom, however, does not refer to matters of complete moral indifference, such as, should I have Cheerios or cornflakes for breakfast? Rather, wisdom is both the *posture* of fearing the Lord, as well as the *skill* of living in God's created but fallen world in a way that yields justice, peace, and flourishing. In any given situation, wisdom beholds the flood of conflicting signals and competing voices. Then it arbitrates between right and wrong. It distinguishes between the worthy and the worthless. It chooses the better path when the better path is hidden by a thornbush. It discerns what people are made of and how they are going to act under certain circumstances. It recognizes the moral ideal and balances that with the politically realistic.

The relationship between law and wisdom can be likened to the relationship between the rules of a game and the strategy you employ to win a game. You have the rules of football; those are fixed. And then you have the coach and quarterback's calculations about how to beat this team on this day on that field. Do you use the running game or the passing game? That's wisdom.

Suppose then that a government wants to build a train track from city A to city B. But following the landscape one way will require them to go through mountainous terrain and put many lives at risk, while following the landscape in another way will require them to build a series of bridges through marshland and will come at exorbitant costs, which means higher taxes. What's the biblical solution? Well, I'm not sure we can say there is one. We can say there are biblical principles we bring to bear on the question, but the answer finally depends on a number of complex calculations involving a host of moral and practical variables. It requires wisdom.

WISDOM IS CRUCIAL FOR APPLYING THE BIBLE TO POLITICS

Most of the political questions citizens face day to day are biblically unscripted. Instead, they occur in wisdom's territory.

Sure enough, wisdom is absolutely crucial to politics in the Bible. Perhaps you know the story about God offering King Solomon anything he wanted: "Ask what I shall give you" (1 Kings 3:5). Solomon asked for "an understanding mind to govern your people, that I may discern between good and evil" (v. 9). He asked for wisdom.

Immediately the narrator turned to telling a story demonstrating that God gave Solomon wisdom—the story of the two prostitutes and the dead baby. Two prostitutes lived in the same house, both with newborns. One rolled over her baby in her sleep and killed it. Each woman then appeared before the king claiming the live baby was hers. Solomon weighed out the situation and then offered a solution: "Divide the living child in two, and give half to the one and half to the other" (v. 25). The real mother panicked, "No, give the child to her." The lying prostitute replied, "Very well, divide him." The exercise revealed each woman for what she was—the real mother or the fake. The king concluded, "Give the living child to the first woman, and by no means put him to death; she is his mother" (v. 27).

The narrator then summarized the story for us: "And all Israel heard of the judgment that the king had rendered, and they stood in awe of the king, because they perceived that the wisdom of God was in him to do justice" (v. 28).

This one verse, I dare say, gives us the Bible's political philosophy in a nutshell. Forget about reading history's greatest political philosophers, like Plato and Aristotle or John Locke and Thomas Hobbes. Read this one verse: the people "stood in awe of the king, because they perceived that the *wisdom of God* was in him *to do justice*" (emphasis added).

Kings, congressmen, ambassadors, generals, police officers, voters, city council members, public school teachers, judges, and juries need *wisdom*. They need the wisdom *of God*. They need the wisdom of God *to do justice*. This is a significant piece of our biblical constitution.

The Bible cares more about whether a government pursues justice by the wisdom of God than it cares about what form of government a nation possesses. Better a king who seeks justice with God's wisdom than a democracy that despises him and pursues folly and injustice. God can use anything.

Listen to the glorious figure of Wisdom in Proverbs 8: "Does not wisdom call? Does not understanding raise her voice?" the writer asked (v. 1). She did call out, and she addressed all people: "I raise my voice to all mankind" (v. 4 NIV). She was interested in Christians and non-Christians, Muslims and atheists, those who read the Bibles and those who didn't.

And what did Wisdom say? She said good government depends on her: "By me kings reign, and rulers decree what is just; by me princes rule, and nobles, all who govern justly" (vv. 15–16). Not only did Israel's kings need her. All who rule on earth do—the Virginia General Assembly, Moscow's city government, the Japanese Ministry of Health, Labour, and Welfare. The people who sit at desks and push pencils and make decisions in each of these agencies will promote the prosperity of everyone they serve by serving according to God's wisdom.

How can this be if these rulers don't acknowledge God? Because whether or not people acknowledge God, both they and this world belong to him. He created it according to his wisdom (see vv. 22–30), which means living by God's wisdom means living according to the warp and woof of the world. To go against his wisdom is to go against creation's design pattern. See how well that works.

Let me offer a few examples of how biblical principles should inform our calculations of wisdom.

Proverbs 10:4 NIV reads, "Lazy hands make for poverty, but diligent hands bring wealth." A wise ruler, no doubt, will look for ways to maximize industry and not reward laziness. Certainly this has implications for welfare policies. How easy it is for a nation's welfare policies to abet laziness and so exacerbate poverty.

However, Proverbs 29:7 reads, "A righteous man knows the rights of the poor." And 29:14 says, "If a king faithfully judges the poor, his throne will be established forever." A good king, like a good shepherd, doesn't leave some of the sheep behind. He seeks to bless and benefit all. He is going to judge them and their circumstances with fairness. He is going to consider the causes of poverty and ask what might contribute to entrenched cycles of poverty.

Wisdom, then, is figuring out how to put these last two points together, and that might change from circumstance to circumstance. Some welfare policies help, and some hurt. We don't want to promote policies that incentivize laziness, but we also want to consider various structural inequities that create cycles of poverty and do justice for those stuck inside of them.

PUTTING LAW AND WISDOM TOGETHER

Let's see if I can sum up everything I've said so far with a picture. First, we should read the Bible politically less like a book of case law and more like a constitution. It gives us a few basics that we need to hold with a firm grip for building our governments and pursuing principles of justice. That constitution looks like this:

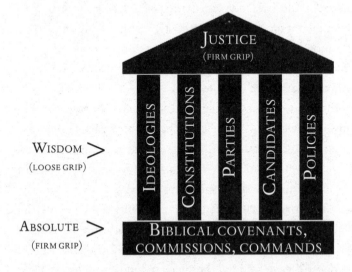

The Bible tells us to hold all its covenants, commissions, or commands with a firm grip. Most of those apply just to God's people. Some of them apply to the nations. And, of course, wisdom is needed to tell us which is which. The Bible also tells us to pursue justice with a firm grip. In between these two is where most of the activity of good government occurs: in the loose-gripped domain of wisdom. Choosing a good political philosophy and good constitution is not ordained of God. It depends on wisdom. In most situations, I would prefer a democracy. On an island of pirates, perhaps not. Choosing which party and candidate to support and which policies to pass also depends on wisdom.

Now stop and think: what happens in courtrooms? Lawyers and judges argue. And often they argue about whether a certain law is constitutional. The Constitution is the standard by which all laws are judged. If a law is shown to be unconstitutional, it gets thrown out. Good lawyers and judges have skill in demonstrating whether a law coheres with the Constitution. They are wise, you might say.

Likewise, Christians will disagree and sometimes argue about whether a certain candidate or policy is more or less "biblical" or at least wise. And what we all need is the wisdom to know whether something is clearly biblical, binding all Christians, or whether it belongs entirely to the domain of Christian freedom.

TRAINING LAWYERS ON STRAIGHT-LINE VERSUS JAGGED-LINE ISSUES

Okay, so it's class time. I want to train you to be a wise constitutional lawyer. If the Bible is our constitution, we need a lawyer's skill in recognizing which political matters are biblical or constitutional, and which are not. My favorite text to assign for lawyer training is Robert Benne's *Good and Bad Ways to Think About Politics and Religion*.

Specifically, Benne referred to two kinds of issues: straight-line issues and jagged-line issues. With the first, there is a straight line from core biblical principles to political policy applications. With the second, there is a complex and jagged line.

I would argue, for instance, that there is a direct path from biblical principle to political application with abortion. Abortion is murder, and the Bible commands governments to protect its citizens from murder. The path is that simple.

As an isolated issue, abortion is different than, say, health-care policy. This is more of a jagged-line issue. Christians might bring biblical convictions to bear in a conversation about health-care policy: we should care for the downtrodden, we should treat all people with dignity and respect, we should seek to remove entrenched cycles of injustice and the poverty that follows, we should ensure the insurers and medical practitioners are fair and honest and don't swindle patients, we should be skeptical of governmental involvement in health care that arguably hurts the quality of care, and so forth. But it's no easy task to add all these principles together in order to yield the biblical or Christian position. Hence, many Christians would admit that the path from biblical principle to political application is more jagged and unclear.

Broadly speaking, we can say that wisdom helps us determine whether an issue is a straight-line issue or a jagged-line issue. Obviously, it's not always clear which is which. That's part of the need for wisdom!

Now, even with a straight-line issue like abortion, questions of political strategy and implementation are significant. Just because we agree abortion is wrong doesn't determine which is the best legislative or judicial strategy in stopping abortion. One Christian might argue for one strategy and another for another. Even here, then, wisdom is needed. Also, not all issues fall neatly into the straight-line bucket or the jagged-line bucket. There's a spectrum between the two.

Yet here is why distinguishing between straight-line and jagged-line issues is important: churches and pastors should bind consciences on straight-line issues, while leaving jagged-line issues in the domain of Christian freedom.

The more something is a straight-line issue, the more the church will institutionally address it. Pastors will talk about it from the pulpit, and a church might exercise discipline over it. The more something is a jagged-line issue, the less pastors should lend their pastoral weight to addressing the matter, and Christians on both sides of an issue should be made to feel welcome. Abortion we address. Health-care policy we don't.

Or think about party membership. Since our church is in Washington, DC, the pastors or elders work especially hard to keep party membership on the jagged side of the spectrum. After all, we want both Republicans and Democrats to get saved. Plus, we don't think we have the biblical authority or competence to make the complex political calculations about the weight of various issues or the likelihood of certain political outcomes that would be necessary to say membership in *this* or *that* party is sin. Party membership remains an area of Christian freedom. But now suppose it's 1941 and our church is in Germany. I think a pastor would be well within his biblical authority to oppose in a sermon the Nazi Party since it called for complete and idolatrous allegiance to Hitler. And a church would be well within its biblical rights to excommunicate a Nazi Party member. Likewise, a church would be well within its rights to excommunicate a member of the Ku Klux Klan today. In both situations, the biblical issues are so transparent that a church is within its rights to bind consciences.

But let me again make a qualification about pastoral speech. Just because a pastor knows that something is biblically right or wrong on a straight-line issue doesn't mean he should propose policy solutions. That would be outside his expertise and authority and subject to the wisdom of those with more competence in those areas, whether Christian or not. My own pastor, for instance, is avidly pro-life. But he won't promote a pro-life march from the pulpit (even though he might participate in one). Standing in the pulpit, he does not want to communicate that Christians, as a matter of conscience, must adopt the political strategy of marches. They might be wise; they might not be. The Bible doesn't come close to saying, and his authority depends on the Bible. Now, you might disagree with his judgment on marches. That's fine. I simply want you to see that there are some political matters a church might address through the pulpit or the membership, and there are some that it should not. John F. Kennedy and K. Owen White, at least in the previous statements, sounded as if they were of the opinion that the church shouldn't address *anything*. I think that's too simple.

Most political issues are jagged-line issues. There are only a few topics that we can put on the straight end of the spectrum, specifically, those issues pertaining to life, family, and religious freedom. By "life" I don't just mean abortion or euthanasia, though those are two examples. I'm primarily talking about the basic call of government in Genesis 9 to preserve the lives of its citizens so that the Cains stop killing the Abels and to establish the basic equality and dignity of all people made in God's image.

The more unhealthy and rebellious a nation is, the more often we can expect opposition from non-Christians on the straight-line end of the spectrum. Meanwhile, on the jagged-line end of the spectrum, we can expect non-Christians to be quite competent, sometimes even more competent than Christians due to God's common grace.

WHY DISTINGUISH BETWEEN STRAIGHT- AND JAGGED-LINE ISSUES?

We need to distinguish between straight- and jagged-line issues for the sake of Christian unity and for the sake of our prophetic witness among outsiders.

Christians should unite around straight-line issues while leaving room for Christian freedom around jagged-line issues. Likewise, Christians should press against the culture on straight-line issues for the sake of justice and for loving our non-Christian friends and warning them of the coming judgment of God. Meanwhile, we might argue for our position on any given jagged-line issue, but we should be much slower to unite our position to the name of Christ, as if we're saying to the world, "This is *the* Christian view on this topic."

Again, abortion presents an easy illustration. I will gladly stand on a rooftop and shout, "Jesus hates abortion!" It's a straight-line issue that the Bible clearly speaks to. I will not, however, do that for my views on inheritance taxes.

I hope you see how crucial it is to maintain these two categories for unity in the church.

So much political dialogue among Christians these days thoughtlessly and divisively treats everything as a straight-line issue. Whether in private conversations among friends or public conversations in the blogosphere, how often do Christians talk as if their position on health care or tax policy or immigration or foreign policy is the only acceptable Christian position, and that all other positions are sin? Wow! Way to raise the stakes and effectively excommunicate everyone who disagrees with you. Way to make *your* political calculation the standard of God's own righteousness. When something is clear in the Bible, let's be explicit and clear. But when the Bible isn't explicit and clear, let's leave room for Christian freedom.

On jagged-line issues, yes, make arguments. Attempt to disciple, even persuade. Write articles and books. Questions of justice *might* be at stake. But remember you don't have the authority of an apostle. You don't write Scripture. Therefore, you should be very reluctant to bind the conscience where Scripture does not—to say, "This is *the* Christian position" or "A Christian *must* vote this way." If your church is ready to excommunicate someone for the wrong position, fine, go ahead and say it. But I hope you'll admit that's not the case for a lot of issues.

Christian liberty is crucial to church unity. When we speak beyond where Scripture authorizes us to go, we risk dividing the church where the Bible does not, and one day we will have to give an account to King Jesus for that. You've heard the saying, "In essentials unity, in nonessentials liberty, in all things charity." That's a good rule of thumb.

Also, uniting the name of Christ to our political cause in matters unaddressed by the Bible risks misrepresenting Jesus among non-Christians. It risks claiming that Jesus stands for something he doesn't stand for. It risks teaching false things about Jesus.

HOW THEN DO WE READ THE BIBLE POLITICALLY?

Let me offer a few comments on reading the Bible politically. It's so easy to misread.

How many times have you observed a zealous young Christian—wonderfully—try to think biblically about some political issue, say, immigration policy. So he digs back into the Old Testament and discovers God's words to Israel about showing compassion to foreigners by reminding them they were once also exiles and foreigners. "Ah," he concludes, "the Bible supports what I want to say about immigration policy." Does it?

Or suppose a Christian congresswoman reads Proverbs 22:7 in her quiet time—"the borrower is the slave of the lender"—and becomes convicted to advocate for laws that abolish all lending. Would that be a good use of Scripture?

How do we read the Bible politically? Here are a few quick principles.

1. Ask which covenantal audience the author has in mind.

All the Bible is relevant for the church and *all* humanity in one sense. But it's a little more complicated than that.

The Bible is structured by covenants, both common and special. And God gave each covenant to a specific group of people. He gave the common covenants to all humanity in common through Adam and Noah. That means Genesis 1 to 11 directly applies to all humanity. He then gave the special covenants to his special people, first through Abraham, Moses, and David, and then through Jesus.

What's crucial is asking which covenantal audience God had in mind in any given text. All the laws you encounter in Exodus to Deuteronomy, for instance, comprise the Mosaic covenant, which God gave to the people of Israel. It wasn't given to the Babylonians. It wasn't given to you and me.

Non-Christians sometimes accuse Christians of applying the Bible selectively because we don't keep all the obscure Levitical laws, say, concerning shellfish or clothes made out of mixed material. We're not being inconsistent at all. Those laws belong to the Mosaic covenant, not the new covenant.

What about the Ten Commandments? In fact, they don't apply *directly* to us, any more than the Chinese or Russian laws against murder or stealing apply to Americans. The Ten Commandments were explicitly given to the people of Israel. Now, it so happens that nine of the Ten Commandments are repeated in the New Testament (not the Sabbath), suggesting they directly apply to Christians (1 Cor. 10:11). And the commandments against murder, stealing, and lying directly impact a government's ability to fulfill its Genesis 9:5–6 responsibilities, which belong to all humanity.

A similar principle applies to the New Testament. Jesus said to "love your enemies" and "turn the other cheek." Does that mean the state should never go to war, or that policemen should never use force? No. Jesus' intended audience here was members of the new covenant in their relationships with one another.

The wisdom literature, such as Proverbs and Ecclesiastes, are closely related to the creation literature of Genesis 1 to 11, which were for all people. That's why non-Christians often find them directly applicable.

We always need to pay attention to which audience the Bible has in mind.

2. Ask what the author's intention is.

Go back to Proverbs 22:7: "the borrower is the slave of the lender." Was the author's intention to establish government-housing policy? I don't think so. His goal was to warn against the sense of enslavement someone in debt will feel, suggesting you might want to avoid it in many circumstances. At the same time, there are surely times when borrowing money is necessary. And a wise government might decide to get involved in various lending practices in order to protect the ones whose circumstances require them to take out loans. So, ask what the author is saying and not saying, and to whom he is saying it.

3. Consider what God has specifically authorized government to do.

In the next chapter, we'll think specifically about what God has authorized government to do. The answer, we'll find, is in Genesis 9:5–6, with a useful elaboration in Romans 13 and in historical episodes such as the stories of Joseph and Solomon.

Anytime we're considering a biblical principle and how it might relate to government, we want to ask the question, has God specifically authorized government to do *that*? He's clearly authorized government with the right to render judgment when lives are at stake. Can we build a case for universal health care from that basic principle? Some might say yes; some might say no. We don't need to answer that question right now, but that's where the conversation needs to happen.

An important part of thinking about the government's God-given authority and jurisdiction is recognizing the difference beween prescribing something or proscribing it, supporting it or criminalizing it. As I suggested above, the Bible may not authorize governments to criminalize every form of sin, but nor does it authorize Christians to support laws that positively prescribe or subsidize sin. Thinking through supporting something is fundamentally different from thinking through criminalizing something.

So a Christian might decide not to support the criminalization of gambling or various forms of sexual immorality, believing that God has not authorized us to do so. But such a position is qualitatively different from a decision to establish state lotteries or same-sex marriage. State lotteries positively support and encourage gambling. Same-sex marriage laws positively support and encourage sexual sin through tax breaks and so forth. Yet does God authorize us to support either? I don't think so.

Which sins has God authorized governments to criminalize? And what activities has he authorized it to support? To answer that we'll need to consider what God specifically commissions government to do.

And that's where we turn next.

GOVERNMENT: NOT A SAVIOR, BUT A PLATFORM BUILDER

There is temptation among some Christians to say that governments don't matter. Only salvation matters. I understand and agree with a part of this thinking. Eternity is longer than anything in this world. Much longer. And so it *weighs* more. Yet saying governments don't matter is (ironically) a shortsighted claim. It's like saying that feeding my children doesn't matter, only sharing the gospel with them does. Right. See how long that works.

Apart from feeding my children, I will never have the opportunity to share the gospel with them. And apart from good governments that establish peace, order, and flourishing through the work of doing justice, Christians won't have the opportunity to point people to the way of salvation.

Just ask many Christians in parts of Syria and Iraq today. Leave, convert, or be killed, the Islamic State said to them in city after city. Though the situation has improved dramatically, for several years it has appeared that "the end of Christianity in Iraq is within sight," historian Philip Jenkins once remarked. Christians were being murdered, raped, enslaved, and turned into refugees by a group that claims to possess state power.[1]

And this is hardly the first time in history when evil governments have threatened to wipe out all the Christians in a region. Islamic invaders nearly extinguished Christianity in North Africa in the seventh century. The Mongol conqueror Tamerlane did the same in central Asia in the fourteenth century. And the ruling shoguns of seventeenth-century Japan would have succeeded in the quest to destroy Christianity there were it not for a few thousand hidden Christians.

Christians like to quote the early church father Tertullian, who famously said that the blood of the martyrs is the seed of the church. Sometimes that's true. A few martyrs can hearten believers and ironically strengthen the church in a certain place. Yet sometimes it's not true. To use one of the previous examples, Tamerlane's armies killed around seventeen million people, or 5 percent of the earth's population at that time. Historian Samuel Hugh Moffett wrote in his book *A History of Christianity in Asia*, "Tamerlane swept the continent with the persecution to end all persecutions, the wholesale massacres that gave him the name of 'the exterminator' and gave Asian Christianity what appeared to be its final, fatal blow."[2]

Whatever troubles Christians might have in America today, praise God for the remarkable freedom and peace we do enjoy. I begin with these historical illustrations to make the simple point: good government matters. More than that, the Bible teaches churches *need* good governments in order for them to do their work. Indeed, this is why God gave authority to human beings to establish governments in the first place.

SERVANTS OR BEASTLY IMPOSTERS?

Fundamentally, God established governments to serve all people, but his own people especially. That may be hard to believe because so many oppose him and his people. Remember the title of this book?

Broadly speaking, two basic kinds of government show up in the Bible: those who knew they were *under* God and those who thought they *were* God or were equal to God. The first kind protected God's people. The second kind attacked them. The first knew they were servants (Rom. 13). The second didn't, and so acted like divine imposters and beasts (Ps. 2; Rev. 13, 17:1–6). The first were more likely to drive inside their God-assigned lanes, the second more likely to drive outside of them.

King Nebuchadnezzar offered an example of the first, at least after the Lord humbled him. This pagan king declared that God's "dominion is an everlasting dominion, and his kingdom endures from generation to generation." He then provided what might be one of my favorite lines about God in the Bible: "None can stay his hand or say to him, 'What have you done?'" (Dan. 4:34–35). It was whenever Nebuchadnezzar was humbled that he stopped questioning God and made a space for God's people, as he did with Shadrach, Meshach, and Abednego after God saved them from Nebuchadnezzar's fiery furnace.

The kings of Egypt and Assyria offered pictures of beastly imposters. They attacked and destroyed God's people. Pharaoh responded to his first encounter with Moses, "Who is the Lord, that I should obey his voice?" (Ex. 5:2). The Assyrian king's field commander, likewise, taunted the people of Israel, "Beware lest [your king] mislead you by saying, 'The Lord will deliver us.' Has any of the gods of the nations delivered his land out of the hand of the king of Assyria?" (Isa. 36:18). They saw themselves as equal to or greater than God, and so their rule was both against God's people and outside of God's guidelines for the scope of government.

No governments are all good or all bad. Even the worst help the traffic lights to work, and the best spend money they shouldn't. God, furthermore, employs both the best and the worst for his sovereign purposes. Think of the death of Christ at the hands of Pilate. Pilate served God in spite of himself (Acts 4:27–28). All governments are God's servants in that sense. Still, beastly governments ordinarily make the work of God's people much harder and sometimes impossible. Christians therefore should study what makes the difference and put their hands to building one kind rather than the other.

Just as we need to learn to read before we can read the Bible, so we need good governments providing peace and safety before the church can do its work. You cannot get to church if you're bludgeoned by bandits on the way. The terrible reigns of the Islamic State and Tamerlane prove the larger point in reverse. Governments really *can* impede the way of salvation. But morally speaking, God intends for governments to build platforms of justice, peace, order, and flourishing for all their citizens so that the people of God can get on with their work.

Think about the purpose of government like the purpose of guardrails on a mountain highway. The immediate purpose of those guardrails is to keep cars on the road. The larger purpose is to help cars get from city A to city B. Likewise, the immediate purpose of government is justice, peace, and order. Everyone should benefit. The larger purpose is to help the church's redemptive purposes. It builds a stage for the story of redemption.

Did you catch that? States play a preservative role in and of themselves, but they exist to serve the larger redemptive purposes of salvation.

THE AMERICAN VERSION OF WHERE GOVERNMENT AUTHORITY COMES FROM

The claim that government gets its authority from God sits uncomfortably with aspects of America's liberal democratic tradition. As we saw in chapter 2, the liberal democratic tradition says that governments derive their powers, in the Declaration of Independence's words, "from the consent of the governed."

Let me try to explain the general American view of government with a story. Once upon a time, you, I, and someone else—let's call him Todd—crawl onto a deserted island after our cruise ship sinks. For a while, the three of us keep to ourselves. We find our own food and generally mind our own business. Yet little by little we discover it makes more sense to work together, both in producing food and in protecting ourselves from the tigers that inhabit the island. At the same time, working together presents challenges. I always demand a larger share of the food. Todd slacks off in his work of watching out for tigers. You can get a little violent after coconuts fall on your head. And so forth. Therefore, the three of us decide to institute a system of rules that govern our life together. Those rules don't touch every area of our lives. I have my religion. You have your art. Todd has his sport. But they govern the parts of our lives that make surviving on this island together possible.

Got the picture? Here are a few lessons that America's founders, like Thomas Jefferson, James Madison, and others, extracted from this kind of story. First, there is a pre-political version of ourselves. That's the three of us while we are minding our own business.

Second, life becomes political when we decide together to form a government for regulating some of our actions.

Third, the regulated areas of our lives we refer to as public matters; the unregulated areas we refer to as private matters.

Fourth, the source of the government's moral authority to make decisions and bind each of us depends on our consent. There's not some other source of authority or moral obligation "out there" that gives the rules that we agree on. The authority and moral obligation of the rules comes from each of us. After all, we agree to do these things together.

Sometimes people refer to this whole process as the forming of a social contract. This does not mean a contract between the governors and the governed. It's a contract that forms the government. You, Todd, and I agree or contract to govern ourselves by these rules. That agreement or contract is the basis of our little government on the island.

Jefferson alluded to such a contract in the Declaration of Independence when he talked about dissolving "the political bands which have connected" a people, and then the right of the people to "institute Government" on principles that seem "most likely to effect their Safety and Happiness."

Now here's where the story gets a little tricky. Suppose you, Todd, and I are discussing our new government, and you guys ask me to record for posterity why we are doing what we are doing. So I write some letters and treatises about the nature of government, and in a few of those treatises I talk about "nature's God" and "the Creator" and "the Almighty" as standing behind everything we do. After all, I personally believe that God is the source of all government authority. The thing is, I know you and Todd don't believe that. And I know I cannot *make* you believe that. Therefore, when the three of us draft the actual constitution that will govern our lives, we agree to say nothing about God. The source of authority in our constitution, we say together, comes from us. So it begins with the words, "We the people do ordain and establish this Constitution." Meanwhile, we also decide that religions with a big-G God like mine are a "private" matter, and that our government should let such religions operate freely while also doing nothing to institutionally support one or another. Finally, we decide that, for the rest of our time together on this little island, all our lawmaking and legal disputes will be worked out in reference to this constitution.

This, in a nutshell, is how many Americans, Christian and not, view the government, its authority, and our obligation to obey it.

THE BIBLE'S VERSION OF WHERE GOVERNMENT AUTHORITY COMES FROM

The Bible offers a different picture, however. The Bible says a government's authority comes from God.

Historically speaking, you, Todd, and I might have crawled onto the shores of that island and decided to form a government. We might have agreed to work together on food production and tiger patrol. In other words, we can tell pretty much the same story as the previous one.

Still, the Bible would draw lessons different from the four provided by the liberal tradition. The Bible says that the authority of government comes from God. It says all three of us are morally obligated to obey that government because God says we must. Listen to Romans 13, particularly my italics:

> Let every person be subject to the governing authorities. For there is no authority *except from God*, and those that exist have been *instituted by God*. Therefore whoever resists the authorities resists *what God has appointed* . . . for he [the one in authority] is *God's servant* . . . he is the *servant of God*, an avenger who *carries out God's wrath*. (vv. 1, 2, 4)

The text is pretty clear. Government represents God. Governments are his servant, his minister. No governing institution exists outside of the larger institutional realities of God's law. Jesus said the same thing in John 19 in his conversation with Pilate: "You would have no authority over me at all unless it had been given you from above" (v. 11).

There is no pre-political you and I because you and I are always under God's rule. Any agreement you, Todd, and I hatch to form a government must abide by God's rules and God's purpose for government. Which means, the obligation the three of us possess to obey the government on Monday morning—even if we ourselves created that government on Sunday night—still depends on God's previous obligations. Our governments, after all, are simply a way of working out in time and space the rules that God has provided.

So let's rewind the tape and watch it again. Hit play. There's the three of us crawling out of the ocean after the cruise liner sank. There's each of us minding our own business, but then deciding to work together. There's us having difficulties working together. I am demanding an unfair portion of food. Todd is shirking tiger patrol. You're getting angry over falling coconuts. Now the three of us are talking about establishing some rules that govern our lives together.

Okay, hit pause on the tape. Think for a second. Who is to say that the amount of food I want is unfair? Suppose I manage to bring a gun onto the island, and I use it to hoard 80 percent of the food for myself and threaten to kill either of you for stealing from my pile. Who is to say that what I'm doing is wrong or unjust? If Todd wants to shirk his share of tiger patrol, who can tell him that he's wrong? And what's so bad about your temper tantrums over coconuts, even if you take it out on Todd and me? From an atheistic perspective, any arrangement the three of us make to form a government between us is entirely pragmatic. It's all a cost-benefit analysis: "Well, I'd like to hoard all the food, but that won't work out for me in the long term. Maybe I should compromise . . ."

From a Christian perspective, however, God says that my

hoarding 80 percent of the food is wrong. It's sin. And God says that Todd's shirking of tiger patrol and your temper tantrums are wrong. Not only that, God authorizes the three of us, as we'll see in a moment, to penalize such wrongful acts.

So hit play on the tape again. Now we see the three of us deciding to write up a social contract and establish a government. That's *how* the government is formed. It's a historical description of what we're watching on the videotape. But morally speaking, as Christians, we know that more is going on than what we can see. The authority of that government, and the moral obligation each of us has to obey it, comes from God, not from the contract. That's *why* a Christian cares about forming a government—to fulfill God's commands. Todd may think we're simply following a cost-benefit analysis about what's best. But as Christians we know the answer at the end of all the whys is God.

In short, we should obey governments *not* as a fulfillment of our contract that we have consented to. We obey government out of obedience to God. To resist it is to resist him.

Will non-Christians establish governments for other reasons and for other gods? Inevitably. I'm speaking to what Christians believe and why Christians must act.

Now, Christians should affirm the line between public and private. I will accept that lesson from the liberal tradition. And there might be some legitimate adjustments between one culture and another in terms of what the government regulates and what it doesn't. But let's be clear. The decisions about what's public and what's private do not depend entirely on the whims of the day. A culture might decide that child abuse is a private matter. But I'd say that that culture would be wrong and unjust to do so. The Bible places child abuse within the government's jurisdiction, as I'll explain in a moment, even if people disagree over what constitutes child abuse. So we must prosecute it and protect children.

Imagine Todd crawls onto the island with his son, and you and I discover that he beats that son. We would then possess a responsibility before God to protect the son. We cannot say, "Oh, that's a private matter."

Conversely, suppose Todd decides to say who we must or must not worship. Hopefully, you will agree with me that it is a private matter, and that he needs to keep his hands off who we worship.

In other words, the line between public and private is not ultimately determined by our consent or agreement.

THE THREE PURPOSES OF GOVERNMENT

What does determine the line between public and private? That is, what should governments regulate and what shouldn't they regulate?

As you can well imagine, I have been thinking through these questions while writing this chapter. In the midst of writing that last section, I took a break from writing and tweeted this remark: "Isn't it a contradiction to say that abortion is a 'private' matter, while paying for them is a 'public' one to be funded by taxpayers?"

What I had in mind was this pro-choice argument: "Abortion is a private matter for a woman and her doctor." I trust you've heard that before. The idea is that pro-lifers might have personal convictions about abortion, but they should not use the strong arm of government to interfere with what's a private decision. So back off!

My tweet meant to ask that if abortion is a private decision, how can you require me and my tax dollars to pay for other people's private decisions? That would seem to make it a public matter, because it involves me and my tax contributions. Hence, there's a contradiction.

A friend then privately messaged me a response. He made the observation that lots of private matters are publicly funded. Think of

Medicaid, the government program that provides health insurance for people who cannot afford their own. Medicaid doesn't require a man with cancer to treat the cancer—that decision is his to make—but it does pay for treatment if he chooses to partake in it.

Do you see the challenge in determining what's public and what's private? You might think government shouldn't be funding Medicaid, and I stand by my point on abortion. Yet my friend's point also stands: some matters blend public and private. And it's precisely here that we find the source of much political controversy: where should the government insert itself, and where should it keep its hands off?

To help us think about that, we need to think about the three purposes of government in the Bible. All three can be found in the opening chapters of Genesis. In chapter 1, God told Adam and Eve to be fruitful and multiply, fill the earth, subdue, and have dominion (v. 28). He made them kings and queens of creation in order to make creation flourish and thrive.

The trouble is, they rejected God's plan and got to work ruling for themselves in chapter 3. Cain graphically demonstrated what human self-rule inevitably produces in chapter 4: murder.

Therefore, for Noah and his family, God repeated the commission he gave to Adam and Eve in chapter 9: be fruitful and multiply and fill the earth. Yet he limited their dominion, as in, "Just because I made you king and queen doesn't mean you can kill people, like Cain did Abel." So God made provisions for human violence:

> And for your lifeblood *I will require* a <u>reckoning</u>: from every beast *I will require* it and from man. From his fellow man *I will require* a <u>reckoning</u> for the life of man.
>
> "Whoever sheds the blood of man,
> by man shall his blood be shed,

for God made man in his own image."

(Gen. 9:5–6, emphasis added)

I italicized "I will require" to catch your attention. Three times God said, "I will require." Government is not something human beings have created or contracted. God's the initiator of rule on this earth. He makes these requirements of us.

What does God require? I underlined the answer: a reckoning. This is how God authorizes human beings to use force against one another in the face of injustice, and the authorization provides the first step in understanding God's purpose for government.

Purpose 1: To Render Judgment for the Sake of Justice

The first and most immediate purpose of government is to render judgment for the sake of justice.

The reckoning here requires parity: life for life. It's not "life for stealing a horse" or "life because you hold different religious views." It's life for life. A principle of mathematical equivalency and fairness is built into God's authorization in Genesis 9:5–6. The implication is that lesser crimes should also be punished with matching penalties. Whatever the severity of the circumstances at play, at the end of the day it's about justice, and God requires it. It's this divine "requirement" to shed blood for blood that provides the government's authority with teeth. It can require you to pay your taxes or drive the speed limit or keep your employer from cheating you. It possesses the threat of force, and that threat is a morally legitimate one, says God. It gives a government the right to defend its citizens from foreign invaders, and it gives them the right to imprison people for life when they take life from others.

The life-for-life principle is perhaps most obviously illustrated in discussions about capital punishment. Now, we can argue about whether life imprisonment or capital punishment is a more just and better way of establishing a "reckoning," but here's a point we must not miss. The punishment given for a crime—whatever form it might take—is not merely about retribution or paying someone back. It's not just about deterring future crimes or rehabilitating the offender. Rather, punishment, most fundamentally, is about affirming the life and worth and value of the victim.

Look again at the last phrase of verse 6: "Whoever sheds the blood of man, by man shall his blood be shed, *for God made man in his own image*" (emphasis added). Taking the life of the killer demonstrates that the life of the person who has been killed really is worth that much. It's that valuable. After all, it was a life in God's own image.

Suppose I lose your diamond ring and say, "Goodness, I'm so sorry. Here's a stick of gum." My guess is that you would not feel justly compensated. You would feel justly compensated if I gave you something of equal value to the ring. Justice must acknowledge the value of your ring: it was valuable and precious and beautiful!

Ironically, the refusal to even consider the possibility of capital punishment, typically argued as a way of affirming a murderer's life, undermines the value of the victim's life. It says, "Sure, your murder was bad, but it can be weighed out against a few years in prison." The mathematical equivalency of blood for blood affirms the value of the shed blood. It yields a reckoning. It doesn't undo the crime, but it acknowledges fully for a watching universe the gravity of what's been done. It offers justice. And justice, the rest of the Bible teaches, is a beautiful thing. It protects the downtrodden, the oppressed, and the hurting.

Are there limits to a government's authority when it comes to rendering judgment? And what if the government uses force excessively and unjustly? Just ask the families of victims of police brutality how they feel about governmental force.

Yet here's another beautiful element of the call in Genesis 9:6 for mathematical equivalency: it creates a governing mechanism that is self-correcting. The verse creates a boomerang effect against any excessive force, no matter the source. If a dirty sheriff shoots a man for a minor altercation in the town saloon, the verse boomerangs back against him, even if he is the dusty cowboy town's lawman.

No person and no governing authority stands *above* Genesis 9:6. The dirty town sheriff, the power-hungry king, the genocidal dictator, nor the racist police officer should be permitted to use force unjustly. Rather, we should work to correct the injustice, even if perpetrated by the one in authority. God "requires" it, says verse 5.

In short, God grants authority to human beings to form governments for the sake of establishing a preliminary, this-world justice.

1 Kings 3:28: And all Israel heard of the judgment that the king had rendered, and they stood in awe of the king, because they perceived that the wisdom of God was in him to do justice.

Proverbs 20:8: A king who sits on the throne of judgment winnows all evil with his eyes.

Romans 13:3–4: For rulers are not a terror to good conduct, but to bad. Would you have no fear of the one who is in authority? Then do what is good, and you will receive his approval, for he is God's servant for your good. But if you do wrong, be afraid, for he does not bear the sword in vain. For he is the servant of God, an avenger who carries out God's wrath on the wrongdoer.

Governments should protect their citizens from threats from the outside and the inside. They should punish the Cains when they kill the Abels, or do what they can to protect the Abels in the first place. They should uphold the value of every single human life, young and old, aging and unborn, rich and poor, minority and majority.

Consider the Child Protective Services government agency. Insofar as CPS seeks to shelter children from violent and abusive parents, it is acting as God's servant and fulfilling its Genesis 9:5–6 mandate. Christians should praise God that we live in a country where the government takes an interest in protecting children from abusive parents. And therefore we should be vocal and known for supporting CPS. CPS workers should find that Christians are the most cooperative. Church pastors, likewise, should not treat reports of abuse against the children of members as an internal church affair, but recognize that abuse belongs to the state's jurisdiction and report those cases.

Purpose 2: To Build Platforms of Peace, Order, and Flourishing

Governments don't possess the authority to render judgment and establish justice for their own sake. The goal is to build a platform of peace, order, and even flourishing on which humans can live their lives.

Let's get into the textual weeds for a second. Think of the context of Genesis 9:5–6. God had punished the world through the flood and just brought Noah and his family off the ark in chapters 6 through 8 of Genesis. Verses 1 and 7 of chapter 9, then, like two pieces of bread on a sandwich, repeat the charge given to Adam and Eve: "Be fruitful and multiply," God said at the beginning and end of the paragraph.

Then notice how the meat of verses 5 and 6 fits inside the two pieces of bread given in verses 1 and 7. The authority that God gave to shed blood for blood (vv. 5–6) facilitates the larger enterprise of filling the earth and ruling over it (vv. 1 and 7). Governments establish peace, order, and some measure of flourishing so that people can fulfill God's greater dominion mandate.

Purpose one leads to and allows for purpose two. Justice leads to and allows for order and flourishing. So says Proverbs: "By justice a king builds up the land" (29:4; also, 16:12, 15). And we see commendable examples of governing authorities doing this in the Old Testament:

- Joseph as prime minister of Egypt helped the nation prepare for famine.
- Israel's law included provisions in its agricultural policy that cared for the poor.
- King Solomon pursued an astute export and import strategy that made Israel prosperous.

These leaders were concerned with more than punishing crimes and administering justice; they were looking to establish a foundation of provision from which the people could pursue God's greater calling. Sometimes people describe government as a necessary evil. But that's not right. Even in a perfect and unfallen world, someone has to decide whether cars are going to drive on the right or left side of the road. Order must be established for people to flourish.

A contemporary illustration of how governments bring peace and flourishing can be found in the work of the US Federal Aviation Administration. The FAA establishes regulations on everything from the installation of rivets on the body of the aircraft to the pilot's command of weather theory.

Is this governmental intrusion? Is this going beyond God's Genesis 9 authorization? You might try doing an Internet search on commercial airline crashes due to pilot error or technical malfunction over the past three decades. You will find dozens of major crashes from airlines of smaller, poorer nations. But you will only find one, maybe two, among US airlines in that time. In other words, the regulations of the FAA arguably save thousands of lives each year. And this is tied to the government's mandate to do justice. Apart from such regulations, it's likely that greedy interests would, from time to time, compromise various safety standards for the sake of financial gain.

In other words, governments exist to build a platform on which human beings can pursue God's dominion mandate. It's a platform of peace, order, and prosperity, albeit one that should always be tied to the more foundational call to produce justice.

Does this mean governments possess a responsibility to fund health care, education, programs like Social Security, or welfare programs for the poor? Two mornings ago I was walking from a breakfast diner to my church building. At East Capitol and 3rd Street, three blocks from the US Capitol building, I walked past a group of fifty or so marchers with picket signs. They were chanting, "Health care is a right. Health care is a right." Not a very creative chant, but welcome to an ordinary day in Washington, DC.

I'm not going to make a case for or against an entitlement like health care. But if you want to make sure that your position is biblically legitimate, this is how you need to do it: try to make an argument from Genesis 9:5–6 and related texts that God authorizes government to provide health care or education for its people on the grounds of justice, as well as peace, order, and flourishing.

For instance, my more progressively minded Christian readers might argue that universal health care affirms the humanity of the economic underclass, making premature death or crime less likely. They might argue that certain systemic injustices have produced generationally entrenched ethnic and class disparities, and that these injustices and disparities require a reckoning.

Meanwhile, my more conservative Christian readers might point to the notion of private property implicit in the dominion mandate and the command not to steal. Then they might argue that once a taxation rate reaches a certain point, it risks becoming state-sponsored stealing, not to mention the injustices undermining the biblical principle of a laborer being worth his wages and various emphases on personal responsibility.

Here is a good conversation. Let's have it! My point is, both perspectives should work to make their arguments *through* the grid of Genesis 9:1–7 and other biblical passages that elucidate its meaning. Either argue that such-and-such entitlement goes beyond God's authorization or is unjust, or argue that such-and-such entitlement falls within the authority given in Genesis 9 and fulfills the requirements of justice. (And when I say "argue," I don't mean in the public square to non-Christians. I mean in the in-house attempt to arrive at your own position, or to persuade other believers.)

It's right here in this argument between the conservative and liberal instincts regarding such-and-such entitlement that we are thrown back to the discussion of wisdom in chapter 4. Remember how the people marveled at the *wisdom* God gave Solomon to do *justice* (1 Kings 3:28)? We need *wisdom* to determine whether *justice* requires entitlement *x*. It's possible that, in some circumstances, justice would require an entitlement, while in other circumstances, it wouldn't. Wisdom might say, "Look at these statistics" or "Consider these trend lines and outcomes." An argument *for* justice *from* wisdom can make use of all sorts of "common grace" material.

Criteria like peace, order, and especially flourishing are somewhat subjective. How much order? How much flourishing? And how do we balance the principles of justice highlighted by the conservative versus the principles highlighted by the progressive? Answering such questions requires wisdom. There's seldom a black-and-white answer that applies across every situation.

For what it's worth, if you find yourself applying a formulaic, black-and-white answer to any and every situation, as in "public education is *always* unjust and wrong," you might be more driven by ideology (which turns wisdom into absolutes) than you realize. Call this a pastoral hunch. Ayn Rand's novel *Atlas Shrugged* demonstrated how ideological libertarianism can reach absurd conclusions when executed in absolutes; Chairman Mao's "Great Leap Forward" in China during the 1950s and '60s demonstrated the same thing for communism. We must avoid formulaic absolutes when it comes to matters of wisdom.

So, what belongs in a government's jurisdiction and what doesn't? What's legitimately public and what isn't? My concern isn't to tell you precisely which areas of life fall into which bucket. It's to help you know how to have the conversation and think through different topics for yourself. You need wisdom for the purpose of justice, and justice must yield peace, order, and the opportunity to flourish.

Here is one more illustration. My wife and I recently updated our kitchen. It was a pretty major job. Walls were torn down, an external door was removed, and a window was enlarged. The refrigerator and oven were moved, as were the water, electrical, and gas lines accompanying them. Our contractor asked us if we wanted to secure the necessary county permits for the job. Our county, like most, requires homeowners to take out permits for these kinds of jobs, which brings several county inspectors into your house both before and after the work. They make sure the work is done according to county code.

"What does it cost to get the permits," we asked our contractor.

"Just guessing, but probably around a thousand dollars," he replied.

"What?!"

My contractor went on and encouraged me *not* to get the permits. Yes, he is a principled man, but he made an argument against permits based on my property rights as a homeowner. He had done work on too many houses where inspectors came and required literally tens of thousands of dollars of unnecessary work.

I was honestly perplexed. Did the government have the right to require me to fork over almost a thousand dollars for updating *my* home?

I e-mailed a LISTSERV I belonged to made up of theologians and ethicists. What did they think?

One ethicist replied with the single phrase, "My precious brother, Romans 13:1–7."

Okay, that was slightly condescending. A friend on the list then texted me separately saying, "Ha ha, you just got Romans 13'd!" Yes, I did.

But I wanted to know, does the government have a legitimate biblical right to charge me this money? I discovered that many people, even Christian friends, simply don't take out permits. After all, the county never knows and nothing happens. I admit that this was a tempting route for me.

Still another brother sent this e-mail: "The purpose of building permits is to provide for the safety of the residents of the county. I could point to horror stories of people doing shoddy work on their houses and creating great danger to the residents of the house and neighbors. Permits offer a check and balance against subpar work from a contractor."

Now that made sense. I thought of the news reports I had heard of breaking-down apartment buildings or housing conditions in poorer neighborhoods where someone had cut corners to save a buck. Now people were injured or a bunch of children were sick due to something like lead exposure.

Building codes and construction permits, one could argue, find their basis in Genesis 9:5–6. Blood for blood, it says. Lives are precious, and governments must protect them. Therefore, my county government wants to make sure people don't take advantage and endanger one another, especially the poor. So, with a little reluctance in my heart, but thanking God for a government that seeks to protect its citizens, I paid for the permits.

Purpose 3: To Set the Stage for Redemption

Finally, we come to the ultimate purpose for government. A good government sets the stage for God's plan of redemption. It clears a way for the people of God to do their work of calling the nations to God.

Here we discover the relationship between God's common-grace gifts and requirements and his special-grace purposes. The special-grace work of the church depends on common-grace gifts and realities. People must learn to read before they can read the Bible. People must eat healthy food and breathe nontoxic air so that they can live, know God, and worship him. Children benefit by having loving parents so that they can better apprehend the love of God the Father. Do you see? God means for the stuff of ordinary, everyday life to serve the purposes of salvation and eternity.

So it is with government. God authorized human beings to form governments in Genesis 9. He then called Abraham in Genesis 12, inaugurating the Bible's great storyline of redemption. And Genesis 9 comes before Genesis 12 for a reason. The first builds a platform and sets the stage; the second begins God's saving work.

The work of government is a prerequisite to redemption.

The New Testament says the same thing. Luke observed:

And he made from one man every nation of mankind to live on all the face of the earth, having determined allotted periods and the boundaries of their dwelling place, that they should seek God, and perhaps feel their way toward him and find him. (Acts 17:26–27)

God has determined the allotted periods and boundaries of nations, and when those nations will rise and fall. Why? That there might be a platform for sustaining human life that people might seek him.

Why should Christians care about good government? Immediately, for the sake of justice. Ultimately, so that there's a platform for salvation. Listen to Paul's request for prayer:

> First of all, then, I urge that supplications, prayers, intercessions, and thanksgivings be made for all people, for kings and all who are in high positions, that we may lead a peaceful and quiet life, godly and dignified in every way. This is good, and it is pleasing in the sight of God our Savior, who desires all people to be saved and to come to the knowledge of the truth. (1 Tim. 2:1–4)

Notice the connection between the king, a peaceful life, and salvation. Paul said to pray for good governments, which provide for peaceful and quiet lives, which allows people to share the gospel and build churches. Christians should care about and pray for good government because they want people to be saved.

The governments of the Islamic State and Tamerlane, from a human standpoint, really did hinder the proclamation of the gospel and the work of salvation. The same is true in today's Muslim nations. It's becoming true in the so-called secular nations of Europe, where some in government want to classify belief in God as a mental illness, or criminalize proselytizing Muslims, or ban homeschooling because it allows for indoctrinating one's children with Christianity. And it's true in America wherever the government opposes religious freedom and the principles of Scripture.

Friend, pray and work for good government. Salvation, in one sense, depends on it.

THE LIMITS OF GOVERNMENT AND RELIGIOUS TOLERANCE

What shall we say about the limits of government? The answer is simple. Christians should seek to limit a government's authority to those places where God has given it. I've already observed that no governing officials can abuse their citizens because no one is above Genesis 9:5–6. That's one limit. Christians might debate whether governments are authorized to provide universal health care, I said. And my wife and I wondered whether God had authorized governments to require construction permits. All these are conversations about the limits of government authority.

My conversation with Zach about same-sex marriage mentioned in the last chapter was also about the limits of government authority. Nowhere does God give the government authority to change his own definition of marriage (Gen. 2:23–24; Matt. 19:4–6). Supreme Court Chief Justice John Roberts agreed: "The fundamental right to marry does not include a right to make a State change its definition of marriage," he said in his dissent to *Obergefell*.[3]

The topic of religious freedom or tolerance also roots in the limits of government. Religious tolerance was the more common phrase until James Madison. Madison felt that "religious freedom" was the stronger phrase, and so he worked to popularize it. However, no government is *free* of religion, as we discussed in chapter 2. Every constitution and law represents the victories or agreements of various gods.

However, Scripture requires us to tolerate one another's gods. The biblical argument for religious tolerance doesn't start with the conscience. It starts with the fact that neither Genesis 9 nor any other passage in Scripture authorizes human beings to prosecute crimes against God. It only authorizes us to prosecute crimes against our fellow human beings.

Listen to Genesis 9:5–6 again: "From his fellow man I will

require a reckoning *for the life of man*," says verse 5 (emphasis added). "Whoever sheds the blood of man," verse 6 repeats.

Notice these verses are explicitly, exclusively, even graphically ("blood") concerned with crimes against humans. That's the jurisdiction. What do these verses *not* authorize us to do? Punish crimes that are exclusively crimes against God. After all, how can a human government establish the extent of a crime committed exclusively against God, such as idolatry or blasphemy or a sin of the heart like pride? How can parity be measured, retribution assessed, recompense meted?[4]

Nor does any other place in Scripture authorize governments to punish false worship.[5] Do the commandments in Deuteronomy 13 to stone those who pursue other gods contradict this claim? Only if one believes the civic elements of the Mosaic covenant explicitly bind nations besides Israel. I don't believe they do.

The first plank in a Christian doctrine of religious tolerance, then, is this: *the state and its citizens must tolerate the worship of those gods whom one does not acknowledge, at least until those gods do harm to oneself or one's neighbor.* Humans do not possess the authority to do otherwise, much less the ability to ascertain the requisite parities of justice in matters related to God. Here we find the grounds for what the First Amendment of the US Constitution calls "free exercise."

There's no invoking of the conscience here, though the conscience is left free to worship as it pleases. The freed conscience is the fruit of this doctrine, not the grounds.

Yet notice there's a limit to toleration: demonstrable harm to a human being. When Christian Scientists refuse medical treatment for their children, therefore, I feel no moral obligation "to tolerate their religion." I believe the state should intervene and protect the children.

What about the growing practice of citing "emotional harm" as an argument against traditional moral principles? A New York judge ruled that the Giffords, a Christian couple who rented out their family farm for weddings, had to pay $3,000 for the "mental anguish" they caused for refusing to rent their property to a lesbian couple. Genesis 9 offers an objective standard for demonstrable harm: shed blood. I'm not saying that "blood" should be the sole standard of harm, but I do think Christian legal minds may need to spend more time figuring out how to make arguments for objective, not subjective, standards of harm.

The second plank in a doctrine of religious tolerance will make more sense after we discuss the doctrine of the church in the next chapter, but let me go ahead and state it now: *governments possess no authority to exercise the keys of the kingdom, and no ability to coerce true worship.*

Not only does Scripture support what the First Amendment calls free exercise, but I would also argue that it supports that phrase in the US Constitution, "Congress shall make no law respecting an establishment of religion." It doesn't say Congress shall not establish a religion. Every law, in a sense, "establishes" a religion. A law against murder, for instance, establishes an element of Christianity, as well as several other religions. But an establishment of a religion is something different. It's an independent institutional authority that declares what a religion believes and who its adherents are. It patrols its own borders and sets its own rules. Congress should not do this for either Christianity or any other religion. As we'll see in chapter 6, Jesus gave the keys of the kingdom to churches. It's the saints who possess the institutional authority to establish "an establishment" of Christianity.

WHAT IS THE BEST FORM OF GOVERNMENT?

If good government serves to promote justice, peace, order, and flourishing and ultimately sets the stage for God's redemption, is there a best form of government we should all be pursuing?

First, there is no abstract ideal form of government in the Bible.

Scripture doesn't approach the topic like a Greek philosopher, as in, "Give us democracy, not monarchy!" Rather, the Bible evaluates every historical government according to whether or not it accomplishes the task that God set for civil governments in Genesis 9:5–6. Is this particular government rendering judgment according to God's understanding of right, thereby preserving and honoring all people made in his image and providing a platform for the redemptive work of his special people?

The Bible also never says anything about *how* governments should be formed. Should we form a government by military conquest? By inheritance? By democratic agreement? Those are the three basic options afforded by history. Again, nowhere does the Bible say.

In fact, God employed several forms of government for his people through the course of the Old Testament: family structures among the Patriarchs, judges from Moses to Samuel, monarchy from Saul to the exile, and then, apparently, the formally independent *qahal* (assemblies) while in exile. No system was sacrosanct.

Now, I do think Winston Churchill was right when he said, "democracy is the worst form of Government except for all the other forms that have been tried." The various structures that Americans associate with liberal government (popular elections, a written constitution, a bicameral legislature, judicial review, the separation of executive and legislative branches, and federalism) have contributed great good to the state of many Americans.

Yet keep in mind that I'm drawing these Churchillian convictions out of the wisdom bucket, not out of the biblical law bucket. For a democracy to work, the right kind of political culture must be in place. There must be a strong tradition of respecting the rule of law. Citizens must prize honesty and eschew bribes. They must trust one another to keep their contracts. They must know how to negotiate, persuade, compromise, and lose votes, yet still submit to the system. Apart from these kinds of public and private virtues, democracy has a much harder time working. It finds itself out of context culturally. Consider, for instance, how well democracy has fared in the post-US-occupied Afghanistan or Iraq, or in the former Soviet republics of central Asia. Not very well. And by no means is it a foregone conclusion that America's political culture will continue to sustain our present democratic republic.

My point is not to say I would prefer a non-democratic government. I wouldn't. But I do want to make sure we as Christians are learning how to distinguish what's absolute (the Bible) and what's prudential (any particular form of government), in part so that we might discern what is best for any given moment.

Second, the best government in the Bible is any government that most wisely and fairly reckons injustices.

Often, the different things that make a democracy a democracy, such as a popular vote, judicial review, a written constitution, and the separation of powers, do fulfill the Genesis 9 mandate. They allow people to be treated as equals and impartially render judgment. These are not biblically sanctioned practices, but *prudent* practices that accomplish Genesis 9 purposes.

But it's not difficult to think of American government practices that did not provide the most reckonings for the sake of its citizens. One might think of the Jim Crow laws, the state and local laws enacted between 1876 and 1965 that mandated racial segregation in all public facilities in the former Confederacy states, giving African Americans a supposedly "separate but equal status" that led to all kinds of economic, educational, and social disadvantages. Jim Crow did not represent the impartial judgment of verses 5 and 6.

But it wasn't just the South or Jim Crow. The Federal Housing Administration, created by Congress in 1934, created a system of maps that rated neighborhoods according to their perceived stability. Neighborhoods the lacked "a single foreigner or Negro" received the highest rating and were eligible for FHA-backed loans. Neighborhoods with blacks were given the lowest rating and were ineligible. And this discrimination filtered through the entire mortgage industry.

Instances of excessive police force against African Americans raise precisely the same issues. Insofar as excessive force characterizes law enforcement, that law enforcement has become unjust. It has not only exceeded its mandate; it has also earned judgment against itself by virtue of the principle of reckoning established in Genesis 9:5–6. Now, I cannot personally sift through the details of various police shootings. I can say that Christians, animated by Genesis 9, should be some of the first to fight against the possibility of unequal treatment of its citizens by law enforcement agencies just as they work for the equal treatment of the unborn.

Let me sum up this second point by saying this about the ideal government in Scripture. It's one that renders judgment according to the criteria of Genesis 9:5–6. It employs the wisdom of God to do justice (1 Kings 3:28: see also 2 Sam 8:15; 1 Kings 10:9; Ps. 72:1–2; Prov. 29:4; Ezek. 45:9). It employs the sword to approve what is good and to punish that which is bad (Rom. 13:1–7). It acts as God's servant. It treats people as ends, not as means.

Third, every human bears some measure of responsibility to pursue the best government.

God's authorizing words in Genesis 9:5–6 apply to all of us. We are *all* responsible for fulfilling this basic requirement of justice, each for his or her part, whether through playing a role in government or through supporting the government.

Most humans in history have possessed a limited range of what they could do to work for good government. What would you say to Greek, Roman, Chinese, or American slaves about their responsibility to pursue good government? Yet insofar as you have *any* opportunity at all to work for good government—maybe you are the king's indentured cup holder, and you can whisper in his ear; maybe you are a democratic citizen in possession of a vote—you are obligated not as a matter of consent but as a matter of obedience to God to work for good government. It's one way you love your neighbor as yourself.

Let's think about our vote, for instance. Whom or what should we as Christians vote for? We should come in with a clear view of what the government has been authorized and ordered by God to do: to exercise judgment and establish justice; to build platforms of peace, order, and flourishing; to make sure people are free and not hindered from knowing God and being redeemed. And we should allow that framework to guide us to the candidates, parties, legislation, or ballot measures we vote for.

We don't want a government that thinks it can offer redemption, but a government that views its work as a prerequisite of redemption for all its citizens. It builds the streets so that you can drive to church, protects the womb so that you can live and hear the gospel, insists on fair-lending and housing practices so that you can own a home and offer hospitality to non-Christians, works for education so that you can read and teach your children the Bible, protects marriage and the family so that husbands and wives can model Christ's love for the church, polices the streets so that you are free to assemble as churches unmolested and to make an honest living so that you can give money to the work of God. Now, you might disagree with government involvement in any of these examples. But it's the grid we need to see and adopt: government renders judgment to establish peace, order, and prosperity *so that* the church might do what God calls it to do.

CONCLUSION

Don't put too much hope in government. But don't give up on it either. Churches need good governments.

A culture and its political institutions might turn against Christianity, but Christians should strive to make an impact as long as they have opportunity. It can get worse. Just ask the Christians in China or Iran.

Here's what I told my Sunday school class on Capitol Hill in the series I did on Christians and government:

> For those of you who work in government, let me embolden you with this charge. We *need* you to make America safe for Christianity. And I'm using the word "need" not to override divine sovereignty, but in the same way you might say a child *needs* her parents to protect and feed her. To those of you who work in politics, thank you for what you do. It might feel like an exercise in futility. But it is critical. Work and pray hard at it.

All of us, likewise, should do three more things.

Pray. Paul urged us to pray for kings and all in high positions so that we may lead peaceful and quiet lives. "This is good," he continued, and "pleasing in the sight of God our Savior, who desires all people to be saved" (1 Tim. 2:3–4). We pray for our government so that the saints might live peaceful lives and people will get saved.

Engage. We render to Caesar what is Caesar's by paying taxes, yes, but in a democratic context we also do this by voting, lobbying, lawyering, writing editorials, or running for office. Even in an empire, Paul, for the sake of the gospel, pulled the political levers he had. He invoked his citizenship and appealed to Caesar. Steward opportunities while you have them. You may not have them forever.

Trust. Jesus *will* win. That is our only source of strength for today and hope for tomorrow.

CHURCHES: NOT LOBBYING ORGANIZATIONS, BUT EMBASSIES OF HEAVEN

In the days immediately after Margaret Thatcher, when John Major was prime minister of the United Kingdom, I spent one semester of college doing an internship in the British House of Commons. One Sunday that semester I attended a conservative evangelical Anglican church in London. After the service an elderly lady asked me what I was doing in London. I said I was interning with a member of parliament. She asked who. I said the man's name. She replied, "Isn't he a Conservative? And you're a Christian?!" I don't recall if she actually said, "Oh dear!" but that was her tone.

Her response caught brand-new-to-Britain, twenty-year-old me by surprise. I had been trained in the United States to think that evangelical Christians lived on the political Right. We emphasized personal responsibility in salvation, morality, and, so, yes, economics. (The fact that minority Christians often leaned leftward had probably escaped my notice at that point.)

However, this woman's generation of British evangelicals believed that Christians should promote policies that cared for the poor, the hurting, and the working class. Therefore, they tended to be pro-welfare state, pro-nationalized health care, and pro-unions. The political Left and Right in Britain did not fall out on different sides of social issues like abortion as in the United States, so they supported the left-leaning Labour, Liberal, and Social Democrat parties.

That conversation blew up some of my political assumptions.

The relationship between evangelical Christians and political parties has become a little more complicated since the early 1990s, both in Britain and the United States. Younger Christians in both countries today find voices on the Left appealing. The divide between globalists and nationalists seems to run on a different plane than the traditional Left/Right divide, almost like a y-axis running across an x-axis. Many of my minority-ethnicity evangelical friends find themselves feeling politically homeless, but then so do some of my majority-ethnicity friends.

In the middle of this shuffling, what I want us to think about is this: who sets the agenda for how Christians think politically?

In many ways, the political parties set the agenda, and we simply follow. It's like a wedding reception where you receive a choice between the beef and the fish. You might want chicken, but that's not an option. Someone else has already determined the menu.

"Can I offer you the Republican meal or the Democrat meal?"

"Well, I'm not sure. Dad, which do I want?"

"We are Republicans, son. Republicans believe in taking responsibility for themselves. Those are our people."

"Okay, that makes sense. Can I have the Republican dish, please?"

Little by little we learn to identify ourselves by that party membership, as we do our nation. "I'm a Republican and an American."

We lock into a sense of party identity, and it becomes intertwined with our faith. It's like a vine that wraps its tendrils around a shrub so that you can no longer tell what's vine and what's shrub. As such, the other party begins to look downright unfaithful, probably immoral. Their moral calculations don't make sense.

One of my goals for this chapter is to encourage us all to stop letting our political parties set our political agenda. Even more, we should not conflate our parties with our faith. Parties are good servants, but bad masters; useful instruments, but awful identities. Instead, I'd encourage us—this is going to sound strange—to switch our primary political loyalties to our local churches. I don't mean the church should tell us how to vote. I mean it's where we will learn a true politics. It's there that we'll discover we want chicken when the only options before us are beef or fish.

A Christian politics always begins with Jesus. He's the King of kings and Lord of lords. And we know his will through his Word.

A Christian politics proceeds through the spoken evangelistic word: "The King is coming to judge all transgressors. Repent and believe, and he will graciously pardon."

A Christian politics then takes root in the individual heart, as we considered in chapter 3. Only a heart that's been remade by the Spirit of God will no longer seek to lord it over others, but will extend mercy even as it has received mercy.

Then, remarkably, a Christian politics should become visible in the life and fellowship of the local church—both in its teaching and in its fellowship. Whether you're a member of this party or that party, the local church is where we learn to love our enemies, forsake our tribalism, and beat our swords into ploughshares and spears into pruning hooks. Here is where we tutor one another in the righteousness and justice of God. Here is where the righteousness and justice of God become tangible, credible, and believable for the onlooking nations.

Every week that a preacher stands up to preach he makes a

political speech. He teaches the congregation "to observe all" that the King with all authority in heaven and on earth has commanded (Matt. 28:20). He strives to shape their lives in the way of the King's law. We then declare the King's judgments in the ordinances, embrace the King's purposes in our prayers, and echo the King's joy and mourning in our songs.

Think through a few areas of political policy. Start, say, with welfare policy. My own church emphasizes "welfare policy," though perhaps not quite with the same terms. Every member of my church promises in our church covenant to "walk together in brotherly love" and "exercise an affectionate care and watchfulness over each other" as well as to "contribute cheerfully and regularly to the support of the ministry" and "the relief of the poor." In addition to giving to the regular church budget, therefore, members give tens of thousands, if not hundreds of thousands, annually to the church benevolence fund. This is one way we care for our members in need. When member Jane found herself homeless, we tried to place her in safe housing. Due to various mental difficulties, she refused the help and chose to sleep in a park instead. So Luther went to the park with her and slept on a nearby bench. He was deeply concerned for her welfare, to say the least.

We also work on "tax policy." Carlos, who spends his working days explaining to US Congress the tax implications of new legislation, has spent many evening hours helping a family in crisis with their taxes. He has worked with the family's creditors and collection agencies because of their uncontrolled debt. Meanwhile, both he and his wife, Sue, tutor their children in various subjects, standardized test preparation, and college application essays.

My church also believes it's important to address America's race problem, or at least, our own race problem. When Patty confessed to me one Sunday morning at church that she struggled to like black people, I encouraged her to have dinner with Tom and Laura. "Tell them everything you just told me," I said. Tom is black.

Tom is godly and mature. And I knew exactly how Tom and his wife would respond. To my half-surprise, Patty did what I suggested. And exactly as I expected, Tom and his wife responded to her with grace, love, and an embrace. Patty repented, and learned to love her brother and sister in Christ.

We could walk through political topic after topic. How about the refugee crises? A pastor friend told me how his church members gave a car to an Iranian refugee who had become a Christian in Iran. They also housed him and discipled him. Now he is a US citizen and has joined the army. Members of my church in my neighborhood, too, have adopted refugee families from Afghanistan.

Here's the larger point: Christians should listen to what Republicans and Democrats have to say on welfare policy, tax policy, racial reconciliation, the refugee crisis, and growing suicide rates. But our thinking shouldn't start or stop there. Our thinking should be more expansive, more complicated, more personal, more humane. Our political instincts should develop by living *inside* the loving and difficult relationships that comprise a church. You might even say our political thinking should be *pastoral*.

Stare for a moment longer, and a little more intently, at several of the previous illustrations:

- Welfare isn't just a policy area; it's a sister in Christ who accepts help, but only on her terms. What are you going to do?
- Taxes aren't just a public matter; it's the financially strapped member of the body sitting at your kitchen table. How do you respond?
- Racism isn't just something we witness on the news; it lurks in our churches and in our hearts. Will you confess?
- Immigration isn't just a topic for politicians; it's someone trying to join your church. Will you open the door?

You get the point. I want our answers to be political and personal and pastoral. And I want us to act for the glory of Christ and by the wisdom of his Word.

That's politics!

May I offer a personal confession? I have had a difficult time knowing how to mentally process recent events in American life that have stoked the fires of racial controversy, whether it be the episodes of alleged police brutality, the election of Donald Trump, or larger conversations about the role of so-called structural injustices. Specifically, I find that my political instincts sometimes (not always) veer rightward, even while my personal affections veer strongly toward minority friends and fellow church members who are decidedly to the left of me. I love them. They are my brothers and sisters in Christ. They are close friends. I assume they have good reasons for thinking as they do, and I assume they can see things that I cannot see due to their experiences. So I find my mind divided, and I am utterly uncertain of the correct political solutions.

Yet I don't think that is a bad place to be. Life in a multiethnic church, in other words, is incubating me in humility, understanding, and a desire for justice. It's teaching me to walk and think more carefully, to speak more circumspectly. It's teaching me to love my enemy and look for the plank in my own eye. It's teaching me a better politics. By God's grace, I trust that I will continue to grow, maybe even catch up in my political thinking to brothers and sisters to the left and to the right of me.

Inside the local church is where a Christian politics becomes complicated, authentic, credible, not ideologically enslaved, real. It's in these real-life situations where you're forced to think about what righteousness truly is, what justice truly requires, what obligations you possess toward your fellow God-imagers, and what you yourself are made of. There's far more than beef and fish on the menu.

Keep in mind that the city where I live, Washington, is filled with

Christians who have moved here because they love politics and want to make a difference. Then add in all the Christian interest groups and lobbying organizations and prayer breakfasts, and you'll find no shortage of Christian political activity. I'm grateful for much of it.

But if you claim to care about politics and you are not an active member of a local church, I'm tempted to think you don't understand politics at all. You are like someone who claims to love cars because you play with Matchbox cars on the floor making "Vroom!" noises. How easy it is to make pronouncements on political policies from afar. Get up, climb inside a real car, and turn on the ignition. Join a church and figure out how to love the person who looks different from you, or who makes a lot more or less money than you, or who even sins against you.

Real politics begins not with your political opinions but with your everyday decisions, not with public advocacy but with personal affections, not all by your lonesome but with a people.

Christians learn politics, in particular, as we work for unity amid all the reasons we give one another *not* to be united. It's in this battle for unity that we should find the first inflections and glimmers of the just and righteous order, one that should make the nations envy.

Remember what I said in chapter 1: in our politics, the saints must first learn to *be* before we *do*.

A CHURCH IS POLITICAL

Let's take a step back now and consider, what is a local church? If it's where we learn, and live, and practice a true politics, then a church is inherently political. No, it's not a base for voter recruitment. It is not a lobbying organization or a branch of this or that party. It is not a place for partisan positions and campaign speeches. Rather, a church is political like an embassy is political.

The US embassy in Buenos Aires cannot command the police forces in Argentina. The US embassy in Beijing cannot give orders to the military of China. Yet both embassies represent the full power of the US government and military. An ambassador speaks for the president. Walk into an embassy building, and they will say you are standing on the soil of that nation. It represents one nation inside another nation.

The church, too, represents one nation inside another. Every member is a citizen and an ambassador of Christ's kingdom and holy nation. We didn't arrive on airplanes, like the US ambassador to Argentina showing up at the Buenos Aires airport. Rather, by the Holy Spirit's indwelling, it's as if we arrive in time machines. The end of history, by the power of the regenerating Spirit, touches down on planet Earth now. We represent heaven's rule as it will be fully revealed in the end times—*now*.

"Your kingdom come, your will be done, on earth as it is in heaven."

One reason people don't recognize the political nature of the church is because of the time delay between the church's promise of judgment and its fulfillment. But make no mistake: unlike the representatives of the NBA or ABC or Microsoft or your high school chess team, we formally represent a king and a judge, the one who rules all of history. We are political. We are emissaries of God's judgment from the future.

A CHURCH IS AND IS NOT A POLITICAL THREAT

Let me unpack what I mean by "political" a bit further.

Picture thousands, even tens of thousands, of time machines suddenly showing up all across the land. The nation gasps. News cameras crowd around them. Government officials and police forces quickly engage these strangers as they climb out of their time machines. It feels like a science-fiction movie about an alien invasion. Yet the people say they are from the future. They represent a coming kingdom, they explain. Interestingly, they speak English, dress like us, and otherwise seem pretty normal.

That said, they admit they want to change the way we live. It almost sounds like, well, what's the word—colonization? For instance, they want to persuade everyone to join them and give primary allegiance to their king. "But no need to worry," they contest. "We have no intentions of overthrowing the government. In fact, we will encourage people to obey the present government." What they mean, though, is that they want people to obey the government for the sake of *their* king. That sounds a little risky. They also explain that each time machine will hold its own weekly meeting, where they will teach everyone who joins to live according to their king's standards of justice and righteousness. As a result, yes, they expect some of their members will oppose some of our businesses and industries (though not by taking up arms). And they expect some of their members will work to change some of our laws (but mainly by working through the rules of the system). They conclude by telling us to think of their time-machine gatherings as embassies from the future that we are all hurtling toward, and that they are trying to give us a leg up on that future now.

Goodness gracious—what do we make of these strange people? Are they a political threat or not? Some of us feel like they aren't. After all, they promise not to take up arms against the government. Others of us feel like they clearly are. They want people to identify with their king and to change the way people live.

Perhaps this illustration sounds far-fetched. But it's exactly what first-century Palestine experienced when the Christians showed up. Two different passages in Acts are worth comparing. First, Acts 19 tells the story of Demetrius, a silversmith, who made silver shrines for the goddess Artemis. Demetrius joined the side that argued that these emissaries from the future, these citizens of Christ's end-time kingdom, were a political threat. He gathered his fellow craftsmen together and complained about Paul: "This Paul has persuaded and turned away a great many people, saying that gods made with hands are not gods." Paul's gospel work gave Demetrius religious concerns: "The temple of the great goddess Artemis may be counted as nothing . . . she whom all Asia and the world worship." Yet his deeper concerns were economic ones: "This trade of ours may come into disrepute" (vv. 26–27). At the conclusion of Demetrius's speech, a riot ensued.

Demetrius had a point. The life and activity of faithful Christians will disrupt false worship. And that disruption often unfolds economically and politically.[1]

Yet that's not the whole story. Christians have no interest in overthrowing the state or the marketplace. The Roman official Festus took up this side of the argument in Acts 25 and 26. The Jewish high priest Tertullus, like Demetrius, accused Paul of stirring up riots (24:5). Yet Festus surveyed the evidence and concluded, "I found that he had done nothing deserving death" (25:25; 26:31). By Rome's lights, Paul was not an insurrectionist who wanted to overthrow the government.

Putting these two episodes together requires a balance:

- Yes, Christians and churches are a threat to the stability of a Roman (or American) way of life; but no, they are not out to provoke civil strife.
- Yes, the presence of Christians in a society will prove to be bad for businesses based on wickedness and idolatry; but no, mobs of church members will not tear down temples, shops, and networks.

- Yes, churches will challenge the idols and false gods that prop up every government, whether the gods of the Roman Empire or the gods of the secular West; but no, they don't try to overthrow the state.[2]

Churches both are and are not a political threat to the civic order. Since no government is free of idols, churches preaching the gospel will always pose some threat. Yet it's not the threat of an invader or insurrectionist; it's the threat of a virus or termites—something that quietly works on the inside and chews away at the foundations, until an idol collapses along with the regime or economy sustained by that idol.

Insofar as churches threaten the gods on which the state relies, they should expect persecution. Persecution is rational. I intended for my science-fiction illustration to give you a sense of that. How would *you* respond if thousands of time machines suddenly showed up? With some trepidation, probably. When Christians say, "Jesus is Lord, and therefore we won't worship Artemis or buy things to support the Artemis industry," we put jobs in that industry at stake. The lobbyists hired by that industry will oppose us, followed by the congressman with Artemis factories in his districts. Have you noticed how corporate America, fearing the loss of market share, has rushed to support the LGBT agenda and threatened the jobs of those who stand in the way?

A CHURCH IS AN EMBASSY OF HEAVEN ON EARTH

So, yes, local churches are very political. Now let's expand on the idea of church as embassy a bit further. This may be the most theologically intense section of the chapter because it deals with church authority, but bear with me. If the state's authority is worth thinking about carefully, the church's is no less so. And it's critical to understanding the separation of church and state, as I mentioned earlier. One possesses the authority of the sword. The other possesses the authority of the keys.

What are the church's keys? Jesus first gave them to Peter and the apostles in Matthew 16. Peter had confessed Jesus as "the Christ, the Son of the living God" (v. 16). Jesus had affirmed Peter and his confession on behalf of heaven. Then he gave Peter the keys of the kingdom to do the same thing: affirm confessions and confessors on behalf of heaven. "I will give you the keys of the kingdom of heaven, and whatever you bind on earth shall be bound in heaven, and whatever you loose on earth shall be loosed in heaven" (v. 19).

Jesus then gave the keys of the kingdom to the local church in Matthew 18. He envisioned a case of church discipline where the church finally had to exclude someone from membership. Jesus concluded the point by authorizing a church to do the same as Peter:

> Truly, I say to you, whatever you bind on earth shall be bound in heaven, and whatever you loose on earth shall be loosed in heaven. Again I say to you, if two of you agree on earth about anything they ask, it will be done for them by my Father in heaven. For where two or three are gathered in my name, there am I among them. (vv. 18–20)

What does it mean to bind or loose? It's the authority to interpret and then to render judgment. It's like a judge who first interprets the law and then he declares his judgment with a pound of the gavel: "Guilty" or "Not guilty." People are then bound or loosed by a judge's decision.

Likewise, the keys of the kingdom give a local church the authority to declare before the nations, "This is/is not a true gospel confession" and, "This is/is not a true gospel confessor." Sometimes I refer to this as the *what* and the *who* of the gospel—confessions and confessors. Or you might say it's all about our statements of faith and church membership directories. Who gets to decide them?

Churches exercise the keys with the *what* of the gospel by their preaching and their statements of faith. Churches exercise the keys with the *who* of the gospel through the ordinances—baptism and communion. Either they receive someone *into* the ordinances, or they exclude a person *from* them.

Baptism is a believer's way of signing the bottom line and saying publicly, "Yes, I'm with Jesus." And it's a church's way of saying, "She's with Jesus." This is why we baptize someone *"into the name* of the Father, and of the Son, and of the Holy Spirit." We put the Jesus nametag on him. We identify him with Christ. It's like a press release to the nations.

The Lord's Supper, likewise, is not merely an individual activity where we close our eyes and enjoy a turbo-charged quiet time in the presence of other people. Rather, it's the family meal where the church demonstrates that it's a family. Listen to Paul: "Because there is one bread, we who are many are one body, for we all partake of the one bread" (1 Cor. 10:17). Partaking of the one bread reveals, shows, affirms that we are one body. It's a church-revealing meal. That's why he was adamant about "discerning the body" and that they "wait for one another" when receiving the Lord's Supper (11:29, 33).

Baptism and the Lord's Supper are the signs and seals of church membership. And church membership, formally speaking, is a church's affirmation and oversight of a Christian's profession of faith. It's a church taking responsibility for you and your discipleship, and it's you taking responsibility for that church.

Church discipline, then, is the flip side of the coin of church membership. What is church discipline? It does not send someone to hell. It's not a way of saying, "We know, in fact, that you're a non-Christian." No, we don't have Holy Spirit X-ray vision eyes. Rather, church discipline is a church's way of saying they are no longer willing to affirm someone's profession of faith and so are removing him or her from the Lord's Table.

The key to understanding the church's authority is in the word *agreement*. At its root, church authority depends on the agreement of two or more believers: "if two of you agree on earth" and "where two or three gather in my name" (Matt. 18:19, 20). If you agree only with yourself, you might be a Christian, but you're not a church.

Perhaps I can explain by going back to the desert-island analogy from chapter 5. Remember how you, Todd, and I ended up on that desert island after our cruise ship went down? We saw how we would form a government. Yet how would we form a church? At least two of us would have to *agree* on who Jesus is and that we each know him. We would then need to agree to regularly gather for declaring the gospel and affirming one another's faith through the Supper. That would make us a church and members of it. If we disagreed on who Jesus is, or if we disagreed on whether we were Christians, we couldn't be a church.

Let me put some flesh and blood on all this. My own church gathers every other month for members' meetings where we receive new members and say goodbye to members moving elsewhere. We also practice church discipline. In one of those members' meetings some time back, the congregation was faced with two separate cases of sexual sin. First, we considered the case of a single man who was sleeping with different women. His friends and the elders had been pursuing his repentance for months. But he had proven unrepentant. So the church decided to remove him from membership and the Lord's Table. We could no longer affirm or agree to his profession of faith.

That same evening we considered the case of a single woman who had become pregnant. Yet she was repentant. Therefore, an elder led the church to thank God for her humility, transparency, and repentance. He explained he was addressing the matter publicly because her pregnancy would soon become obvious, and he wanted to encourage the church to embrace her and rejoice with her over the child. In his words, "As a church what we want to do now is to rally around her, to love her and support her in any ways that we can. Christ's church is a family. We want to be a family that is open and loving and supportive, recognizing that we all are here only because of the grace and mercy of God. So please continue to love and encourage her as our sister. In particular, if you're a mom, she would love for a few of you to reach out to her to help her as she prepares for the good but difficult work that's ahead of her. She's here with us tonight and would love your continued prayers and encouragement." Unlike the young man, the congregation happily affirmed her profession.

We just covered a lot of church doctrine really quickly: the keys, the ordinances, church membership, church discipline, and the nature of the church's authority.[3] All of that was necessary for two reasons: for understanding what the institutional church is and for understanding the separation of church and state. People quickly affirm the separation of church and state, but they don't give much thought to what a church actually is.

Here's a one-sentence definition: a church is a group of Christians who identify themselves and each other as followers of Jesus through regularly gathering in his name, preaching the gospel, and celebrating the ordinances. All this they do by the authority of the keys.

And it's those keys that give a local church an embassy-like authority. At one point in college, I lived in Brussels, Belgium. My passport expired. So I went to the US embassy to replace my passport. The embassy didn't *make* me a citizen on that day. But they did possess an authority that I as an individual US citizen do not possess: the authority to formally recognize me before the nations as belonging to the United States and give me a new passport.

So it is with the local church. It doesn't make you or me Christian. It formally recognizes us as Christians through the church's act of agreement. It baptizes us into Christ's name so that we can gather in his name. And keep in mind, the "it" of the church is *us*.

The state, however, has no authority to recognize who the people of God are. It has no authority to say, "Here is right doctrine" or "false doctrine"; or to say, "Here is a true church" or "a false church." Its authority comes from Genesis 9 and subsequent passages. A church's authority comes from Matthew 16, 18, and 28. The state preserves our lives; the church works for our redemption. The state builds a stage; the church enacts a play and names the key players.

Thinking about the church's authority should help us to see that Christianity is not a religion for individual operators, every saint acting like the captain of his or her own ship in the broad seas of this world. It's not a faith for free agents. Christianity is a faith to be lived together. We hold onto one another. We lock arms. We are a body, mourning and rejoicing with every other part. And the local church is where we live out what it means to be a body, a family, a temple, a flock, a people, the pillar and foundation of truth. Did you notice how many of the metaphors for the church in the Bible are corporate metaphors? Don't tell me you belong to the family if you're never at the family dinner table.

Christianity, by nature, is political. It requires righteous deeds and just lives, but righteousness and justice are measured, in large part, by our loving lives together. Hence, Christianity comes with both accountability and authority for every Christian, the accountability and authority of citizens. We are—remember—citizens of the kingdom of heaven. It's inside the life of the local church that each of us exercises that citizenship authority and accountability, as demonstrated in my church's members' meeting.

Gathered together, furthermore, we are embassies of that kingdom, outposts of Christ's rule scattered about the nations.

Can the authority of the church be abused? Surely, it can and is, just as the authority of princes, policemen, pastors, and parents is too often abused. Churches most often abuse their authority by requiring more than Scripture requires. They bind consciences where Scripture doesn't. They make members feel guilty or like "bad" Christians if they don't conform to their man-made rules and traditions. This is anti-gospel.

But just as unhealthy marriages don't cause us to throw out the binding nature of marital covenants, so unhealthy churches should not cause us to leave behind the local church.

A CHURCH IS NOT COMPETENT TO WIELD THE SWORD

So every church is political. Every church is an embassy of heaven. But no church is competent to wield the sword. Therefore, churches should ordinarily not seek to influence government policy *directly*. Doing so, in effect, is a breach of the separation between church and state. It risks misidentifying Jesus' name with human wisdom. It risks abusing the consciences of church members. And it risks undermining Christian freedom and unity.

A US senator once invited my church's senior pastor to his office for advice. The senator was a member of the church, and his was the last vote needed in the Senate to pass a constitutional amendment requiring a balanced federal budget—a major vote, no doubt. But he felt undecided. He said to my pastor, "My colleagues are pushing me. The party whip is pushing me. The press is hounding me. You're my pastor. How should I vote?"

My pastor, wisely, responded, "Brother, I'll pray that God gives you wisdom."

Years later, recounting the story to me, my pastor told me, "It's not like I didn't have an opinion on the constitutional amendment. I had a very strong opinion."

"So why didn't you say something?"

"Because," he replied, "my authority as a pastor is tied to the Word of God. I *know* I'm right about the Bible. I *know* I'm right about the gospel and Jesus' promised return. And I'm happy to address any political issue that meets the criteria of being biblically *significant* and *clear*. Yet the constitutional amendment in question was neither biblically clear nor significant. Therefore, I'm going to preserve my pastoral authority and credibility for the things Scripture has told me to talk about."

My pastor went on to explain that he knew it was a satanic trap set just for him. Here he was, a young and new pastor on Capitol Hill, who happened to have a deep interest in politics. Satan would have loved for him to think he could have *influence*. He could *be somebody*.

Yes, God had called him to be somebody, somebody who preaches the gospel and shepherds a flock!

Here is how I would defend my pastor's closed mouth and what I hope many evangelical pastors would learn. First, pastors need a clear sense of priorities. The church's most powerful political word is *the gospel*. And the church's most powerful political testimony is *being the church*. There is more political power in the gospel and in being the church than there is in electing a president, installing a Supreme Court justice, or even changing a constitution. If you don't understand that, you should not be a pastor. Change jobs. An excellent president or constitution might make a decades-long impact. An exceptional president or constitution might be felt for centuries. A faithful pastor and church, however, work on the time scales of eternity. They don't just pass laws. Through God's Word and Spirit, they change hearts. They raise the dead. They give sight to the blind. They usher people into true righteousness and true justice and true love. The man whom most historians consider the greatest president, Abraham Lincoln, did no such thing, at least not directly.

Second, I'm not saying that pastors should never address constitutional and public policy matters. My pastor also said to me, had the senator been asking him about the Thirteenth Amendment (outlawing slavery), Fourteenth Amendment (rights of citizenship for all races), or the Fifteenth Amendment (voting rights for all races) he certainly would have spoken up. The gospel has implications, and those who are justified will pursue justice. Faith shows itself in deeds. But in most instances trying to directly influence government policy involves you in more than just "putting on" deeds. It involves you in competencies you don't possess, and it says more about Jesus than you have the authority to say.

I briefly mentioned this in chapter 3, but our discussion of the keys gives us more theology to understand the point here: When pastors or churches tie their names to a piece of governmental policy, legislation, or nomination, they effectively tie the name of Jesus to that endeavor.

This is why I sometimes call the church a "sign maker."

The institutional church hangs signs with Jesus' name on them over the *what* and the *who* of the gospel, like my church did in the membership meeting by taking it off the young man but keeping it on the sister. No, this doesn't happen every time an individual Christian supports a candidate or piece of legislation, though there is some risk of that. But whenever a church acts formally or officially, which typically we do through the mouths of our pastors, we tell everyone, "This is where Jesus stands."

Over the course of centuries, we can look back and discern moments when we wish churches had taken a stand on government policy. We wish American churches would have been clearer, say, on slavery or civil rights. We wish South African churches would have stood against apartheid. And perhaps there are governmental matters on which churches today should speak more decisively. Regrettably, such omissions are best discerned in hindsight.

So, yes, churches can sin and prove faithless *by not speaking up in matters of government policy when they should.* There is a time and season for everything: a time to speak and a time to stay silent. Which means that once in a great while churches should speak directly to government policy or to particular candidates.

Yet more often, I think, we in America risk speaking when we shouldn't. For instance, I have watched churches unite their names and therefore the name of Jesus to a Supreme Court nominee, to presidential candidates, and to legislation in Congress. And nearly every time I want to ask, "Are you sure? Do you really want to stake the reputation of Jesus and the gospel to that nominee or candidate or reform?" What if the nominee turns out to be an embezzler? What if he votes differently on the court bench than you expect him to?

The point is, we have the wisdom of God in Scripture. Let's speak decisively from *that* book and stake Jesus' reputation on it. Most matters of governmental policy, as we saw in chapters 3 and 4, depend on human wisdom. Most are what we called jagged-line issues. We want Christians who are wise like Solomon to work in those domains, yes, but let's maintain the distinction between church and state. As churches, we should not pretend we have divine wisdom when we don't. And let's not bind the consciences of church members and other Christians when all we have is human wisdom and human tradition.

Instead, American Christians need to work harder at promoting Christian freedom when it comes to candidates, causes, and policy.

My point here is *not* that churches are "spiritual" and "not political." I think I have made that abundantly clear. Rather, my point pertains to occupational competence and authority. I'm happy for you to give me informal medical or legal advice. But unless you're a doctor or lawyer, we both know your counsel isn't worth much. Licensed doctors possess medical competence. Bar-certified lawyers possess legal competence. So we go to them and trust them. And notice their competence is tied to an authority, whether the authority of the American Medical Association or a state bar.

Likewise, if you want to ask my personal opinion on some Supreme Court nominee or executive order, I might offer my personal thoughts. Yet I will do so privately, and I will tell you explicitly that I'm *not* speaking as a pastor and I'm *not* speaking for the church. I certainly won't take out an advertisement in the local newspaper to offer my opinion.

A CHURCH IS NOT PARTISAN

Just as a church should not seek to wield the sword and influence government policy directly, so a church should ordinarily not be partisan. That is, it should not identify itself with one political party or another.

My points here parallel the last section. At stake is the separation between church and state, the reputation of Christ, the consciences of church members, Christian freedom, and Christian unity.

Likewise, there are exceptions. Churches in China might indeed take a stand against Communist Party membership. I mentioned the examples of Nazi Party membership or Ku Klux Klan membership earlier in the book, both of which should lead to excommunication.

But notice the stakes here: unless you are ready to deny or remove church membership to someone for his or her party membership, a pastor or church generally should not endorse or denounce one party or another or candidates from said party. When a church does, it effectively ties the name of Jesus to that party and subverts the mission of the church to being a branch of that party. Non-Christians will begin to view that church as a lobbying wing of a party and Christians as political operatives for that party. Talk about undermining the gospel!

Why should pastors ordinarily *not* endorse or denounce parties or political candidates? Think about why the Holy Spirit makes someone a pastor or overseer:

- to give life to the dead by proclaiming the gospel,
- to draw a line between life and death, between the church and the world, and
- to lay out the path of obedience.

This is why Paul told Timothy not to preach, but to preach the Word (2 Tim. 4:2). It's why he also told Timothy, "Keep a close watch on yourself and on the teaching. Persist in this, for by so doing you will save both yourself and your hearers" (1 Tim. 4:16). A pastor's occupation is conscience-binding. And he should only bind the conscience of his hearers with the Word of God. It is not his political opinions, calculations, or best guesses that call into existence the things that are not and then give order to this glorious new creation. (Ezek. 37; Rom. 4:17, 10:17; 2 Cor. 4:1–6; 1 Thess. 1:5; James 1:18, 21; 1 Peter 1:23.)

Other than in extraordinary circumstances, therefore, no, I do not think pastors have the authority to reveal the mind of God, to divide the church from the world, or to fasten the gospel and the name of Jesus to candidates, leaders, or parties.

A CHURCH IS PROPHETIC

Perhaps you are wondering, isn't the church supposed to be prophetic? Shouldn't we present a witness to the nations of the way of righteousness? Not only that, but doesn't becoming such a prophetic witness require us to instruct and disciple our members in all matters of life, especially in the morally and religiously significant matters of politics?

Yes! A church is a prophetic witness. And a church must therefore disciple its members in the way of righteousness and justice. This is what I have been getting at throughout the book by describing the church as a model political community. We are to demonstrate for the nations the way of true righteousness and justice.

But that's different than presuming to have institutional competence and authority where we do not.

Perhaps it's worth rehearsing one more time the distinction in chapter 3 between straight-line and jagged-line issues. Straight-line issues have a clear path from biblical principle to policy application. Jagged-line issues require us to zigzag between one principle and another, doing our best to find the path of wisdom and righteousness.

There is a straight line between Romans 13 and teaching a church to pay its taxes. There is a jagged line between various biblical passages and any argument you might want to make for a flat tax. You might be utterly convinced in your mind about a flat tax, and I'm happy for you as a Christian to write an article making the case for it: the Bible affirms private property in the commands not to steal; no one is entitled to another person's wealth; there's nothing intrinsically wrong with having more wealth; the claims that the rich must pay their "fair share" never explain why that's "fair" but rather look like state-sponsored jealousy and populist pandering; high taxes hurt the means of wealth production, which ultimately hurts the poor; the Old Testament tithe was a flat tax; and so forth. Fine. I'd even be willing to say you're making your argument from the Bible. But can we agree it relies on a number of assumptions, connections, and logical deductions, and that good Christians will make different arguments from the Bible?

So now another Christian points to the fact that the poor are made in God's image; that governments pursue justice in order to protect that image; that later passages of Scripture couple justice with caring for the downtrodden and disenfranchised, which places an additional moral burden on those with more resources; and so forth. This, too, is a biblical argument. Who is right? They're both reasonable arguments. Both arguments use wisdom to make their various connections. You might be convinced you're right, but recognize the distinction between your wisdom and what's clear about God's wisdom. Yes, theology generally works by drawing implications from Scripture. But after several jagged turns in the road, we should acknowledge our limitations. I'd implore you (1) to leave all but the clearest issues in the realm of Christian freedom, and (2) to not formally connect it to the church's message or a pastor's word.

Let's go back and think further about endorsing or denouncing a candidate. You might be utterly convinced that a Christian must vote for candidate Joe against candidate Jane. Fine. But now suppose another Christian assesses the political and historical landscape differently. He agrees with your moral principles entirely, but he doesn't think your assessment of what's at stake in this election is correct. Meanwhile, other moral principles compel him to vote for candidate Jane.

Will you grant him the Christian freedom to do so? Will you resist binding his conscience? Will you maintain Christian unity?

Your vote for candidate Joe always depends on not just a *moral* assessment, but a *sociological* assessment about what social forces are in motion in an electorate; a *historical* assessment that treats one interpretation of the past as correct and presumes to know which past events will shape the near future; a *political* assessment about the strength of various political actors; an *institutional* assessment about how various legislative bodies and courts and other non-state actors are pitted against one another; even a *statistical* assessment about the likelihood of events turning one way or another. How good are you at crunching all that data? Does your ability to conduct these assessments and render a judgment yield a conclusion that's as plain and clear as preaching the Bible?

All your predictions and calculations might be right. I'm simply pleading for you to make space for other Christians to disagree with you, to leave these matters in the realm of Christian freedom, to preach *the Bible*, and to lower the emotional temperature on these kinds of conversations.

The prophetic power of the gospel and the church will grow as we disciple one another toward being a just and righteous people. So teach biblical principles. But don't wade into public policy tactics and then bind the conscience.

The church's most powerful political (and we could add prophetic) word is in proclaiming the gospel. If you don't understand that, you should not be in church leadership of any kind.

The historian Samuel Hugh Moffett knew better. His book, which I mentioned in the last chapter, chronicled the terrors of Tamerlane the "Exterminator," who nearly vanquished Christianity from parts of Asia in the fourteenth century. Moffett offered an unexpected conclusion about what killed Christianity in Asia. It didn't finally result from persecution. It didn't result from not enough Christians going into politics or not seeking to transform the culture. It resulted from Christians not evangelizing. He wrote:

> What finally withered the proud advance of Christianity across Asia was not the persecution of a Tamerlane, though the permanent effects of that ravaging destruction still linger. More crippling than any persecution was the church's own long line of decisions . . . to compromise evangelistic and missionary priorities for the sake of survival.[4]

Bad government really will hurt the church and hinder the church's witness. It's true. Let's work for good governments. Still, even more crucial is that churches must not stop evangelizing, no matter what.

Just as the church's political (and prophetic) word is in sharing the gospel, so its most powerful political (and prophetic) witness is its life together. In addition to the kinds of testimonies I mentioned earlier in the chapter, I think of my friend Gary. Gary has never been attracted to a woman, but feels attraction exclusively to men. Yet he agrees with Scripture that God created marriage for a man to share with a woman and physical intimacy for the marriage bed. He assumes, therefore, that he will be single for the rest of his life. Gary's longtime friends and fellow church members Rodney and Sarah know about Gary's same-sex attraction. They love him and enjoy spending time with him. Plus, they want to encourage this brother in the faith. Therefore, they decided to share a home with Gary and do life together. They eat most dinners together. They often drive to church together. And so forth. In this all three are helping one another learn the crucial value of Christian friendship, living as Christ intends for us to live.

Now, if churches across America for the last one hundred years had handled people struggling with same-sex attraction like Rodney, Sarah, and Gary have, do you think the debates over homosexuality and gender might be a little different today? At the very least, I suspect our gospel witness would be dramatically strengthened.

THE CHURCH IS MULTINATIONAL AND MULTIETHNIC

Christ died for people of every nation, tribe, peoples, and language (Rev. 7:9). The universal church is therefore multinational and multiethnic. Our local churches should also aspire to be multinational and multiethnic, as circumstances permit.

It's tough work, admittedly. We more easily trust people who look like us or share our national or tribal identities. That's the natural posture of the fallen human heart. The problem worsens as we begin to make much of ourselves because we belong to a certain group, and to belittle others because they don't. We self-justify and then exclude. That's a denial of the gospel.

When Peter stopped eating with the Gentiles, was he thinking in ethnic terms? "They're not Jewish like me." Or was he thinking in old-covenant legal terms? "They're not circumcised like me." Paul's challenge to Peter focused on the latter (Gal. 2:14, 18), but the latter entailed the former. Either way, Peter was effectively denying the gospel of justification by faith alone, said Paul (Gal. 2:16). To divide the body of Christ ethnically, downplay those divisions, or ignore those divisions undermines the gospel.

How tragic, then, that white Christian America gave itself over to a gospel-denying separatism for so long, forcing blacks to start their own churches and denominations. I believe American churches have made progress compared to where we were in 1850 or 1950. But we have some way to go.

I remember bragging to one of my pastors, Thabiti, that I didn't think of my good friend Christopher as black. Thabiti challenged me: "Huh, that's interesting, because Christopher certainly experiences life as a black man in America. And you've never asked him about that? You must not be a very good friend." Ouch. But yes, that makes sense.

I remember conversing with James, a Korean American brother, about his becoming an elder in our church. He had spent a decade as the pastor of another church and had been incredibly fruitful in our church. Yet there had been a series of delays in his nomination, and we were reflecting on that fact. Multiple unique factors were at play, but it was hard not to think about the fact that Asian Americans, as a general pattern, feel overlooked in majority-white organizations, including churches. They especially feel overlooked for leadership positions. One book called this "the bamboo ceiling."[5] Whites happily hire Asian Americans to do some types of work, but statistics suggest they're comparatively slow to promote them into positions of leadership, whether as CEOs or as pastors.

Here's a practical tip: if you belong to the majority ethnicity in your church, ask your minority friends what it's like to be the minority in your church. I've asked this question dozens of times ever since my conversation with Thabiti, the last time a week ago with another Korean American brother. His reply was "It's great, because this is the sort of church where people regularly have those conversations." Praise God. That's a little bit of progress. But we have further to go still.

How do the single minority women in your church feel? It's easy for them to feel unattractive by white American norms and therefore ignored by the men. How can our churches better care for them? What values do we encourage in our churches' dating cultures?

What about the music? Does it merely reflect the styles and preferences of your own cultural group? For decades now—frustratingly—church-growth books hopped up on the latest marketing strategies have encouraged pastors to grow their churches by deliberately targeting "social demographic units." So this church appeals to white college-educated Baby Boomers; that church appeals to white millennial hipsters. In the process they unwittingly reinforce the natural social divisions that characterize humanity.[6]

Or think about your church's Sunday morning or small group prayers. Do they reflect the concerns of minorities in your city? Our elders have discovered how easy it is for whites to be completely oblivious to the local concerns of African Americans in Washington, DC, to say nothing of other groups. That, of course, is the result of watching different news channels, reading different websites, living in different neighborhoods, maintaining different groups of friends, attending different birthday parties, watching different movies, and generally living in sealed-off cultural enclaves. As I heard another pastor say, don't expect to build a multicultural church unless you're living a multicultural life. Moreover, if you are in a monoethnic church in a multicultural context, it may be that your church is more partisan than you realize.

The solution to racial supremacy (at worst) or ignorant insensitivity (at best) starts with the gospel of justification by faith alone. God's justifying verdict is a covenantal one.[7] It declares us to be right before his throne and gives us standing in his kingdom among his people. It removes the need for that kind of self-justifying or group-justifying. It declares us to be different parts of the same body. So personal or structural hurts experienced by Christopher or James or single sisters are hurts for all of us.

Yet not only are we members of the same body and family, we're also citizens of the same kingdom. Up until the mid-1990s, our church had an American flag on the platform. No one thought that that was a sin. We're dealing here in matters of prudence. But members of the church began to wonder if it subtly communicated the wrong message to international visitors, especially if they were non-Christians. As Christians, the pastor observed in one conversation, we have more eternally in common with our fellow believers from Brazil and Bangladesh than we do with non-Christian Americans. The flag question came to a head one night in a deacons' meeting (this was before our church had elders). It was a tear-filled meeting. Nearly all the deacons were World War II veterans. One man pulled out a poem he had written to the flag as a child and read it. But then these old white men decided unanimously to remove the flag. They wanted our church to be a gathering of Christians before it was a gathering of Americans.

Today, one of my church's most successful evangelistic ministries is the international student ministry. And I thank God for the role those World War II veterans played in preparing the ground for that ministry.

Remember, our churches are embassies of Christ's kingdom, time machines from the end of history. And each one has the privilege and responsibility, depending on its setting, to display something of that awesome multinational and multiethnic assembly.

THE CHURCH IS ULTIMATE

Finally, the church is ultimate. Now, our individual churches will come and go. Yet Christ's church—*the* church—will remain. It will prevail against partisan politics, the rage of the nations, and hell itself.

"He who sits in the heavens laughs" (Ps. 2:4).

Christ's churches therefore do not depend on the state's permission. The gospel provides its own permission, and churches follow the gospel's mandate, not the state's.

You may recall from chapter 4 that the ultimate purpose of government is to serve the church. It builds a platform on which the church can do its work. The church, too, serves government as a model of justice and righteousness in both word and deed. But the ultimate purpose of the church (and every individual church) is not to serve the government or the nation. It is to worship God and to prepare people for the worship of God. Churches do this, in part, by teaching members to be good citizens. But the worship of God is ultimate, not the state or the nation.

Non-Christians will sometimes heap praise onto Christians for the good deeds they do. The Bible predicts this will happen (Matt. 5:16; 1 Peter 2:12), and we can thank God when it does.

But don't let this fool you. Some churches begin to chase that praise, like a dog's nose turning toward the waft of beef. Their sense of mission even changes. "We exist to transform the city, redeem culture, change the nation."

Hold on. Did Jesus really go to the cross as a payment for sin simply so that crime rates would go down?

I don't want to create an antithesis between faith and deeds. Yes, Christ died so that we and our neighbors would live righteous lives. But remember that this present age is passing, and that the church has begun to live in and for the next age.

To say the mission of the church is to transform the culture or redeem the nation is to fall for a prosperity gospel. It puts people's hopes in temporal things, not eternal ones. Not only that, it undermines a congregation's motivation to work for both temporal and eternal things. After all, cultures, nations, neighborhoods, crime statistics, and presidential administrations will come and go, get better and get worse. Why should I tie my hopes to something so transitory? I give up. I think I'll go play video games.

Churches lose their culture-transforming power when they make cultural transformation their primary focus, pastor John Piper rightly observed.[8]

If you want a church filled with people who care about their neighborhoods and nations, the only *lasting* foundation is to help them set their hearts on eternity. True love of neighbor is born out of a love of God. Likewise, the ambition to work for temporary forms of justice will only grow in the soil of a belief in God's eternal justice. I want to work for justice *now,* because it will reflect, even imperfectly, his coming justice *then.* But if there is no coming justice then, why work for it now?

Which means, if you want an outwardly engaged church, you must continually emphasize the fact that the church's upward engagement, not its outward engagement, is ultimate.

CONCLUSION

A fitting conclusion to this chapter is from a sermon introduction the senior pastor of my church gave the Sunday immediately following the 2016 presidential elections. The room was tense. I had just done an extended question-and-answer time on the election during the Sunday school hour in my class on Christians and government. It went fine, not great. The pastor then began his sermon with several remarks about his boyhood and how he had to learn what it meant to empathize with other people. Then he said this:

> Some members of our congregation are happy with the results of this last week's election, some don't care, and some are scared. It's our job as a congregation to live out the covenant we've taken before the Lord and to show that the Christ we share is more important to us than the politics we don't. This church has survived close elections before. It was here when Teddy Roosevelt was elected and when his cousin Franklin defeated President Hoover. We survived Truman v. Dewey, Kennedy v. Nixon, and Nixon v. Humphrey—all close and contentious elections. I was here when we survived Bush v. Gore, and in those days we had had Mr. Gore's scheduler as our deacon of sound while the Republican Senate Majority leader sat right down there! I pray that we as a congregation can actually see the gospel displayed as we love those who voted differently than us this past Tuesday. And part of that can mean some very difficult conversations directly with those with whom you have some pretty deep political differences. But part of loving them means being willing to hear them out and believe the best.
>
> I know some seem compelled to have more of a Democratic church, or a Republican church, but I think it's actually our best gospel-strategy to grow as Christians and to reach Capitol Hill and this District by working hard against identifying our church with opposition to either party. We prayed for Bill Clinton and we prayed for George Bush and we prayed for Barack Obama—and we will now pray for Donald Trump.

If culture is coarsened or some members of our church or community have lives that are made more difficult, we will, as we've always done, work to bind up the wounds and encourage their continued discipleship and witness until the Lord returns or calls us home. We will pray for goodness and justice and right to triumph, but we will harbor no illusions that if Gore or McCain or Hillary Clinton had been elected, then the Fall would have been reversed. In our politics, the victors and the vanquished live in a fallen world, even though they experience the fall differently. Pray that we learn well from listening to each other's histories, as I've tried to learn. And pray that God would give us wisdom in knowing how best to respond to those that we're wondering if we should regard as our enemies.

Once again, the church's most powerful political word is *the gospel*. And the church's most powerful political testimony is *being the church*.

CHRISTIANS: NOT CULTURAL WARRIORS, BUT AMBASSADORS

There are at least three wrong paths Christians in America might take today in their approach to politics and the public square.

Wrong path number one is *disengagement*. Here Christians isolate themselves from civic life and focus only on their lives together. They tell themselves this is the "spiritual" thing to do. The prophet Jonah wanted to go nowhere near the deeply immoral Ninevah. Gratefully, for Ninevah's sake, God would not let him and required him to preach a political message about God's coming judgment. The city repented.

Many white South African churches thought they could avoid engaging with the nation's apartheid regime. So they adopted an "apolitical" and "neutral" posture. After the regime fell, South Africa's Truth and Reconciliation Commission observed that this supposedly apolitical approach allowed churches "to be misled into accepting a social, economic and political system that was cruel and oppressive." The "fears of white church members," it continued, led them "into sins of omission."[1] These churches thought they could avoid politics, but their neutral stance in fact endorsed an evil and unjust political status quo. In so doing they compromised their gospel witness.

Whatever you think of America's public morality today, churches must not disengage. If you and I were standing in front of a whiteboard, I'd write down the words *love* and *justice* for you. God commands us to seek justice and to love our neighbors as ourselves. No, not every battle is worth fighting, but the call to love and justice alone should keep Christians engaged—somehow. Cynicism and separation are not options for us.

Wrong path number two is *capitulation*. This is not the path of neutrality but of positively endorsing the world and its ways. And how promising this path looks. It wins friends and offers immediate political status. Its short-term prospects are great. The prophets and priests of Jeremiah's day therefore cried "Peace, peace" when there was no peace (Jer. 6:14). Paul, too, pointed to a people who knew God's righteous decree but practiced and gave approval to those who defied God's decrees (Rom. 1:32).

An extreme example of capitulation are the pastors in the German Evangelical Church (est. 1933), also called the Reich Church, who aligned themselves with the policies of the Nazi Party. A subtler example is liberal Christianity's accommodating itself to the sexual ethic of the day.

To Christians on the political left I would say, grant no peace to the Democratic Party's position on abortion. Fight against it. Make noise. To those on the right I would say, make no peace with any vestiges of white supremacy in the Republican Party. If you work in law enforcement, for instance, you have a great opportunity to be one of the most vocal in opposing it. Christians on both sides of the aisle will need to think carefully in coming years about how to make peace with friends identifying as LGBT while also affirming God's purposes for marriage and sexuality.

Daniel and his friends Shadrach, Meshach, and Abednego offer great examples of not capitulating. These high-ranking government bureaucrats worked hard for the king, but they also refused the king's idolatry: "Be it known to you, O king, that we will not serve your gods or worship the golden image that you have set up" (Dan. 3:18).

Wrong path number three is *worldly engagement*. There is a way of engaging that's right on the substance but wrong on the strategy or tone. As Michael Gerson and Peter Wehner documented in their book *City of Man*, the Christian Right in its heyday often comes in for criticism on this front.[2] The movement stood up for good things, but its language tended to be apocalyptic. It gave earthly political outcomes—a vote on a law, an election, or a Supreme Court case—an outsized importance. Too many exclamation points and all cap sentences tell our non-Christian fellow citizens that our policy agenda is more important than the gospel itself. It says THIS ELECTION IS THE MOST IMPORTANT THING IN THE WORLD! It communicates that we're *really* just a branch of this or that party. It says that God is not so big, after all. That is why we have to scream.

Something quietly hiding underneath the floorboards of this third error is utopianism. Utopianism is the belief that perfect justice is possible in this world and that we can bring heaven to earth now. Yet utopianism, whether of the Christian or the non-Christian variety, often produces injustice. The utopian mind-set relies on its own strength instead of God's. It overestimates what can be done in this world and so forces its way. It exploits and abuses people in the name of a greater good.

In some ways, this last temptation is the most likely danger for the generation of Christians raised on the heroic stories of William Wilberforce and Hannah More, Harriet Tubman and Martin Luther

King Jr. Indeed, a temptation for me when writing a book on faith and politics is to find such stories about the glorious things that Christians can accomplish for the public good.

"Look at what William Wilberforce did to abolish Britain's slave trade! So get involved, work hard, and have faith, young culture warriors."

Such stories are inspiring and wonderful. Praise God for the Wilberforces and Tubmans and Kings. They helped to end horrific injustices.

Yet just as cynicism is not an option for Christians, neither is triumphalism. The biblical perspective on political engagement requires something a little more complex. Complexity never makes for a rousing campaign speech. Crowds don't like nuance. But what if that's what the Bible offers us?

Former Fox News commentator Bill O'Reilly opened his book *Cultural Warrior*, "At times you *have* to fight. No way around it. At some point, every one of us is confronted with danger or injustice."[3] That's true, so far as it goes. There is a time and a place to fight. Yet the picture Scripture offers is less cultural warrior and more ambassador. Ambassadors know how to fight, but they also know how to be diplomatic. They're not just trying to win a war; they're trying to represent a whole other kingdom.

MATTHEW'S OTHER TEXT ON TAXES

This is the picture Paul provided when he referred to us as ambassadors with a ministry of reconciliation (2 Cor. 5:18–20). It's the vision Jesus presented when he referred to us as sons of the kingdom who represent the heavenly Father.

You are probably familiar with the episode in Matthew's gospel where Jesus said to render to Caesar what is Caesar's when asked about paying taxes (Matt. 22:15–22). Do you know the other text in Matthew that refers to taxes? He told us we're sons who are free from taxes. Yet then he told us to pay them for diplomacy's sake. Talk about complex. Here it is:

> When they came to Capernaum, the collectors of the two-drachma tax went up to Peter and said, "Does your teacher not pay the tax?"
>
> He said, "Yes."
>
> And when he came into the house, Jesus spoke to him first, saying, "What do you think, Simon? From whom do kings of the earth take toll or tax? From their sons or from others?" And when he said, "From others," Jesus said to him, "Then the sons are free. However, not to give offense to them, go to the sea and cast a hook and take the first fish that comes up, and when you open its mouth you will find a shekel. Take that and give it to them for me and for yourself." (17:24–27)

It's a slightly confusing text. The tax collectors asked if Jesus planned on paying the two-drachma tax, which is the tax used for the upkeep of the temple. Yet Jesus extended the lesson beyond the temple by referring to the kings of the earth. Then he said two different things to Peter. And it's in these two things that we find the *complex* biblical perspective we need.

On the one hand, Jesus said that the sons of the kingdom are free. That's us as Christians. We are not ultimately bound by the rules of the temple, the kings, or the kingdoms of this world since this world order will soon pass away.

On the other hand, Jesus did not wish "to give offense." He wanted to be diplomatic. Plus, the present rule of the temple, as well as the kingdoms of this world, was established by God. They were legitimate. So he told his disciples to pay the tax.

How do we put these two hands together? We need to recognize the overlap of two ages: the age of the fall with its institutions and the age of new creation with its institutions. As Christians, we live in both ages simultaneously.

Here's an illustration from ethicist Oliver O'Donovan. The Soviet Union, which was falling apart through the year 1991, was formally pronounced dead on December 26, 1991. In its place sprang up the Russian Federation. Imagine then that it is October 1991, and you're an official of the up-and-coming Russian government. An official of the old Soviet regime asks you to do something, and you think to yourself, *That's ridiculous. This is exactly why you guys couldn't keep the lights on!* Nonetheless, you don't want to show open contempt for the present regime, because it will create unnecessary trouble and you'll look like an anarchist. Plus, you feel utterly confident that power will soon change hands and that you'll be running things in a month or two. The old order is vanishing, a new one is coming, and so you decide to show respect by doing what the Soviet official has asked you to do.

Jesus, too, knew that the present authorities of this world had no future. Therefore, he didn't need to respond with either contrite obedience or angry defiance. His response was somewhere in between.[4] It was complex.

Paul adopted exactly the same attitude in 1 Corinthians 7. If you're a bondservant, he said, get your freedom if you can, but realize it's not the end of the world if you cannot (vv. 21–22). "For the present form of this world is passing away" (v. 31).

Let me try to whittle down the lesson for us: respect and honor the legitimate institutions of this present age. Let them do their jobs and work for their good. But realize that they are passing, and do not give them your ultimate allegiance and hope.

More concisely: work for love's sake, but don't let your hopes get too high.

No, that won't stir up a crowd. No nightly news shows for me, I guess. But I think it is faithful to Scripture.

INVESTING AT KENT ELEMENTARY

My friend Eric adopted such a faithful posture in all his work through the Kent Elementary School Parent Teacher Association. When their oldest child reached kindergarten age, Eric and his wife carefully considered whether homeschool, a Christian school, or the public school Kent Elementary (not the real name) was best. They chose Kent because it was a block from their home. At the time, Kent was not in good shape. The facilities were run down. It lacked teachers. Test scores were middling. And few of the neighborhood residents sent their children there. The students who did attend had uninvolved parents.

Eric and his wife, however, decided not only to send their children to Kent, but to pour themselves into the school. "As we did the cost-benefit analysis of going to Kent versus a better school, we knew that living a block away would allow us to be present in the school and the community. My wife could drop in to teach art or Spanish. I could easily meet with the principal or teachers. And having parents present is half the formula for any school's success, whether public or private."

Eric joined the Parent Teacher Association. He recruited other parents to join. Eventually he became the president. Wisely, Eric did his best to support the school principal and tried not to work at cross-purposes with him. "I described the PTA as the wind in the sails of the boat of the school. We're not the professionals. We don't have the time. But as parents in the community we have a responsibility to come alongside and help the school. That's the role we took."

Likewise, Eric's overtures were received by a flexible principal who was willing to partner with Eric and the PTA board. In fact, the PTA helped the principal do some of the things he wanted to do but couldn't due to the bureaucratic and political constraints on him. The parents in turn used their various vocational skills and connections to help the school. The grant writers wrote grant applications. The fundraisers raised funds. Someone at the park service worked on outdoor education.

I personally recall how multiple members of my church bought their Christmas trees through a Kent Elementary fundraiser several Christmases in a row. I felt a little guilty for buying a cheaper tree elsewhere!

Gradually, the PTA built up its own budget of about $300,000 for this school of three hundred kids. They hired a science teacher, a physical education teacher, a language teacher, and an art teacher. Once those teachers were in place, the principal found ways to absorb them into the school's budget. The PTA also undertook building beautification projects. They renovated the playground and the gardens, and undertook other landscaping projects.

Little by little, Kent earned a great reputation in the city. Test scores rose. The facilities improved. The neighborhood developed a strong sense of ownership of the school, which contributed to the neighborhood's own sense of community. Parents became excited to get involved. Eric's two oldest children began as kindergartners and have both graduated out of the school. His third and youngest child is now entering the third grade.

"It's like farming," Eric said. "Growth doesn't happen overnight. It took blood, sweat, and tears. And it had to start with a commitment from me and my wife. DC Public Schools did their part in working to get good teachers. In the end, it took a joint venture to better steward everyone's resources."

Kent is in many ways a school-revitalization success story. It's a mini-Wilberforce narrative. I want it to inspire you to get involved wherever you live: in a school, in a city council, in writing letters to the editor, in a crisis pregnancy shelter, in a homeless shelter, in a neighborhood revitalization project, or in any number of other ways to honor the institutions in place, and, in so doing, do good.

THE SISYPHEAN NATURE OF POLITICS

But that's not the end of the story.

In the last few years, Kent has begun to refuse to acknowledge any birthdays or holidays like Thanksgiving or Christmas. If children do sing holiday songs, they are instructed to change the words, like "Merry, merry, merry *winter*" instead of "Merry, merry, merry Christmas" There is no pledge of allegiance or opportunity for patriotism. Instead, the school sticks to pushing black history month (good) and Gay Pride (not good) on bulletin boards and in school-wide assemblies. They've also adopted a curriculum that downplays learning facts and instead teaches children to express themselves.

Eric discovered after the fact that his second-grader's teacher, whom Eric befriended, was reading transgender stories to his daughter's class in circle time. The teacher never told the parents he was doing this, so they weren't able to give their input. "It feels like we helped build this school," said Eric, "but now DCPS is starting to cut us out."

The principal with whom Eric had worked for years had retired, and Eric had helped to bring in a new principal with impeccable credentials. After the hire, however, Eric learned that she was a lesbian with an aggressive social agenda. Now, Eric said, he feels divided. "I plan on meeting with her and extending an olive branch, saying I'm here to help. But I also want her to keep parents in the loop." He said he is entering his youngest daughter's third-grade school year with apprehension. "If the school really imposes this progressive agenda in a way that won't allow us to be involved, we will have to pull her out of the school."

I recognize that not every reader will agree with Eric's decisions about sending his children to a public school in the first place, particularly one with an aggressive social agenda, but let me refer to the last chapter's discussion on making room for other Christians' political judgments. Here, I want to draw out three lessons.

First, we are to live as ambassadors, not as cultural warriors. Eric is an excellent example. He is a strong Christian who has tirelessly engaged one of the key political institutions of this present age, a public school. He has sought to do his children and neighbors good. No, his precise calling may not be yours, but all of us are called by Scripture to love, honor, obey, and do good, as we'll see in a moment.

Second, we need to remember that politics in this world will always be Sisyphean. Do you remember Sisyphus? He was the king in Greek mythology who was condemned by the gods to roll an immense boulder up a hill, watch it roll down, and then repeat the act for eternity. So it is with our political accomplishments in this world. Build the freest nation in the world, and then watch it enslave its subjects, abort its babies, or maybe even persecute Christians. Down the hill the boulder rolls. The Wilberforce stories inspire the soul, but don't forget the realities and upside-down judgments of Ecclesiastes either:

> I saw under the sun that in the place of justice, even there was wickedness. (3:16)

> He who quarries stones is hurt by them, and he who splits logs is endangered by them. (10:9)

Eric has quarried stones and split logs to help build the school. Now, it's working against his children. Several weeks after my conversation with Eric, his brother told me that the new principal is adding to the school uniform selection. Students will still have the choice of a green or white shirt, but they can also choose a rainbow shirt that says "Equality."

This makes me think about Abraham Kuyper and the Netherlands. Christians often point to the example of Kuyper as a model for Christian public service. He served as prime minister from 1901 to 1905 and is a remarkable example of a life well used for the kingdom in many other ways. Read his material and learn. But also realize that following World War II the Netherlands took a hard turn toward secularism and today is one of the most godless countries in the world. Work to do good while you're here, but know that nothing lasts. This isn't heaven.

One of my fellow church members, who works for a congressman, said over lunch recently, "I'm just grateful to be a disposable congressional staffer working for a disposable member of Congress. It's a brief opportunity to do good and to stave off evil." That sounds about right. Try to leave your corner of earth's garden in better condition than when you got there, but watch out for rolling Sisyphean boulders.

Eric understands this. Gratefully, he hasn't just invested himself in Kent. He invests himself in our church—serving as a deacon, employing church members at his company, consistently giving of himself generously. His hope and treasures are stored up in heaven, not on earth. Therefore, he can keep a loose grip on the school.

Again, I would say, engage in your church as Eric engages. Do not place your ultimate allegiance or hope in anything you can accomplish. But be willing to leave any particular project behind if necessary, even after investing blood, sweat, and tears.

When we add these first two points together a third emerges:

recognize that political success for a Christian equals faithfulness, not results. God calls us to efforts, not outcomes. When a Christian confronts a nation and its leaders, whether in a Senate bill or in a gospel tract, opposition will come. But that does not change our task: Christians must speak faithfully as prophets and priests on behalf of Christ.

Speak faithfully, and then expect the lions. Our witness will be vindicated over time, occasionally in this world, certainly in eternity.

Here are twelve more lessons for Christians on how to engage politically and live as ambassadors, not as culture warriors.

1. Join a church.

That's not the first thing you expect to hear on political engagement. But this is the cumulative lesson of the last chapter. If the church's most powerful political testimony is *being the church*, you should join one. Submit your discipleship to a congregation's oversight and fellowship. Partake of those signs of kingdom citizenship, baptism, and the Lord's Supper. And learn everything that Jesus commanded by sitting under good preaching. Following repentance and faith, the political life begins here.

For instance, I remember one evening when Doug and Brady joined my family for dinner. Both men are single. Both are members of my church. One had an abusive father. One had an absent father. And one of my daughters that evening blessed us all with an ornery attitude. She had been that way all day, and I was tempted to be impatient with her. Yet aside from all the other reasons not to be impatient with my daughter, it occurred to me that Doug and Brady were watching me. I had the opportunity to demonstrate and define how a Christ-following dad should respond to difficult children. They had seen the outlines of such a father drawn through the church's teaching ministry. I had the opportunity in my home to color in those lines.

What gave me that opportunity? The fact that I am a baptized, Lord's Supper–receiving member of a church. A church had marked me with "the Jesus nametag" of the ordinances, effectively saying to these men, "Here is a Christ follower. Watch him to know what Jesus is like."

Suppose, however, that I spoke to my daughter abusively. Doug and Brady would have learned a very different lesson: "Oh, I guess Christian dads can be like other bad dads. There's no difference."

Or suppose, following this second scenario, that they challenged my abusiveness and asked other mature members to challenge my abusiveness but I refused to change. Therefore, the church might finally remove me from membership. In that case, Doug and Brady's conception of a Christ-following dad would be protected and redeemed.

The bottom line here is this: it's in the gathered and scattered life of a congregation that we learn and rehearse and live out a new politics. That is our first form of political engagement. It grows those inside the church. It serves as a witness to those outside the church. I cannot tell you how many people have become Christians, in part, through watching the gathered and scattered life of our church. How did Jesus say the world will know we are his disciples? By our love for one another (John 13:34–35).

At the risk of annoying you, here are three short books to help you along these lines (and notice the subtitles): my own *Church Membership: How the World Knows Who Represents Jesus*, Mack Stiles's *Evangelism: How the Whole Church Speaks of Jesus*, and Mark Dever's *Discipling: How to Help Others Follow Jesus*.

2. Fear God and get wisdom.

The apostle Peter told us to "fear God. Honor the emperor" (1 Peter 2:17). And fearing God comes before honoring the emperor in every sense.

Fearing God is the beginning of wisdom, says Proverbs, and successful political engagement depends on wisdom. "By me kings reign," said Wisdom, "and rulers decree what is just" (Prov. 8:15). Ambassadors, to be sure, are men and women of wisdom.

The fear of God and wisdom give us the right heart posture. It defeats the fear of man. It enables us to play the long game and make the tough decisions. Sadly, pastors and politicians too often play only for short-term gain. Leaders of the land prove constitutionally unable to do the politically costly thing. They fear the next election or church leadership meeting too much.

The person who fears the Lord will put a career on the line in order to do the right thing. She knows there is something greater than a career. He doesn't worry about being called names.

The fear of God and wisdom recognize that Jesus is Lord over parties and party bosses, armies and nations. Germany's Confessing Church, watching the Nazi cloud slowly creep across German skies, reasserted Christ's lordship in the 1934 Barmen Declaration.[5] In article 2, they declared:

> We reject the false doctrine that there could be areas of our life in which we would not belong to Jesus Christ but to other lords.

They continued in article 3:

> We reject the false doctrine that the Church could have permission to hand over the form of its message and of its order to . . . the prevailing ideological and political convictions of the day.

No, Hitler is not lord of the church. Christians rightly grant the state authority in some areas of a church's life: building codes, child-protection policies, nonprofit requirements, if a church wants such a status. But the state does not possess authority over a church's membership or message. The Confessing Church made this clear in article 5:

> We reject the false doctrine that beyond its special commission the State should and could become the sole and total order of human life.

Within a year of the Barmen Declaration, the Confessing Church realized that Nazism offered nothing more or less than a new religion. They declared in a 1935 synod, "We see our nation threatened with mortal danger; the danger lies in a new religion." They also said Christ's churches "will be called to account" by their heavenly Judge "if the German nation turns its back on Christ without being forewarned." Their task was to warn. They feared God. They were ambassadors for another king. Shortly after making this latter statement, the Gestapo arrested seven hundred pastors. Some members remained under surveillance, others were imprisoned, and still others were sent to concentration camps.[6] Soon the Confessing Church was outlawed.

Do American Christians possess such courage and fear of God in the face of the prevailing ideological and political convictions of our own day? Or do we pander to power? John the Baptist did not pander to Herod. He spoke truth and lost his head. Certainly, there is a place for Christian leaders to befriend the mighty. But I worry about any Christian leader who is not willing to offend the mighty on behalf of the Almighty, even if it means losing political access, or worse.

It seems like once a month my own senior pastor, Mark Dever, is reminding our Capitol Hill congregation not to respond to darkening changes in our culture with panic or alarmism. To do so is to contradict the Bible's teaching on ordinary Christian discipleship. It exposes a latent utopianism. It might even suggest we have swallowed a kind of political prosperity gospel.

Instead, Dever reminds us, a heart that fears the Lord trusts God, not circumstances. We must remember that everything we have is God's grace. We should not become sour toward our employers, friends, family members, and government when they oppose us. Like Paul, we can sing even in prison, knowing that our sins are forgiven and that our vindication awaits. Christ's victory is certain, and the gates of hell will not prevail against the church.

There should be no anxiety or desperation among the saints as we engage in public life. Love your church. Love your nation. Even love your party. But remember that whether your church or even your nation rises or falls, Jesus wins. Confessing Church member Dietrich Bonhoeffer knew precisely that, even as Hitler shot him.

3. Obey and honor the government.

Again, Peter said, "Fear God. Honor the emperor" (1 Peter 2:17).

And Jesus said, "Render to Caesar the things that are Caesar's" (Matt. 22:21).

And Paul said, "You also pay taxes, for the authorities are ministers of God, attending to this very thing. Pay to all what is owed to them: taxes to whom taxes are owed, revenue to whom revenue is owed, respect to whom respect is owed, honor to whom honor is owed" (Rom. 13:6–7).

The Bible illustrates the posture of honor and obedience in the way Joseph served Pharaoh and how Daniel and the three Hebrew boys served Nebuchadnezzar. Except when the king called them into idolatry, they served vigorously. Paul, too, showed respect for the rule of Rome in Acts.

I also think of my fellow church member who works in the enforcement office of a federal government agency. Over dinner he explained how some employees in the agency were frustrated by the recent change in administration. "Why are they frustrated?" I asked.

"Because they are being asked to follow the rule of law," he replied.

Excuse me?

He went on to explain. "Congress enacts laws, and then it's up to the various government agencies to determine how to apply them. Sometimes my agency has taken such an expansive view of its authority that they've gone well beyond the law that Congress enacted. As a consequence, the courts have struck down many of my agency's rules as going beyond what the law provides." The new leadership in my friend's agency meant to apply the law as well as they could according to the terms *specified by Congress*.

What a wonderful illustration my friend, as a fairly high-ranking government official, is of obeying the government by honoring Congress's law as specified. How all of us, too, should obey and honor the government, maintaining the rule of law.

Christians make the best princes and citizens, said Martin Luther. Indeed, they should.

4. Make use of whatever political stewardship you have.

Part of obeying the government, however, is to use whatever share you have in government, whether or not you're an agency head.

As I said in chapter 5, Genesis 9:5–6 applies to you. It applies to everyone. Like this: "Listen John, Sally, Omar, Zhang Wei, whoever sheds the blood of man, by man shall his blood be shed. Got it? With whatever political stewardship you possess, work to this end."

So we don't just obey government because we're under it. We help and serve the cause of government insofar as we are in it. There is something vaguely democratic about government in the Bible because we're all commissioned by Genesis 9:5–6 to pursue justice.

To be sure, Paul never would have thought of joining hands with Caesar to make law. But he did use the stewardship he had.

He appealed to Caesar, knowing that his status as a Roman citizen afforded him protections and a say in his own trial.

Whatever stewardship you personally have in the cause of government, you as a Christian, like Paul, should use it. If you have been born as a prince, you should use that stewardship. If an American citizen, vote as an American citizen. For some, the stewardship might be small indeed. But even the subject of a monarch can be a good neighbor and honor the king. By honoring the king, you uphold the system of justice that seeks to reward the good and punish the bad.

Different opportunities and resources will require different levels of engagement from individual to individual. In a democratic nation like ours, rendering to Caesar means rendering to democracy what belongs to democracy. A failure to vote, if one is capable, is arguably a failure to love one's neighbor and, therefore, God.

This means there's no room for apathy in a Christian's posture toward the state. As the general public becomes more apathetic, Christians should remain civically informed and engaged. So vote. And do so in an informed way.

5. Know your political culture's supreme values (or idols) and look for common ground.

Every culture has some values that it prizes above all others. Os Guinness wisely observed that "freedom is unquestionably what Americans love supremely, and love of freedom is what makes Americans the people they are." He continued, "From its very beginning, the United States was blessed with a sturdy birthright of freedom. It was born in freedom, it has expanded in freedom, it has resolved its great conflicts in a 'new birth of freedom.'"[7]

Both the political Left and Right win arguments by appealing to freedom. One appeals to the freedom to define marriage; the other appeals to freedom of the marketplace. The pro-choice argument has always possessed this tactical advantage over the pro-life argument: it is grounded in the language of freedom. After all, we are a nation that values freedom over life itself. Didn't Patrick Henry once say, "Give me liberty or give me death"?

Now, a Christian's supreme political value should always be justice. We thought about that in chapter 5 and will consider it further in the next chapter. It's not enough to say that such-and-such law will produce freedom. Christians should be interested in knowing whether something is a *just* freedom. When a culture treats certain things as primary that the Bible would treat as secondary, that culture has created a dangerous idol. Eventually, that idol will imprison and destroy, as idols always do.

Here we find one of the greatest challenges for making political arguments in the public square. On the one hand, every good politician and pastor knows how to make arguments based on finding common ground with his opponents. "You believe in freedom. I, too, believe in freedom. And I agree that laws against pornography will curtail one kind of freedom. But let's think about the freedom of the countless women who have been enslaved by sex-traffickers, and how pornography contributes to this problem."

On the other hand, you always risk affirming a people in their idolatry by doing so. "Why not let people remain free to marry someone of any gender they please?"

The bottom line here is that Christians need good judgment and wisdom. Do I lean into this argument or into that argument? Which brings me to the next lesson . . .

6. Be a "principled pragmatist" in your public-square arguments.

Throughout this book, I have been having an in-house conversation with you. I have relied on biblical arguments and treated you as someone who believes the Bible is God's Word. And this is where

Christians must begin all their thinking about politics and policies. We must start by asking God what *he* intends for us and for the world, lest we let some other god set the terms.

Yet, once we have our in-house conversations, we need to think about how to have conversations with outsiders. Along these lines, a friend recently asked me if I was a "classical liberal" or a "principled pluralist" or something else. In case a label might help, let me call myself a principled pragmatist. By that I mean, *for the purposes of biblical justice and within the bounds of biblical morality (principled), make whatever arguments work (pragmatist).*

No, I'm not referring to philosophical pragmatism. I'm talking about being wise. Wisdom, after all, is pragmatic. It's concerned with what works. Remember the verse that I said gives us the political philosophy of the Bible in a nutshell: "They stood in awe of the king, because they perceived that the wisdom of God was in him to do justice" (1 Kings 3:28). That should be our outward public posture as Christians. That's principled pragmatism: wisdom to do justice.

Does invoking statistics about human flourishing win the argument? Use them. Does invoking points of consensus with your opponents' supreme values help you win? Then do it. Does showing the contradictions in their positions help you win? Then expose the contradictions.

But be leery of being too captivated by any political worldview. Your tight-gripped principles should come from Scripture, not ideology. That said, cull what's good from liberalism, what's good from conservatism, even what's good from nationalism. Learn to find the good and leave the bad.

For instance, those who self-identify as feminists can sometimes make an idol out of personal identity and female empowerment. And this idol might lead to a biblically unjust policy recommendation, like abortion. Still, God created women in his image as fully equal to men. And a worker is worth *her* wages (Lev. 19:13; 1 Tim. 5:18). Indeed, the Lord opposes those who unjustly withhold wages (Mal. 3:5; James 5:4). Therefore, I would encourage pro-lifers to join forces with pro-choicers in arguing that women should receive equal pay for equal work.

Now, whether or not you agree with me on this particular recommendation, you can see the larger point: wisdom (being pragmatic) commends co-belligerence across party and tribal lines. I think Tim Keller was right when he said that "Christians' work for justice should be characterized by both humble cooperation and respectful provocation."[8]

So are we quick to listen and slow to speak? Can we show respect in debates? One sign that you identify more with your ideological tribe than you do with Jesus is that you cannot hear what's good when it comes from another tribe. You assume that everything that people on the other side of the aisle say must be wrong.

By encouraging you to be pragmatic, I'm encouraging you to do what you can to win. Win the debate. Win the election. Win the court case. Not for your own sake, but for love and justice's sake. So be wise. Be shrewd. Study. Learn from the masters of persuasion. Mimic them. Make better arguments. Win!

7. Be willing to invoke God in your arguments.

This point overlaps with the last one, and it's long enough and possibly important enough to be its own chapter. Still, I'm stuffing it in here as one more point on how to engage a public square that is a battleground of gods, even if it takes a bit more explaining.

The idea of a social contract, which is the justifying ethic that often underpins Western constitutional republics like ours, fashions citizens who feel obligated to only make common-ground arguments. Christians in particular make three kinds of common-ground arguments: what I call the Luther approach (which appeals to conscience), the MLK approach (which appeals to natural law), and the sociologist's approach (which appeals to statistics).

Let's start with the Luther approach, which appeals to conscience.[9] Think of Luther all the way back at the Diet of Worms: "To go against conscience is neither safe nor right."

For instance, several years ago President Obama's Affordable Care Act sought to require employers to insure employees for abortion. Churches and Christian organizations immediately objected, arguing on the grounds of religious freedom that it unjustly burdened the conscience to insure an employee's abortion. Now, I agree with that, but notice what's going on. Religious freedom isn't the real issue. It's a backup issue. The real issue, for a Christian, is murder. We don't want the state to require us to fund something we believe is murder. Yet Christians also realize that not everyone believes abortion is murder. So we make a backup argument that appeals to the common ground— our societal agreement not to burden one another's consciences. I won't burden your conscience if you won't burden mine. Deal?

The second approach popular with Christians is the natural law approach. The founders sometimes used this approach. Martin Luther King Jr., too, famously took this approach in his *Letter from the Birmingham Jail*. He wrote, "A just law is a man-made code that squares with the moral law or the law of God. An unjust law is a code that is out of harmony with the moral law. To put it in the terms of St. Thomas Aquinas: An unjust law is a human law that is not rooted in eternal law and natural law."[10] King assumed his readers would recognize, at some level, that certain eternal moral laws are bound up in creation itself. Therefore, he could persuade them by appealing to the eternal laws. So, yes, natural law appeals to an outside, transcendent law, but it presumes that every human being can apprehend and agree to it on terms they recognize. A recent example of a brilliant natural law argument can be found in the book *What Is Marriage? Man and Woman: A Defense* by Sherif Girgis, Ryan Anderson, and

Robert George. All three authors are Roman Catholics who believe what the Bible teaches about marriage. But the book's argument aims at persuading people who don't believe in the Bible.

The third approach is the sociologist's approach. Suppose I want to argue that marriage matters, particularly for the good of children. I could point to the various studies that show that children raised by a single parent are three times more likely to be physically abused than children raised by two married parents, four times more likely to be abused if raised by cohabiting parents, and ten times more likely to be abused if raised by one parent and a live-in boyfriend or girlfriend.[11] Shouldn't we therefore support public policies that promote married two-parent homes?

All three approaches aspire to be broadly accessible to people from different worldviews and religions. All three are geared to a pluralistic public square. And despite whatever weaknesses each might have, all three can be useful for different occasions. Remember, we should be principled pragmatists.

Yet all three also share the same weakness, and this is a subtle but crucial point. All three lack the force of conviction because the very thing they are good at—finding common ground—affirms our modern intuitions that all authority and moral legitimacy rests in every individual's consent. Unless I can be convinced something is true *on my terms*, it must not be true. And so you owe it to me to convince me on my terms. Ironically, the very attempt to *persuade* risks *hardening* people in the deeper certainty that they are right.

We all know from experience how this works. How well have your arguments over politics and religion with friends or family members worked? Are they typically persuaded or hardened? I remember sitting in a coffee shop with Jacob discussing same-sex marriage. He wanted to persuade me. I wanted to persuade him. Throughout the whole conversation, I sensed he was simply using my arguments to get better at making arguments for his own position.

Don't misunderstand. I'm not saying we give up the Luther approach, the MLK approach, or the sociologist's approach. There is a role for each. Yet to compensate for their shared weakness I think we should add one more weapon to our arsenal: the Polycarp approach. The Polycarp approach doesn't look for common ground. It recognizes that every once in a while it's good to show up and simply announce, "Behold your God," like the Old Testament prophets did.

Polycarp was a pastor in second-century Smyrna (modern-day Turkey). In 155 he was arrested and asked by a Roman proconsul to worship the emperor and curse Christ. Polycarp replied, "For eighty and six years have I been his servant, and he has done me no wrong; how can I curse my King, who saved me?" The proconsul threatened him with being burned at the stake. Polycarp replied that the proconsul could only light a fire that lasted for a moment. God threatened both of them with an eternal fire that would never go out. The proconsul ordered his death, and Polycarp burned at the stake.[12]

The philosopher Nicholas Wolterstorff has observed that Christians in the West don't resist governmental incursions like Polycarp did. We "will not declare that Christ is our king." Instead we appeal to religious freedom. We are more Luther than Polycarp, said Wolterstorff. "No Polycarps among us." To a non-Christian, furthermore, our approach might sound like self-interest. Appealing to conscience is exactly what they do. Yet might biblical faithfulness require something else? Wolterstorff thought so: "Fidelity to Christian scripture requires that Christians join Polycarp in declaring that Christ is our sovereign."[13]

No, Polycarp's strategy didn't work in the short-term for Polycarp. Yet his martyrdom, together with a host of others, eventually lent credibility to the claims of Christians. More and more conversions to Christianity followed. When Christians invoke the name of God or Christ in public argument, we communicate that not only is Jesus our King and Lord, but he is theirs, even if they deny it.

Hear Psalm 2 again: "Now therefore, O kings, be wise; be warned, O rulers of the earth. Serve the LORD with fear, and rejoice with trembling" (vv. 10–11). The psalmist was not searching for common ground. He was saying, "God is, and you should take heed. This is reality." It is the word of an ambassador sent by a king whose chariots are about to round the last mountain bend.

Are Polycarp's and the psalmist's words antidemocratic? Is there an inevitable tension between the democratic "We the People" and the prophet's "Thus says the Lord"? Arguably the most famous political philosopher of the twentieth century, John Rawls, thought so. He said we are morally obligated to only bring arguments that everyone can understand on his or her own terms. We *must* make arguments where there is an "overlapping consensus," Rawls said.[14]

I, however, am calling Rawls's requirement a Trojan horse for small-g god idolatry. Sometimes a government will have to make decisions where there is no consensus. For example: what is marriage? Do I need to convince Jacob on Jacob's terms, or does Jacob need to convince me on my terms? Whose gods make a decision in the public square on this question? Someone's must.

Taking the Polycarp approach does not mean carving out a space for religious speech in the public square. It means admitting that the public square contains *only* religious speech. Jacob comes with his religious speech; I come with mine. And we both should admit it.

No, I don't think we should try to force anyone to worship anything. I don't think we can. Instead, I am saying that everyone should enter the public square admitting who his or her gods are. Then everyone should employ his or her best arguments—common ground or not—for why his or her version of justice will make for the best laws.

What might the Polycarp approach look like practically speaking?

Here is an e-mail that illustrates. A pastor friend of mine sent it to the principal of his children's school. It leverages both the Polycarp and the Luther approaches. He explicitly named Jesus Christ as the foundation of his beliefs, yet he also searched out common ground by appealing to free speech. The principal had written an e-mail to the parents of the school expressing her grief over a racist incident that had occurred earlier at a bus stop. She also expressed how glad she was that certain flyers at the bus stop had been taken down. My friend replied as follows:

Dear Hailey,

Thank you for alerting us parents to the vile incident that happened today and encouraging us toward good resources and conversation with our children and fellow parents about how to respond . . .

As the pastor of one of our community's local churches, I've tried to create opportunities for our congregation to talk about the evil and the prevalence of racism and interact with perspectives outside the majority culture. This past year we held an on-going series on "Racism and the Church," considering the topic from a variety of perspectives: the Asian American experience, racism and law enforcement, immigration, and the African American experience. We had clergy of color, multi-ethnic and inter-racial couples, as well as majority culture representatives speak to us on the challenges they've faced. We intend to continue and build on those conversations in the coming year.

I offer this so that you will understand that as a faith community, we stand with the community as a whole in both rejecting racism for the evil that it is, and working to combat racism wherever we find it, but especially within ourselves. Dialogue, conversation, and careful listening across racial lines is a crucial step in that work. As Christians, we also believe that it is fundamental to the message of Jesus Christ, who came to heal our divisions both with God and each other.

However, I am concerned by something that I read in your e-mail, and that is the apparent approval of the suppression of free speech. In our country, even vile and hateful speech is protected speech, unless it rises to the level of harassment or threat. Clearly the two men yelling at the innocent student constituted harassment and should not be tolerated.

But the flyers, vile as they are, were posted in a common area used by the community at large to advertise all manner of events, associations, and ideas. To encourage or approve the tearing down of lawfully posted speech in a public area just because we find it offensive is not the message we want to send to our children, nor is it the way we want to teach them to respond to speech they disagree with. . . .

Our response to vile speech, and the response we teach our children, must not be suppression of speech, but the education of better speakers, with a more compelling message than that of hate and bigotry. Our response must be to create communities in which such vile speech gains no traction and finds fewer and fewer who are willing to listen to, much less entertain, such ideas.

I know that is your goal within our community, and I stand alongside you in that effort . . .

Sincerely . . .

The letter affirmed free speech, but it did not come across as self-interested. It found common ground, but it also affirmed a higher and transcendent demand: the message of Jesus Christ. It took a strong stand against wrongs "out there," but also acknowledged the planks in his own eyes: "working to combat racism wherever we find it, but especially within ourselves."

All in all, my friend's e-mail struck me as politically astute and pastorally wise. It was ambassadorial.

Incidentally, the principal called my friend after he sent this e-mail. She said how much she appreciated it. She acknowledged she hadn't given such careful thought to the issue of free speech. And she invited my friend to join the Parent Equity group that meets at the school to think through matters related to race and ethnicity in the community.

If the public square is a battleground of gods, we fool ourselves to pretend otherwise. Pretending that everyone enters in a non-sectarian fashion is to participate in a mass delusion. I'm trying to sell you my Trojan horse, and you're trying to sell me yours. I don't think we should give up the search for common ground. That's democracy and living amid pluralism. But perhaps it is time to begin honestly acknowledging our perspectives. "Look, my God does in fact make a demand on us, but I think you'll find that his demands lead to our peace, good, and flourishing. As for your gods, how are they doing? Which category of statistics would you point to in order to argue that America is improving and that people are happier?"

Without a doubt, the Polycarp approach, too, has its costs. Just ask the martyred Polycarp! It will immediately close ears, especially in our present public square. Nearly everyone today suffers the mass delusion of "neutrality." I am simply pointing to the direction I would like to see Christians push public conversations, little by little, with prudence and discretion. Start by exposing everyone's gods or at least helping people to see the worldview backdrop of their policy positions. Then name our God as the real God and appeal to the conscience, the unchanging laws of human nature, and statistics to argue that his ways are better and most just.

And how much better it would be if healthy and hospitable churches were sitting in the background testifying to the same truths.

8. Practice convictional kindness.

Here's one more word about these public conversations. I like the phrase "convictional kindness" from Russell Moore's book *Onward:*

Engaging the Culture Without Losing the Gospel.[15] We should act according to our convictions, but we must do so kindly.

Peter admonished us, "Keep your conduct among the Gentiles honorable, so that when they speak against you as evildoers, they may see your good deeds and glorify God on the day of visitation" (1 Peter 2:12). The integrity of the messenger matters. Does your conduct before the world mark you as a credible spokesperson for Christ—doing good works and being humble and repentant about your shortcomings?

The quality and tone of our speech also matters. James offered advice for all our speech including in political engagement: "Let every person be quick to hear, slow to speak, slow to anger; for the anger of man does not produce the righteousness of God" (1:19–20). Paul put an even finer point on it: "Let your speech always be gracious, seasoned with salt, so that you may know how you ought to answer each person" (Col. 4:6).

If you participate in social media, does your tone edify or convey care? Or does it lambast and belittle? How will it affect your evangelism?

Our arguments should seek to persuade rather than to score points. One clear indication that you are simply seeking to score points is that you paint the other side in the worst light imaginable. You point to their worst-case-scenario stories. Your side will cheer when you do this, but the other side knows exactly what you're doing: you're shaming them. As a result, your tactic widens the divide. Instead, represent your opponents in the best possible light. In time, you will earn credibility and respect, and you might learn something as you work to represent them fairly.

By this token, we should remain genuinely open to persuasion, particularly in the jagged-line or wisdom territory. Non-Christians often have competencies we don't. They may understand cause-and-effect relationships in economics better than we do. They may have a scientific background that informs our thinking about energy policy. They may understand the situation on the ground in Ukraine more fully than we do. In cases like these, humility demands that we engage in genuine inquiry. Not only is this the right thing to do, but it will have a marked effect on how we are perceived.[16]

9. Do not attribute your interpretation of historical events to Providence.

Christians sometimes try to win political arguments by claiming to "know" what God is or is not doing in history. But this can be a subtle form of idolatry. "The secret things belong to the LORD our God, but the things that are revealed belong to us," says Deuteronomy 29:29. To presume to know what God is doing behind the scenes is to presume to be God.

Historian Mark Noll's fascinating book *The Civil War as a Theological Crisis* gives multiple examples of Christians in the American North and South both interpreting the events of the Civil War in their favor. Both ascribed motives to God that fortified the rightness of their cause, whether in a battle lost or won.

The North believed that the South's desire to perpetuate an evil system provoked God's displeasure, and so God was bringing an end to that system. The South interpreted its defeats as an act of God's discipline against the righteous.

I likewise recall church leaders in America interpreting Hurricane Sandy in 2012 as God's judgment against the nation's moral transgressions.

Was God doing any of these things? Perhaps. Or perhaps God was doing a million other things. Abraham Lincoln profoundly observed in his second inaugural address that both the North and the South "read the same Bible, and pray to the same God; and each invokes His aid against the other." Yet the prayers "of neither has been answered fully. The Almighty has his own purposes."

When we claim to *know* what God is doing in history, speaking where Scripture does not, we risk projecting our own ideological and partisan preferences onto God. In effect, we substitute our wisdom for God's, and thus become idolaters.

10. Know your own party's strengths, weaknesses, and idolatrous trajectories.

We must hold our party affiliations with a loose grip. Otherwise, we will domesticate our faith to our party. Therefore, it's a good idea to know your party's strengths, weaknesses, and idolatrous trajectories.

Let me give you my own evaluation of the two main American parties. You don't need to agree. I just want to give you an example of the kind of evaluation I would encourage every Christian to do.

A biblical strength of the Republican Party is its emphasis on personal responsibility and not looking to government as a service provider. A biblical strength of the Democratic party is its interest in representing the disenfranchised and downcast.

An idolatrous trajectory of the Republican Party is its tendency toward an amoral libertarianism, which can function according to the utilitarian principle of sacrificing the few for the sake of the many. Its good emphasis on individual responsibility can overlook larger structural realities and deny implicit biases. And these blind spots or idolatries—and it can be one or the other—end up leaving behind the poor, the foreigner, or the minority. This is unjust.

An idolatrous trajectory of the Democratic party is toward a secular godlessness that literally boos God at its national convention while also treating government as the godlike savior for all of life's ills. Many in the party have bought into the god of self-definition and self-expression, a religion that denounces and screens out biblical morality. The party's platform and practices prize the "liberty" of sexuality and lifestyle decisions over the life and liberty of an unborn person.

Whether you identify with the Democrats or the Republicans, the gospel frees us from being over-identified with either. Instead, it equips you to enter either party as an ambassador. It enables you to be a better party member by affirming the good, denouncing the bad, and pushing your party toward justice.

As with the KKK, the Nazi Party, or the Communist Party, I do believe a time can come when Christians should no longer affiliate with a certain party. Yet keep in mind there is a distinction between your own personal judgment on that matter and a church's judgment in its membership decisions. And until your church is ready to make that much more difficult decision, Christians should show respect, care, and love for one another across party lines.

11. Be prepared on occasion to disobey the state.

Think of Daniel and the three Hebrews who refused at separate times to bow down and pray to Nebuchadnezzar's false gods at the threat of their lives. Or think of Peter doing the same when standing before the Sanhedrin: "We must obey God rather than men" (Acts 5:29).

There are rare times that Christians must disobey the state and perhaps even rarer times when we might overthrow it.

Earlier we said that every human being is commissioned by Genesis 9:5–6 and that there is something vaguely democratic about government in the Bible. One implication of this is that we should work to uphold Genesis 9:5–6 even when a government doesn't.

Ask yourself, does Genesis 9:6 apply to Adolf Hitler? "Whoever sheds the blood of man, by man shall his blood be shed." Or is a dictator like Hitler *above* the reach of that verse's accountability? Christians sometimes debate whether the German pastor Dietrich Bonhoeffer was right to participate in an assassination plot against Hitler. For my part, I think Bonhoeffer—since he had the opportunity—may have had a positive Genesis 9:6 *duty* to participate. Hitler had shut down every possible peaceable avenue of removing him, and Hitler was *not* above Genesis 9:6. Nor is any government.

It's rare indeed when Christians and citizens generally might think of overthrowing a government. All sorts of other considerations come into play. If, in all likelihood, your attempts at overthrow are going to get your family and friends killed and nothing more, your insurrection may not be just. Just war theory applies here too. Your revolution is unjust unless you can put a better government in place. Otherwise, the anarchy you create will lead to all sorts of other injustices. But, in principle, a government that is not sustaining human life but positively hurting, abusing, and destroying its own people is a government that, we might argue, has earned the judgment of Genesis 9:5–6.

That is the biblical case for a revolution. It's not the mere withdrawing of consent, as Thomas Jefferson said. Obviously, any action you take against a government will be judged by God's final government on the Last Day. Make sure you're ready to give that account.

Slightly more common are those instances when a Christian will have to decide whether to obey a law that requires him or her to disobey God's law. Of course, it's not always so easy to determine when that is. You're a court judge who is asked to perform a same-sex wedding. Do you? Probably not. You're a court clerk who is asked to type up the license for the same-sex marriage that just occurred. Do you? I'm honestly not sure.

The best advice I can give you if you find yourself in such a situation is, talk to your Christian friends and especially your pastors. Many such scenarios will have to be treated on a case-by-case basis.

There's much more that needs to be said here. But hopefully you're getting the broad outlines. God has given government a job to do, and its authority only falls inside the jurisdiction that God has established. When the government drives outside of its lanes, or requires sin inside its lanes, you have no moral obligation to obey. Further, when a government habitually and characteristically works against its God-given mandate, it may well be time to fire the government.

Incidentally, praise the Lord that we live in a country where there are so many peaceful ways to fire the government before you ever have to resort to civil disobedience or revolution. God does not promise his people a country as good as America has been.

12. Pray for the government.

Paul instructed us to pray "for kings and all who are in high positions, that we may lead a peaceful and quiet life, godly and dignified in every way" (1 Tim. 2:2). We should pray not only for the governments we like, but for the ones we don't like.

If we're to pray for the king so that we may live peaceful and quiet lives, another implication follows: we should also pray against unjust governments. I love Philip Ryken's illustration about one praying church in Aberdeen, Scotland, named Gilcomston South Church. He served there as a pastoral intern. Here's Phil telling the story:

> Back in 1992 it was typical for a member of that church to thank God for the way he had brought down the Iron Curtain of communism in eastern Europe. From the way that they prayed, it was clear that they believed that their prayers had something to do with the collapse of the Soviet Empire. I was tempted to pull one of them aside and say, "You know, it was a little more complicated than that. The global economy had something to do with it, not to mention the arms race and the spiritual bankruptcy of communism. It took more than your prayers to pull down the Berlin Wall."
>
> I was tempted to say such a thing, but I knew better. Who is to say what part a praying church actually plays in world affairs? To go to Gilcomston on a Saturday night was to know what was

going on in the world. The prayers of God's people really are at the heart of what God is doing. When the true history of the world is finally written, we will discover that Christians like the ones in Aberdeen had a profound influence on world events.[17]

CONCLUSION

Let's go back to where we began this chapter. Scripture calls us to politically engage for love's sake, but don't set your hopes too much in the politics of the world. Our political hopes must remain in Christ's kingdom and in his church.

A pastor friend recently shared with me the story of a seventy-five-year-old woman in his church. When he asked her to shelter a young homeless woman for the night, she replied, "Oh, Pastor, James says faith without works is dead. She can not only come into my home; she can share my own bed." The woman then spent several months in the older woman's home. She went to drug rehab. She literally slept in her host's bed.

This older saint understood Christian politics. It began with her own life decisions and then spilled outward. Faith gave way to deeds.

Yet there was no room for triumphalism either. Just last week—the pastor told me as I write—the younger woman died of a drug overdose.

Politics in this world, as we said, is Sisyphean. "Vanity of vanities! All is vanity," said the author of Ecclesiastes (1:2).

Here are two questions for you: First, is it possible that God has good purposes even in the futility of drug overdoses and so many other political failures? Second, will you love and seek justice among your neighbors around you, even if you don't see results, for the glory of God, the vindication of his people, and the good of your neighbors?

I love the series of tweets my fellow elder Isaac posted the day after a large group of white nationalists marched in Charlottesville, Virginia. Isaac is black. He tweeted:

> Waking up to see what has occurred in Cville; that's where I met Meg (my white wife) and proposed to her. We love that town.

Then,

> Seeing what's happening there causes me to groan in such a way that reminds me that I am made for a house not made by hands (2 Cor. 5:1).

Finally,

> So I'll work down here, push the battle line forward if only an inch, but my hope will not be that work. My hope is God, my exceeding joy.

Inside our church, Isaac works to help the majority culture better understand the concern of minorities. He gives special talks. He holds book discussion groups. He targets minority brothers to disciple as potential elders. He spends time with knuckleheads like me. Outside our church he writes on issues of race. He performs evangelistic spoken-word poetry at local bookstores for unbelievers. And more. Inch by inch. For the joy set before him.

Isaac is a politically engaged Christian, yes, but also a wise one. He's not looking for access to the powerful. He's discipling the ordinary, the normal, the underwhelming, just like his Savior Jesus did. He's not trying to change the world. He's living out a changed world. He's starting small, knowing that the kingdom of God is like a mustard seed.

A Christian's engagement in politics thus has both higher stakes and lower stakes than we might initially think.[18] The stakes are higher in the sense that we are all duty-bound to represent Christ well in the public square. Both the words we use and the results we achieve are a part of the solemn work of glorifying God and enjoying him forever. But the stakes are also lower in the sense that no political result on this earth is final.

We make sincere efforts to persuade others to our points of view. But we do not fear losing, because we know that our God has already won. Every political result that plays out in this life is under God's sovereign control and is being worked out for the good of those who love him and who are called according to his purpose (Rom. 8:28). This knowledge liberates us to be the kind of happy ambassadors who are always faithful, and sometimes (with God's help) effective.

JUSTICE: NOT *JUST* RIGHTS, BUT RIGHT

"Well, Mr. Leeman, why do you want to teach the second grade?" the principal asked.

Second grade? Is that what she's interviewing me for? I'd never thought about teaching the second grade. *Do I even like seven-year-olds?*

Eventually I stammered, "Well, the second grade is crucial because you're still establishing foundations, and, you know, foundations are important." I don't remember what I said after that.

I had never taken a single college course on education. My undergraduate and graduate degrees were in political science. But I had heard the DC public schools were desperate for teachers and giving out temporary licenses. I was twenty-four, single, and interested in a yearlong adventure while applying for more graduate school. So I attended a DCPS job fair and put in an application to teach high school social studies.

Only the elementary school called.

The principal didn't ask any further questions. Instead she spent the next fifteen minutes describing her philosophy of education. She reached the end, smiled, and said, "And, Mr. Leeman, I think you would fit very nicely at our school. I hope you will accept the teaching position." She was at the end of a long career and out of steam.

So no coursework on education. No certification. No second question. No background check. No phone calls to my references. Only a fifteen-second glance at my résumé. And, lo and behold, several weeks later I was in a classroom with twenty-six second-graders.

One girl in my class was Hispanic. The rest were African American, as was every other adult in the school save two. The school was tucked in between federal government office buildings and Section 8 federal housing projects. The students came from the projects. Today the school is rated at the very bottom (12th percentile in the nation on math, 9th percentile on English).

I was completely in over my head. For the first month, the school had no curriculum for me to follow. No books. No pencils or paper. Just me, a blackboard, twenty-six little chairs, twenty-six little desks, and twenty-six precious and beautiful seven-year-olds. I was never given a teaching assistant. The principal stepped into the classroom for a few minutes only half a dozen times during the whole year.

Gratefully, my church provided me with basic school supplies for all the children. And a woman from the church came in to assist on a number of occasions. I made up my own worksheets.

Many of the children were being raised by their grandmothers, most by single mothers who were clearly working themselves to the bone. They'd show up a few minutes late to pick up a child, out of breath and apologetic.

One mother regularly dropped off her boy around ten in the

morning. She would be high on drugs. A school administrator told me he was a "crack baby," the term we used in the nineties. It feels insensitive to say it now. He couldn't be contained at his desk and would often run around the classroom, poking the other children, oblivious to my pleading. Many days I had to walk him down to the school office. He'd sit in the office for an hour or two, and then they'd send him back. There was nothing they could do either.

I never desired to teach for more than a year. I think that, somewhat selfishly, I just wanted the experience. It was easily the hardest year of my life workwise. Thankfully, the children seemed to learn their double-digit addition and subtraction. Their reading improved ever so slightly. I don't think I hurt their education, but I don't know how much I helped it either.

A few weeks before the school year concluded, a friend in journalism called and told me about an international economics magazine looking for a managing editor. She knew the publisher and would call him on my behalf if I was interested. I was. A few days later I found myself sitting at a long mahogany table surrounded by wingback chairs across from a couple of white DC insiders in expensive shirts and shoes. A contemporary all-glass wall was on one side, a ninth-floor view of downtown Washington on the other. The office assistant offered me a choice of beverages in a glass with ice. No metallic-flavored school hallway drinking fountain here. I distinctly remember leaning back in the tall chair and noticing something else the school didn't have: air conditioning.

I spent the next couple of years at that magazine. I didn't keep up with the children and felt a little guilty about that. Picture me instead sitting in a nice DC restaurant with friends recounting the adventures of that harrowing year. After a few crack-baby stories, they would congratulate me. "That's great, Jonathan. It's really neat you did that." Look at me. I'm the white hero.

CAN AMERICA HEAL
ITS DIVISIONS?

I began this book with illustrations of how contentious and divided America has become. We're divided over immigration, health care, the host of policy issues that give rise to the debates between nationalism and globalism, marital norms, LGBT equality, transgender politics in the high school locker room, religious freedom, and more.

The politics of race, the backdrop to my year teaching the second grade, offers another obvious illustration of America's division today. Was I able to parachute in and helicopter out of that school because of my own individual talent and skill? Or because I had access to a whole host of resources and networks that my African American students and colleagues did not have, such as a supportive two-parent home, college professors and employers who gave me the benefit of the doubt because I'm white, and friends in downtown DC jobs who could make phone calls on my behalf? Let me restate the question: were a host of individuals to blame for the tough state of this public school and its neighborhood (absentee fathers, drug-addicted mothers, tired principals)? Or did larger systemic injustices set the stage on which the entire narrative of my year was set (underresourced schools, white privilege, discriminatory mortgage lending practices and white flight, harsher criminal sentencing against blacks than whites for drug use, leading to those absentee fathers)?

You can interpret this story in one of two ways. And I assume readers will go one way or the other. Based on surveys, if you are a white conservative Protestant, you are more likely than any other demographic category (minorities, non-Christians, and others), to blame the individuals themselves. If you are a black conservative

Protestant, you are more likely than any other demographic category to blame "the system."[1] The first groups says this is a personal responsibility issue. The second group says it's a justice issue.

The larger point I want to draw out here is that behind every political division in the nation is a different view of justice. Pick any point of division you want (abortion, immigration, race politics, or others), and behind that division you'll find at least two sides with different versions of what justice requires. My public school story, for instance, will trigger the justice reflexes of some, not others.

If we live in a divided age, as the title of this book says, it's in part because we have different views of justice. And these different views of justice make it very difficult to talk to one another. Instead, two sides bark at each other like scared dogs. Students on university campuses bemoan "microaggressions," demand "safe spaces," and violently confront conservative speakers. Professors end up in neck braces. Meanwhile, white nationalists march in Charlottesville, Virginia, and elsewhere. Not only do disparities exist, we seem to be shouting about them more and more.

"So I feel a deep sense of dread," said a writer in the foreign policy magazine *The American Interest*, "that our social fabric is too corroded to channel disagreements through political institutions; that the American creed is battered and broken." He concluded, "Great countries can fall apart. I don't know what that would look like for America. And I don't know how to stop it."[2]

I don't know if America's divisions today are run of the mill or if the nation stands on the precipice of a cataclysmic division, where rule of law gives way. My own instinct is that our nation's relative wealth masks the depth of division. If the economy were to collapse, we would discover what the country is really made of.

Either way, do you think America possesses the tools to heal its divisions? It depends on where we look for justice.

A NATIONAL MISSION STATEMENT

America's primary tool for healing divisions and pursuing a unified vision of justice has always been to assert and reassert our shared belief in equality, liberty, and natural rights. You hear these assertions in inaugural speeches, school classrooms, and movies.

Yet we've also long recognized that the goal of unity through this vision of justice was something of a test. For instance, the Civil War tested that unity. So said Abraham Lincoln in his 1863 Gettysburg Address. His 272-word speech began,

> Four score and seven years ago our fathers brought forth on this continent, a new nation, conceived in Liberty, and dedicated to the proposition that all men are created equal. Now we are engaged in a great civil war, testing whether that nation, or any nation so conceived, and so dedicated, can long endure.

Consider the question that the speech wants us to answer: can a self-governing nation dedicated to both freedom and equality *endure*? The great civil war was testing that proposition.

When Lincoln asked his question, he was looking back "four score and seven years" to 1776 and the Declaration of Independence. The Declaration had also declared the "self-evident" truth "that all men are created equal." The trouble was, the author of the Declaration himself hadn't really owned that proposition. He owned slaves. The Constitution hadn't owned it. It counted slaves as three-fifths a person for the purposes of determining the number of representatives in the House. And several generations of slave-holding Americans hadn't owned it. Justice had not prevailed.

So Lincoln was asking, would the nation finally own the proposition that all men—meaning *all* people of *every* color—were created equal?

He concluded the speech by calling for "a new birth of freedom." This new birth would prove that self-government ("government of the people, by the people, for the people") actually works ("shall not perish").

Together Jefferson's Declaration and Lincoln's Address present America's mission statement on justice: we are a people dedicated to the principles of equality, freedom, and natural rights.

IS A DEDICATION TO FREEDOM AND EQUALITY ENOUGH?

What do you think: Is our national vision statement on justice enough to heal our national divisions? Do we just need someone to repeat the Gettysburg Address?

Or let me sharpen the question: Can you and I, *no matter which gods we worship*, justly govern ourselves together based merely on a shared commitment to the principles of freedom, equality, and individual rights? Can three hundred million of us do that?

I think the answer is no.

Apart from a fear of God, the hope of the Declaration and Gettysburg is a misplaced hope for a nation. Christians should not merely be interested in equality, liberty, and individual rights, but in a just equality, a just liberty, and a just set of rights, *as God defines just*.

I'm not saying it's time to wrap the cross in an American flag. I'm not saying we need a constitutional amendment that affirms the God of the Bible. I am saying we need to stop and acknowledge reality again and to beat the drum I've been beating throughout this book. Everyone has a God or god whom he or she worships in everything. Every God or god comes with his or her own brand of justice. And therefore every God or god comes with his or her own conceptions of equality, freedom, and rights.

Pick your God or gods; out will come your views on justice.

Pick your conception of justice; out will come your views on equality, freedom, and rights. We might find overlap with the gods of others. But there are no religiously neutral brands of justice, equality, freedom, and rights available to us.

The advocates and opponents of Jim Crow's separate-but-equal laws all affirmed something called equality. But clearly they meant different things by the word.

The pro-lifer and the pro-choicer both agree on something called freedom. But they disagree on whether a woman has the freedom to terminate her pregnancy.

Conservatives and progressives agree that gays and lesbians possess a right to marriage. But they disagree profoundly on whether they have the right to marry someone of the same sex.

Behind both sides of all three pairs, at least functionally, are different views of justice and different gods. America's past has its share of false gods, such as the god of white supremacy. Perhaps the most famous gods today are the god of me and the god of my group. Both these gods rage mightily against the Lord and against his Anointed.

Which means, we can affirm with Lincoln and Jefferson the "self-evident" truths about "inalienable" rights and the equality of all people. But that doesn't mean we won't end up as a nation divided. The more everyone's god of me or my group reigns, the more we will slide deeper into tribalism.[3]

I want to spend the rest of this chapter comparing two different brands of justice and the gods behind them. It's almost like looking at two universes. Is the goal here to figure out how to "Christianize" America? No, it's to help Christians understand how to stand for the justice of the true God and not to align themselves with the justice of some false god. There is no third option.

JUSTICE AS RESPECTING RIGHTS

The reigning conception of justice in America we inherited from the American founding is justice as respecting rights. I have rights. You have rights. Justice means affirming and protecting those rights as far as we can without interfering with someone else's rights. Rights make right. Courts exist, among other reasons, to adjudicate when different people's rights come into conflict.

Defining justice as respecting rights seems like a nice, pragmatic compromise for maintaining the peace between people of different worldviews and religions. We cannot agree on who God is. But we can respect one another's rights, right?

Well, it's not that simple. Who or what establishes which rights are right? Sometimes our gods will agree on which rights are right. At other times they won't, which is when the battles begin. As we've thought about throughout this book, hidden inside of a person's view of "rights" is a god and that god's definition of right and wrong.

Chai Feldblum, an Obama-appointed commissioner on the Equal Employment Opportunity Commission, essentially agreed. Feldblum is a lesbian. She spent the 1990s working to overturn the government's ban on gays and lesbians in the military, and the 2000s for LGBT equality in the marketplace. She believed Christians in the wedding industry, for instance, should not be able to turn away gay customers. "Once individuals choose to enter the stream of economic commerce by opening commercial establishments, I believe it is legitimate to require that they play by certain rules."[4] So the Christian baker must bake the cake for the homosexual wedding. The bed-and-breakfast owner must accommodate the lesbian or unmarried straight couple.

Feldblum acknowledged that her moral values and the moral

values of evangelical Christians contradict each other head on. It's a zero-sum game, she said. One has to win, and one has to lose. It simply won't work to pretend we can find neutral common ground. Feldblum did not count her lesbian identity as "religious." She made a distinction between "belief-liberty" and "identity-liberty." But she conceded that both of these things play the same role in a person's life. Both are crucial to identity formation and both determine our politics.

She wrote, "If I am denied a job, an apartment, a room at a hotel, a table at a restaurant or a procedure by a doctor because I am a lesbian, that is a deep, intense and tangible hurt." And that hurt, she said, isn't alleviated just because she can go down the street and find another vendor. No. "The assault to my dignity and my sense of safety in the world occurs when the initial denial happens. That assault is not mitigated by the fact that others might not treat me in the same way."[5]

For Feldblum, identity is ultimate. Identity is god. There is nothing deeper, more profound, more unmovable. Therefore, identity is the source of righteousness and right. If my sense of identity demands it, it must be right.

Her politics then follow her religion of personal and group identity. The rights of gays and lesbians trump the rights of Christians and religious liberty: "In making the decision in this zero-sum game, I am convinced society should come down on the side of protecting the liberty of LGBT people." Indeed, she found it "difficult to envision any circumstances" in which courts should side with religious freedom over LGBT identity.[6]

On this battleground of gods, whoever's god can scream the loudest, most malign the other side, and secure the most votes wins. It's a test of sheer power. If my god can beat up your god, my god's understanding of right gets to define everyone's rights. My god gets to determine what justice is.

Is justice in such a system therefore merely about who has the most power?

Sometimes people refer to Feldblum's brand of thinking as "identity politics." Identity politics, broadly speaking, begins with the common-sense observation that our lives and beliefs are shaped by the groups we occupy—whether those groups are based on gender, race, class, sexual orientation, or something else. And then it makes moral and political claims based on those group identities.

In its best forms, identity politics, at least when it comes from the Left, gives a voice to the oppressed and raises the public's consciousness of their oppression. It works to create empathy for people on the margins. Christians should support that objective. Further, it's helpful to acknowledge that we all speak from our perspectives, whether majority or minority, Christian or not.

In its more secular forms, however, identity politics is where a post-religion, post-philosophy, post-truth, postmodern world goes to find its source of *all* belief and morality. Secular identity politics tells us our beliefs and morality are *all* socially constructed. God is dead; capital-T Truth is too. Which means, there is scarcely a common humanity to speak of, and there are no morally impermissible groups. Yet we still need something to believe, some moral standards to guide our lives.

Where do we get them? From our tribe. Our tribes give us meaning, purpose, value, a code. People on the political Right and political Left do this. It's not as if only progressives play this game while conservatives maintain some objective posture. We all live and identify with our tribes, and those tribes coexist in a perpetual state of war, like a Mad Max movie. Indeed, what we think of as "I" or "myself" is a composite of all the tribes we inhabit: the values and words we learned from this family, that ethnic identity, that nation, that high school, that professional group, and so forth.

Two consequences follow. First, conversation between tribes

stops. We speak different languages, after all. "They're not 'woke.'" "They're tearing down our history."

Second, tribes often attribute to each other the root injustices. You indict me for being bigoted and oppressive. I accuse you of totalitarianism and trying to control the way I think. And we're back at the shouting match.

When you remove the God of glory and the God of judgment who created all humanity in his image, this is where the story of freedom, rights, and equality culminates. I dare say, the American Experiment, divorced from God, makes same-sex marriage, transgender-bathroom debates, and the end of religious tolerance inevitable. Every person becomes his or her own god. Every citizen possesses the right to "define one's own concept of existence, of meaning, of the universe, and of the mystery of human life."[7]

Conservatives decry this line from the Supreme Court case *Planned Parenthood v. Casey*, but I'd say it's perfectly consistent with the values of the Declaration and the Gettysburg Address when they are divorced from God. If God is not judge and I am not created in his image, then, yes, I have every right to define my gender, my existence, my everything.

Though I can hardly prove the point, my guess is that the American Experiment slowly changed the nation's moral intuitions in a way the founders never would have predicted. The values extolled in a public square for two hundred years will eventually define that nation's basic sense of morality. And for two hundred years Americans have listened to school teachers, Independence Day speeches, patriotic stories, calls to arms, and movies in which the hero defiantly yells "Freedom" against English oppressors. They all say the same thing: "Our commitment to rights, freedom, and equality is what makes us great. We will even give the ultimate sacrifice of our lives on the battlefield for them." Once, Americans might have lived their lives with a broader array of moral intuitions, such as a belief in honor, loyalty, respect for authority, and the sacred.[8] But slowly, bit by bit, from one generation to the next, those older intuitions, those basic moral categories which need no argument, are fading away. Less and less do they make sense to us. The only moral categories that come to predominate are a belief in liberty, proportional fairness, and not harming others—the three values that animate social justice. So if you were to say to most Americans today, "That's degrading" or "Don't emotionally defile her" or "You owe him respect" or "Please obey" or "Honor your body" or "It's inappropriate to dress and act that way," the words mean almost nothing. Our moral register simply doesn't recognize the categories.

JUSTICE AS ADMINISTERING WHAT GOD SAYS IS RIGHT

Time to look at a second universe. What does the Bible say about justice? Christians throw the word around a lot these days, so I want to be careful here. Slowing down for a moment will help us in the long run. Let's start with five qualities of biblical justice.

1. It entails judgment.

The Hebrew word that my ESV Bible translates as "justice" 125 times is interchangeable with the English word "judgment." It's the noun form of the verb "to judge." Justice in the Bible, first and foremost, is an activity, and it's the activity of *judging* or *applying a judgment*.

2. It entails righteousness.

The term doesn't refer to just any judgment, but judgment according to God's righteousness. Almost half the time you see the word *justice* in the Old Testament the word *righteousness* is next to it, as when the psalmist said to God, "Righteousness and justice are the foundation of your throne" (Ps. 89:14). The two words together are what grammarians call a *hendiadys*—two words connected by an "and" that explain each other and together mean something bigger, like *nice and cozy*. The biblical ideas of justice and righteousness are locked together and are mutually defining, even when they don't appear together.

Therefore, putting points one and two together, I often insert either the words *righteous judgment* or *administering righteousness* in my head when I see the word *justice* in the Bible. If Isaiah says that "the LORD is a God of justice" (30:18), I think to myself, *The Lord is a God of righteous judgment.* When Proverbs says, "By justice a king builds up the land" (29:4), I understand that a king builds up the land by administering righteousness.

If you want a definition of *justice* from a biblical perspective, either *righteous judgment* or *administering righteousness* might be the simplest. The slightly longer definition provided in J. Paul Nyquist's book *Is Justice Possible? The Elusive Pursuit of What Is Right* is also helpful: justice is *"the application of God's righteous moral standards to the conduct of man."*[9] I like that definition because it helps us see that justice is not just a courtroom word, where a judge literally judges. We want to exercise justice—apply God's righteous standards—in our families, with our neighbors, with our fellow church members, in relation to the disadvantaged, and so on. That is doing justice.

3. It is a quality.

Justice is not just an activity but a quality. When we speak of a just balance or a just law or a just person, we mean that balance or law or person's life accords with standards of righteousness.

4. It is personal and relational.

Speaking of "standards," it occured to me that words like *standards* or *laws* or *formulas* can sound impersonal. And standards can be impersonal, as when Scripture refers to "just balances." But the broader idea of justice in Scripture is personal and relational. How is that? Justice begins with God, and God, by nature, is personal and relational. All God's attributes, including his righteousness, are therefore personal and relational. Whenever God exercises judgment, he does so according to his own *internal* and *personal* standards. Further, he does so in a manner perfectly suited to the relationships between his three persons and perfectly suited to his covenantal relationships with human beings.

5. It is covenantal.

That brings us to a fifth point: biblical justice is covenantal. God established and defined his relationship with *humanity in common* through the "common covenants" given through Adam and Noah. And he established and defined his relationship with his *special people* through the "special covenants" given through Abraham, Moses, David, and Christ.

When asking the biblical question, "What does justice require?" we need to think about which covenant is in motion. Justice requires slightly different things according to the standards—or, better, according to the divine vows—of God's different covenants. One set of God's vows binds people through the covenant with Noah, another through the covenant with Abraham, and so forth.

WHAT KIND OF JUSTICE DO GOD'S COMMON COVENANTS REQUIRE?

Let's take a closer look at the common covenants. What kind of justice do they require?

We considered in chapter 4 the government's job to pursue justice based on Genesis 9:5–6, which is one element in the Noahic covenant (Gen. 9:1–17). God said he requires a "reckoning" for shed blood based on the fact that people are created in God's image. The standard here is parity (blood for blood) for anything that brings harm to an image-bearing human being. That's what a government and its citizens need to keep their eyes on.

Sure enough, God indicted Israel and its leaders later in its history for not upholding this basic level of justice through the prophet Ezekiel: "Her princes in her midst are like wolves tearing the prey, shedding blood, destroying lives to get dishonest gain. . . . The people of the land have practiced extortion and committed robbery. They have oppressed the poor and needy, and have extorted from the sojourner without justice" (Ezek. 22:27, 29).

God has covenantally identified himself with all humanity through his image. To attack or demean or abuse or exploit someone created in God's image is to do these things to him. It's like laughing at someone's reflection in a mirror. You're laughing at the person. God's image in us is a suit of armor or a force field. It protects each of us.

Moreover, it gives us value and worth. That aborted fetus, that homeless man on the street, that person struggling with gender dysphoria, that member of the opposite political party, that Muslim—God has identified himself with all of them by creating them in his image.

All these lessons certainly apply in the courtroom, where a judge can require blood for blood. But the implications extend well beyond the court. The constitution writers and legislatures in a good government will want to ensure that all of a nation's laws affirm the value and worth of God-imaging human beings.

Suppose, for instance, that both high school dropout rates and unemployment rates begin to increase. A just government would want to investigate such matters. After all, being created in God's image involves growing in knowledge and working. And if something structural is preventing a portion of the population from growing in knowledge and from working, those structural factors have effectively created an injustice. Or, at least we could say, the impulse to correct the problem is a just impulse.

My fellow church member Chelsea teaches at a public high school where the dropout rate was 46 percent several years ago. Chelsea knows from Genesis 9:5–6 that each one of these students has been created in God's image. Therefore she works both inside and outside of her classroom to help decrease that dropout rate. I asked her to explain what exactly she does:

> I host Bible studies in my classroom after school with snacks; buy lots of meals at Chipotle/Subway for hungry students; bring kids to church; keep a loaf of bread with peanut butter and jelly in my classroom mini fridge for kids to make sandwiches for lunch; keep fruit snacks and granola bars in my filing cabinet; bought a couple students toiletries; buy a lot of school uniform shirts; collect uniform-approved sweaters from church members and keep them in the classroom; keep super glue and needle and thread handy for all the ripped pants and broken glasses; made a lot of posters and went to a lot of basketball and football games to cheer on students whose parents never came . . .

This sister is administering God's righteousness in her work—doing justice by treating these teenagers as God-imagers, many of whose lives have been shaped by layer after layer of injustice.

I'm not of the opinion that an unequal distribution of resources is inherently unjust. God gives more to some, less to others, as he sees fit. Think of Jesus' parable of the stewards, where one man has five talents, another two, another one. Still, the image of God in every human being should elicit a special concern for the disenfranchised and downtrodden. "The righteous care about justice for the poor" and, "If a king judges the poor with fairness, his throne will be established forever," says Proverbs (29:7, 14 NIV). We need the wisdom of Solomon to do this well. Government intervention can hurt as much as it can help. The point is, the brand of justice assigned to governments in the Noahic covenant seems to be broader than mere retribution. It charges a government with a concern for the poor, the oppressed, and the sojourner, like Ezekiel said.

Indeed, all this images God's own justice. "The LORD works righteousness and justice for all who are oppressed" (Ps. 103:6); and "the LORD will maintain the cause of the afflicted, and will execute justice for the needy" (140:12; see also Deut. 24:17–18; Ps. 10:18; 82:3; Isa. 1:17, 23; 10:1–2; Jer. 5:28; 22:13–16).

FIRST RIGHT, THEN RIGHTS

The fact that we were created in God's image also means that a just government will work to protect its citizens' rights. Nineteenth-century Dutch theologian Herman Bavinck drew this point out of God's common and special covenants: "God makes a 'covenant of nature' with Noah and a 'covenant of grace' with Abraham, acts by which he again, out of sheer grace, *grants to his creatures an array of rights* and *binds himself by an oath to maintain these rights*" (emphasis added).[10]

In other words, the idea of natural human rights didn't start with secular, anti-Christian Enlightenment thinkers in the eighteenth century. It goes back to God's covenant with Noah. People have rights because God created them in his image. Governments should respect people's rights *because* people are made in God's image and are of inestimable worth.[11]

Yet here is what's crucial for American Christians to recognize. True justice doesn't start with our rights. It starts with God's righteousness and his understanding of what's right. We do justice by doing what's *right*, which includes respecting people's *rights*. First right, then rights. The order is crucial. What God says is right is the root; rights are the flower.

To put it another way, we should never stop asking what makes rights right. The answer for a Christian must be that rights are right because God says they are right. That's why human governments should respect our rights.

When Americans talk about justice merely as respecting one another's rights, they cut off the roots to the flower (to borrow from David Elton Trueblood). Eventually those flowers will shrivel and die.

"I have a right to an abortion."
"I have a right to my prejudices and my hate."
"I have a right to marry whomever I please."

Really? Says who?

When we disregard what God says is right, then anyone can say which rights are right and which aren't. There is no rebuttal. There is no public and accepted righteousness or standard of right.

Rights are wonderful gifts when a society is virtuous, possessing a godly standard of right. Less so when it becomes unvirtuous.

TWELVE LESSONS ON DOING JUSTICE

Remember also from chapter 5 that Genesis 9:5–6 has been given to all humanity, not just the officeholders in our governments. Christians in their private and public lives, therefore, should take an interest in upholding the image of God in other people. Here are twelve practical suggestions on doing justice by the standards of the common covenants.

1. Recognize that justice involves punishing the oppressor and lifting up the oppressed.

My sense is that people on the political Right emphasize justice as punishment, while those on the Left emphasize it as lifting up the oppressed. The Bible emphasizes both. We see this in Psalm 72's description of the just king: "May he judge your people with righteousness, and your poor with justice. . . . May he defend the cause of the poor of the people, give deliverance to the children of the needy, and crush the oppressor" (vv. 2, 4).

What office do you hold? Voter? Senate staffer? Church elder? Teacher? Parent? Do you use your office not just to oppose wrong, but to lift up those who have been afflicted? To defend the needy? Do you peel your eyes for such opportunities? Is that characteristic of you? Or do you have lots of excuses?

Keep in mind, when you're in power, you have a vested interest in maintaining the status quo. That can make it harder to see various forms of injustice. Often, it will be those on the periphery who call attention to those injustices. A Christian in a position of authority should continually work to cultivate the selflessness of Christ by listening to such voices and searching out injustices, even if it means disrupting the status quo and upending one's own power. Bible scholar Leon Morris observed that justice in Scripture isn't about "adherence to custom" or "a retention of the older order"; rather it's "nothing less than revolutionary dynamite."[12]

2. Recognize that different spheres call for different kinds of actions.

Suppose I'm not convinced the present immigration laws are fair. What does doing justice look like here? It might simultaneously look like three things according to three different domains. As a subject of the nation's laws, I apply God's righteousness by obeying and enforcing the present laws impartially. As a citizen and voter, I apply

God's righteousness by seeking to change the law. As a Christian, I might apply God's righteousness by addressing any perceived injustice in the present laws through acts of charity or personal help.

Chelsea, who works in the high school with high dropout rates, addressed the problem one way while teaching in her classroom and another way with girls after school.

3. Recognize that obligation to "do justice" increases as proximity increases.

The closer you are related to a situation of injustice—closer geographically, closer relationally, closer in terms of formal responsibilities—the more morally culpable you are if you do not ensure that wrongs are turned to rights. We learn this from Boaz's example at the end of Ruth, as well as Paul's comments about a man's responsibility being for his family in 1 Timothy 5.

The members of my church who live in my suburb possess more of an obligation to attend our town council meetings than members who don't live in our suburb. And even that obligation among us might differ according to different stewardships that God has given each of us.

4. Apply good laws fairly and impartially.

In the context of applying the laws that exist, doing justice means "equal treatment and a fair process. No bribes. No backroom deals. No slanderous judgments. No breaking your promises. No taking advantage of the weak."[13]

5. Vote for laws that treat people as creatures made in God's image.

In the context of making new laws, doing justice means treating people as God-imagers. Back in 2012, two measures on my Maryland state ballot gave me the opportunity to exercise such righteous judgment. Question 6 read, "Establishes that Maryland's civil marriage laws allows gay and lesbian couples to obtain a civil marriage license." Question 7 called for "the expansion of commercial gaming in the State of Maryland . . . to increase from 15,000 to 16,500 the maximum number of video lottery terminals that may be operated in the State." I voted against both of these because I believe from Scripture that both same-sex marriage and gambling harm people. It hurts their image-bearing nature.

6. Distinguish means and ends.

Sometimes justice requires a fair process, as in the courtroom where it calls for impartiality. Sometimes it calls for a certain outcome, as in overturning laws for abortion. When it's the former, one cannot be flexible on means or process. When it's the latter, one can be very flexible on process.

7. Support God-grounded civil rights.

The civil rights movement has always included both theological and secular voices. When Martin Luther King Jr. claimed that "the arc of the moral universe is long, but it bends toward justice,"[14] he was implicitly saying that a God of justice would finally resolve all things. However, the more recent and popular writer Ta-Nehisi Coates, an atheist, claimed the moral universe doesn't bend toward justice, but toward chaos.[15]

Certainly Christians can learn from Christians and non-Christians alike. I've learned from Coates. But insofar as civil rights takes an anti-God direction, building exclusively on human identity and removing God from the foundation of justice, civil rights will push toward idolatry. The same is true of any white reactions to the movement.

A better path is to continue insisting that all people have been created in God's image, a glorious truth that affirms both equality and difference. Read John Perkins's *Dream with Me: Race, Love, and the Struggle We Must Win* for a recent expression of that approach. Drawing from Genesis 1, Perkins, who led voter registration and school desegregation efforts in the 1960s, wrote, "We do not give people dignity; God gives it to them."[16]

The secular approach to race and ethnicity either insists that everyone should conform to one objective cultural norm (perhaps the more common conservative error?), or insists that everyone is different and that we cannot understand one another (perhaps the more common progressive error?).

The Christian path affirms both our common humanity and our created differences. It requires color-blindness with respect to our oneness in Adam and (if believers) in Christ (Gal. 3:28). It requires color-consciousness with respect to our different experiences, histories, and cultural traditions, as well as the unique ways different people can glorify God (1 Cor. 12:13–14; Rev. 7:9).

The secular path tries to create empathy but offers little basis for it. It only speaks in the language of power and self-assertion.

The Christian path, built on our God-imaging unity with all people or our Christian unity in the gospel, offers the grounds for empathy. Within the church especially, we discover the ability to weep with those who weep and rejoice with those who rejoice. All these people of every color are my brothers and sisters. Discriminate against him or her, and you discriminate against me.

8. Suspect your own capacity for injustice.

As fallen sinners, we self-justify and excuse ourselves quickly. But we are all capable of injustice. Something I've noticed about my conservative and liberal friends alike is how sensitive everyone has become to the slightest critique, particularly critiques of our tribes. But Christians justified in the gospel can shed such defensiveness. Instead we can listen, learn, reconsider, and confess.

I appreciate my friend Andrew Walker's counsel: "Read those you disagree with. Sometimes those you disagree with will have something very thoughtful to say. This will help you learn that your ideological opponent is not an enemy or a horrible person. Also, you must develop empathy as a political instinct. To get a hearing from the person you disagree with, it's important to understand as much as possible where they are coming from, and what in their past has shaped them. You will never be persuasive if you fail to demonstrate empathy."[17]

9. Suspect your own potential for prejudice and implicit biases.

This is a more specific version of the last point. Certainly I hope every Christian would know to repent of any self-conscious prejudice and racism. Yet we should also watch our hearts for implicit biases—our unconscious fears or aversions toward different kinds of people. In some ways, our brains are built to make associations and form biases. A young child learns to associate a hot stove with "no touch." Yet how easily a natural preference for "our group" slides into a sinful sense of superiority or disdain for another group, particularly those of different ethnicities, accents, skin colors, or gender.

Paul Nyquist listed several examples of implicit bias in his book *Is Justice Possible?*

- Asian Americans have higher cancer rates than any other ethnic group, but are the least likely to receive recommendations for cancer screenings.
- Doctors who are shown two identical patient histories and asked to make a judgment about heart disease are much less likely to recommend cardiac catheterization to black patients.
- African American students are far more likely to be suspended than white students.

- Real estate agents will show African Americans fewer apartments to rent or houses for sale.
- Résumés with an African American-sounding name must be submitted to 50 percent more companies to yield the same number of calls.[18]

I've heard multiple black professors report they have to work extra hard on the first day of class to convince the students that, yes, they are smart enough to teach the class.

My goal here is not to indict your heart. It's to encourage you to examine it. As Christians, we should be the first to stop self-justifying and the first to self-indict when necessary. Our prejudices and biases are so natural, in fact, that repenting of them is a lifelong project.

10. Build loving friendships across ethnic and class lines.

Remember how I said biblical justice is personal and relational, since our just God is personal and relational? For most people like me in the middle class and ethnic majority, understanding the frustrations and injustices experienced by people on the margins and in the minority will prove difficult apart from personal relationships. And token friendships won't do. Instead, all of us must develop meaningful and loving relationships across ethnic and class lines. It's only in the context of such relationships—I predict—that you will discover that the requirements of justice are never as simple as textbook platitudes.

We often think of personal empathy and love as clouding the impartiality of justice. Hence, that Roman figure Lady Justice wears a blindfold. And, yes, justice must be impartial. Yet love is precisely the thing that helps us recognize the weight of other people's God-imaging *value*. It's when we love someone that we recognize how precious in God's sight he or she is. Love and empathy, we might even say, are prerequisites of justice, apart from which our judgments will always be imbalanced. The loving person seeks justice. The unloving person doesn't. God's justice is indeed impartial, but his eyes are wide open. And his judgments are never separated from his love.

The takeaway lesson is this: if you would be just, build meaningful friendships with people who don't look like you, sound like you, or shop in the same kinds of stores. Apart from meaningful relationships with people from different groups that involve your heart, your affections, and your love, you will most likely possess an incomplete picture of that group. And, as such, your calculations about "what's just" will more than likely be skewed, partial, and unjust.

11. Search out structural injustices.

Scripture says that not only can individuals be unjust, so can legal and social structures. Think of how Haman convinced Ahasuerus to enact a genocidal campaign against the Jews in the book of Esther (3:7–14). Think of how Jesus condemned the lawyers for loading burdens on people that are too hard for them to bear (Luke 11:46). Think of the preference shown to the Hebrew-speaking widows in Acts 6 or to the rich in James 2. As the prophet Isaiah wrote, "Woe to those who decree iniquitous decrees, and the writers who keep writing oppression, to turn aside the needy from justice and to rob the poor of my people of their right" (Isa. 10:1–2).

Structural injustice should be no surprise for Christians. Sinful people will pass sinful laws, erect sinful institutions, and devise sinful social practices. Or, at the very least, we easily establish policies or practices that unconsciously burden a certain group, such as an office manager who requires employees to work on Saturdays without giving special consideration to an Orthodox Jew (the Roman government did better).

Furthermore, suppose we acknowledge that not only can processes be unjust, but outcomes can be unjust. What then should we make of so many American ghettos? They were created at least in part by the discriminatory practices of banks, insurers, the Federal Housing Authority, and "white flight."[19] The residents of such neighborhoods today continue to suffer the effects of past injustices, which, at some level, is unfair.

Now, no human being possesses the ability to address every injustice even in one's own city. Plus, few Christians will have the opportunity to address bad laws, policies, or outcomes in a broad and systemic way. But recall this book's emphasis on *being* before *doing*. Each one of us, as Christians, has the opportunity to live and love in view of such systemic inequities. Admittedly, it's easy to simply ignore the existence of the poor, the abused, or the discriminated against. We're preoccupied with our own problems and pursuits, after all. Yet a heart indwelt by God's Spirit should have an increasing measure of difficulty in overlooking the image of God among the hurting. And little by little that burden to administer God's righteousness should impact our daily decisions in one way or another.

Three elders and about seventy members left my church on Capitol Hill to plant a church in one of the more economically depressed neighborhoods in Washington, DC. Many of them moved there. Their goal is to live and love these DC neighbors who have been created in God's image. James, one of the church elders, told me about picking up a teenager named Theo for church. He immediately knew some time had passed since Theo had washed his clothes. Then he asked Theo if he had eaten. Nothing that day. So the first stop was James's house, where James and his wife washed Theo's clothes and fed him.

Theo, to be clear, bears the same image of God that James does. One man is not better than the other. But generations of hardship and sin placed these two men in dramatically different positions. James's actions toward Theo are actions of compassion and love, but they are also actions of administering God's righteousness toward someone made in God's image.

12. Support the criminal justice system and its officers, but also work to improve it.

It's easy to focus on problems in the American criminal justice system. But for every miscarriage of justice, our nation's police officers, judges, and prison administrators perform hundreds if not thousands of ordinary and daily acts of justice. We should thank them and praise God who causes his rain to fall on the just and the unjust (Matt. 5:45). It's easy, in other words, to take for granted how much peace and safety and security Americans do experience. One might try living in war-torn Syria, or buying a home in a city controlled by the Mafia and run on bribes. By God's common grace, nearly all Americans still believe in the rule of law. And our law officers and courts fulfill their God-given assignments. We should thank God for them and support them.

That said, our criminal justice system knows the consequences of corruption, prejudice, and folly. Christians can therefore look for ways to help. Nyquist's book *Is Justice Possible?* offers a number of practical steps in the political arena (know the issues and research candidates' positions), in the judicial arena (advocate for the wrongly incarcerated and advocate for judicial reform in bail, overcriminalization, proportionate sentencing, prison rape, and civil rights), and the personal arena (minister inside prison walls and volunteer outside prison walls). Start there to learn more.[20]

I think of my former fellow elder Jeremy. One day Jeremy saw an African American friend pulled over by several police officers. So he pulled up behind the entourage just to watch and keep everyone accountable. I wish I had Jeremy's love and courage.

Meanwhile, our church invited member Homere, as a relatively new member of the DC police department, to share his prayer

Justice: Not *Just* Rights, but Right

requests on a Sunday evening. As he described how dark the world is that he faces every night on the streets, the congregation grew in empathy for Homere. We longed for his good and for his ability to do good. More than that, we approached the throne of grace on his and the whole department's behalf.

WHAT KIND OF JUSTICE DO GOD'S SPECIAL COVENANTS REQUIRE?

So far, I have been talking only about "common covenant" justice. What can we say about the justice required by God through his special covenants?

Here we stumble on one of the most remarkable features of justice in the Bible. In the context of his special covenants, the justice and righteousness of God produce salvation, vindication, and justification for his people. Remember, I said earlier that justice is covenantal. God's justice and righteousness, with respect to his people, is a husband making and keeping his marital vows to his wife, even at great cost to himself.

Is this because God's people are righteous and just? No, it is because God has specially united himself to his people, like a man to his wife. He paid her debts and granted her all his wealth. In the very face of their faithlessness, God said, "And I will make for them a covenant on that day . . . And I will betroth you to me forever. I will betroth you to me in righteousness and in justice, in steadfast love and in mercy" (Hosea 2:18,19).[21]

God's shows his righteousness and justice by proving faithful to his vows and maintaining his bride in righteousness (Rom. 3:21–26).

For the people of God, then, God's justice produces redemption. Isaiah told us, "Zion shall be redeemed by justice" (Isa. 1:27; see also 30:18; 42:1, 3–4; Hos. 2:19–20; Matt. 12:18). And the psalmist prayed,

"Hear my voice according to your steadfast love; O LORD, according to your justice give me life" (119:149).

Where does justice begin for the new-covenant Christian? How do we administer righteousness? First and foremost, we *do justice* by putting our faith in Christ: "The righteous shall live by his faith" (Hab. 2:4; Rom. 1:17). Remember how Nyquist defined *justice*: applying the righteousness of God to the conduct of man. The righteousness of God is applied to us first by trusting Christ. Isn't that remarkable?

Second, we *do justice* through evangelism. We proclaim the good news of God's righteous judgment on display in Christ's life, death, and resurrection, and then we call people to repent and believe. This applies God's righteousness to others, and it helps them grow in righteousness. Want a just neighborhood? Share the gospel. When people become Christians and join a church, they begin to participate in the life of true justice and righteousness that should typify our churches.

Third, we *do justice* by working to correct injustice, especially among the hurting and disenfranchised. Common-covenant and special-covenant responsibilities overlap here. Justified people do justice in the ways previously defined. So the apostles asked Paul "to remember the poor," which was "the very thing" Paul "was eager to do" (Gal. 2:10). Paul in turn told Titus, "Show yourself in all respects to be a model of good works" (Titus 2:7). And Titus in turn should teach the church: "Remind them to be submissive to rulers and authorities, to be obedient, to be ready for every good work" (3:1, see also, vv. 8, 14).

In those three steps we see the political life of a justified and just person.

If you have seen or read *Les Misérables*, you know that the cold and calculating police inspector named Javert prided himself on being a man of justice. He spent most of the storyline chasing down Jean

Valjean, who had broken parole. Valjean's story effectively began when he received an extravagant act of mercy, after which he spent his life doing mercy and sacrificing himself for others. For instance, he tried to rescue a prostitute and then, when she died, he raised her daughter. Scripture just might label these two characters in an unexpected way. It would appear that not only was Valjean a man of mercy and compassion, his work to rescue the victims of injustice showed him to be a true man of justice. God's command to do justice is at the same time a command to show love, compassion, and kindness.

- "Learn to do good; seek justice, correct oppression; bring justice to the fatherless, plead the widow's cause. (Isa. 1:17; see also 1:23; Jer. 7:5–7; Ezek. 22:29).
- "What does the LORD require of you but to do justice, and to love kindness, and to walk humbly with your God? (Micah 6:8, see also Prov. 21:3; 28:5; 29:27; Amos 5:22–24).

In the words of civil rights activist John Perkins, "True justice is wrapped up in love." They are "intimately tied together."[22]

Christians do justice by caring for the materially disenfranchised and the spiritually downtrodden in every way—physically, socially, emotionally. Yet we do justice most of all by pointing people to their Judge and would-be Redeemer and calling them to repent and believe.

A MORE ROBUST PRACTICE OF JUSTICE

I began the chapter with my story of parachuting into an inner-city school before helicoptering out. To me the story represents the veneer of justice that is easy for Americans to adopt. The biblical picture of justice is more multilayered and robust.

First, a Christian vision for justice begins with our lives together inside the church. Think of Acts 6, where the Greek-speaking widows (but not the Hebrew-speaking) were being neglected in the daily distribution of food. An ethnic injustice was in play. So the apostles encouraged the church to appoint seven men to oversee the distribution. The congregation's response, it turns out, was an ethnically sensitive one: every man they chose had a Greek name.

My own congregation hasn't experienced anything as dramatic as widows going hungry. But we have felt all the tensions of race and class that come with living in America today, particularly in Washington, DC. And these tensions have grown the more ethnically diverse we have grown.

For instance, our elder board has diversified more slowly than the congregation, in part because of the lag time between getting to know men over several years and then appointing them as elders. But maybe it's also in part due to our own implicit biases for other whites? Either way, minorities have attended for a Sunday or two, felt unrepresented in the leadership, and left.

So how do we, as mostly white elders as of this writing, work to help our elder board better reflect a more diverse congregation? There are some short-term decisions we can make, like regularly asking members from a different class or background to lead different elements of Sunday services. This encourages these members to realize they can aspire toward leadership, where they will be received. But the harder work is two-fold.

First, there is the long-term work of spending time with brothers from different ethnicities and classes, discipling them into leadership. For my part, therefore, I spend an inordinate share of my discipleship time with younger men from different backgrounds than me. I do that both to address the larger structural imbalance in the church, as well as to fight against implicit biases inside of me. I've learned this pattern from the other brothers around me.

Second, our elders have spent a lot of time discussing how our criteria for leadership might be white or Western. For instance, our whole board recently discussed whether we were slow to recognize potential Asian American elders since brothers coming out of an Asian context tend to view and engage with authority differently than some of us do. We had to sort through, "What's biblical, and what's just our cultural expectations of leadership?"

Beyond all this, the impulse to justice inside a local church means working against any form of discrimination, lifting up those who have been abused or discriminated against, seeking to repent of an abusiveness in one's own leadership, becoming aware of the sacrifices the majority culture asks minority cultures to make simply by joining, and more.

I'd say this impulse even includes its own kind of identity politics: identifying with the hurt or abused or discriminated against. My friend Isaac who is African American was holding his white wife's hand on the way to church. A white man accosted Isaac, called him the N-word, and implicitly suggested their marriage amounted to rape. Meanwhile, two other white women from our church were walking just behind and witnessed the whole affair. They pulled Isaac in and encouraged him to keep walking. Isaac then shared with the church and we all prayed. His grief, our grief. Our rejoicing in suffering, his rejoicing in suffering.

So a more robust vision of justice starts inside of the life of the congregation. Then it spills outward. And it spills outward, first, with evangelistic impulse and purposefulness. That's not to say we shouldn't do good to outsiders for other reasons. It's not to say we must share the gospel every time we do a good deed. It's simply to say that our friends and neighbors and children will only experience lasting righteousness and flourishing and love in the obedient knowledge of God. And so we love and act most justly toward them when we do everything with respect to God, as Augustine taught so well.

Second, our outward turn must account for large-scale realities. For some Christians this might mean taking a job or using vacation time to combat broader "headline grabbing" injustices. I think of Clare from my own church who took a year after college to move to Guatemala to do data monitoring and evaluations on child sexual assault. I think of Thomasine, also from my church, who moved to Ghana for a couple of years to fight slavery in the fishing industry. Chesed, a next-door neighbor and close family friend, has helped facilitate connections between refugees from Afghanistan and members of our church. Dave, a friend of mine from another church, uses his vacations to fly to Thailand and work against the sex-trafficking industry there. He's done this seven years in a row.

Accounting for larger-scale realities more commonly means examining where you live, work, or go to church and asking yourself if there's anything you can do to address long-term entrenched patterns or policies that cause some groups to be overlooked or disenfranchised. Drawing from the previous examples of implicit bias, a real estate agent might consider how to address the widespread pattern of treating minority and majority clients differently. Doctors might investigate why Asian Americans receive less cancer referrals even if they contract cancer at a higher rate. Law enforcement officers or teachers might look for ways to address such biases in their work. My friend Matt is a partner at a DC firm. He was asked to join the diversity committee. The firm wanted to promote diversity by making a big deal of Martin Luther King Day. That's fine. But much more crucial, Matt proposed, is for the partners to start looking for strong minority associates, taking them under their wing, and grooming them toward partnership. It's a long-term solution, but it will build something more solid that lasts. It doesn't simply paint the veneer of reconciliation.

As we continue to pursue a Christian vision for justice, we must address political policies and projects. Most Christians already have a vision for this, and we've talked about it in earlier chapters. Folks on the Right tend to work against issues like abortion. Folks on the Left tend to work against racial matters. It's deeply frustrating to me, as I said in the introduction, that Satan has managed to so successfully divide Christians and churches, particularly along ethnic lines, through our differently weighted justice burdens. The first step to restoring trust is reclaiming our joint membership in the gospel. The second is to drop the defensiveness and better listen to one another. Imagine if majority and minority saints began to work together here? Might the saints not push back the kingdom of darkness a pace or two? In my estimate, the greater responsibility to listen, learn, and move in belongs to the majority. But let every saint heed the call of the gospel to unity, love, and justice.

I appreciate the example of Republican Senator Tim Scott working together with Democrat Senator Cory Booker to stimulate jobs for younger Americans by offering tax credits to employers who offer apprenticeships for younger job applicants. They proposed paying for this program by curtailing the printing of government publications that are already available online. And I'm quite sure the world would benefit from fewer government publications! They have also partnered together to work on issues surrounding mass incarceration.

I know little to nothing about these two men otherwise, but I do pray the saints would follow that kind of bipartisan example. And I rejoice that many have already begun.

CONCLUSION

I confess, I'm not immediately optimistic about America's race problem, as well as its other points of division. We keep reasserting our shared beliefs in rights, equality, and liberty. But hiding inside of those words are different gods with their different views of justice. The principles that unite America, ironically, divide it.

And that's the bigger issue here. Our challenges on race are just one illustration of it. Equality, liberty, and individual rights are good gifts from God. But apart from God they lack the ballast to keep a nation united. There is no appeal to what's right and the Maker of right. Therefore, the nation rages against the Lord, just like every other nation since the nativity of nations.

Can we force the nation to adopt our definition of *right* in the public square? No, of course not. But that doesn't mean we should stop speaking up for it and living by it. Our political success, remember, depends on faithfulness, not results.

I do have hope and trust in the work of Christ and his Spirit in the church. Our churches have the solution: gospel love and gospel justice. One leads to the other. In love, God the just became God the justifier. While we were yet sinners, Christ died for us (Rom. 5:8). In so doing he removed the barrier between us and God, and then the barrier between us and one another. Our fate and hope and life in no way hangs on the favor of the nations.

Gospel love and gospel justice together untangle knots, neutralize acids, and dissolve the most intractable clogs. Love alone will cause us to choose justice, to beat our swords into plowshares and spears into pruning hooks. To turn the other cheek and walk the extra mile.

Shouldn't our churches be the first places on the planet where we witness these things? Where, as I said in chapter 1, we achieve and cherish Lincoln's just and lasting peace? We should live this way inside. We should turn to do the same outside. The church's work, finally, is in no way contingent on the favor of the nation toward Christianity. We might be popular or unpopular. But our political task is the same: love your neighbor, share the gospel, do justice.

FINAL THOUGHTS

Why the Battle Might Get Worse, but Our Political Hopes Can Remain Unchanged, Untroubled, Untouched

I went to a Washington Nationals baseball game yesterday with my wife and kids. We had a great time: pretzels, cheese fries, cotton candy, lemonade. No one got a hot dog though.

During the seventh-inning stretch a woman sang "God Bless America." People stood. Some removed their hats.

I have to admit, that song feels a little strange to me. Which God? What kind of blessing? It's sort of like the words "In God we trust" on our dollar bills. Are we talking about the same God? And trust how?

I see advantages and disadvantages to those kinds of civic expressions of belief and trust in God. On the one hand, it's the church's job to pronounce the name of the Almighty. Also, such civic expressions can feel like hypocrisy.

On the other hand, a nation and its rulers should remind themselves often that they will appear before the judgment seat of Christ, so that each may receive what is due for what has been done in the body, whether good or evil (2 Cor. 5:10). The psalmist warned:

Now therefore, O kings, be wise;
    be warned, O rulers of the earth.
Serve the LORD with fear,
    and rejoice with trembling.
Kiss the Son,
    lest he be angry, and you perish in the way,
    for his wrath is quickly kindled.
Blessed are all who take refuge in him. (Ps. 2:10–12)

Notice to whom these lines are addressed: the kings and rulers of all nations, including ours. And as voters, aren't we those rulers? Perhaps it's good that the faintest glimmers of this warning show up every time someone looks at a dollar bill or hears that song.

LOVE OF NATION

I do want God to bless America, land that I love. I want him to bless it with peace and justice. I want the nation to know the blessing that comes to citizens and leaders who take refuge in him, as the final line of the psalm says.

Some of my more globally minded friends wonder if it's okay to love your country. As with many forms of love, there's healthy and unhealthy versions of love for country.

I love America analogously to how I love my own church. I don't love my church to the exclusion of other churches. All our churches share one gospel and one God. We belong to one family. We're on the same team. Nonetheless, it's the members of my own church whose names I know, whose children I watch in the nursery, whose classes I teach, whose lives I'm a part of. My love for all God's people is exercised *there*, among *them*, even with all our shortcomings and sin.

It should be the same with our love for our nation. We should not love it to the exclusion of other nations. We all share one God and belong to one common, God-imaging humanity. God has determined the periods and the boundaries of America and every other nation so that people may find their way to him (Acts 17:26–27). Nonetheless, it's the citizens and statues and buildings and holidays and artists and landscapes and baseball games and cheese fries and hospital delivery rooms of our nation whose names we know. Our love for humanity should be exercised *there*, among *them*, even with all our shortcomings and sin.

HOPE FOR THE NATION

None of us knows what's ahead for the nation. The battle might temporarily grow fiercer. It might temporarily improve. We do know the nation will rage against our God and against his Anointed. The Anointed One, his son Jesus, promised that they will do this until he returns.

Yet the political hopes of the church can remain unchanged, untroubled, untouched. After all, our life is a supernatural life, and our work is a supernatural work, my pastor has said. We cannot raise the dead or give sight to the blind. That was true in the 1790s and the 1950s, and it's true today. Our work therefore is no harder or easier than it's ever been. It has always depended entirely on God.

We should not be naïve about the forces of darkness arrayed against us. But fear and withdrawal make no sense for the church. We press on as we always have.

Yet, if I'm going to have any hope for the nation, I cannot place it in the nation. I will place it in healthy churches.

People often extol the genius of the American founders and the wisdom of the Constitution. And let's give honor where honor is due. Unless you count the tiny republic of San Marino whose documents apparently go back to 1600, America possesses the oldest written constitution in the world. It has needed some fixing along the way, particularly after the Civil War. But it's generally proven more durable than anything found in the old and great nations of Russia, China, Germany, Egypt, or elsewhere. Not only that, America has arguably proven to be among the most prosperous, strong, and free nations in history.

Yet it seems to me we should give as much credit to the childhood pastors and Christian parents of the American founders as to the men themselves. Nearly every founder was weaned on the moral virtues of Christianity, even if many of them eventually rejected its doctrines. They inconsistently applied the lessons, but they were taught to regard human beings as created in God's image, each person worthy of dignity and respect. They inherited an understanding of rights and the conscience and equality from a faith that, yes, they variously kept at arm's length. They took the flowers, even if they cut them from the roots.

God's common grace grants many a nation better than it deserves, but I have little confidence that America will long remain strong, prosperous, and free without any concept of God's righteousness and justice somewhere in the background. That's not because I believe in a civil prosperity gospel: obey God and the nation will be blessed as his chosen people. It's because I believe the way of God's righteousness and justice is the way of wisdom. And prosperity and flourishing ordinarily come to the wise. The nation can be strong apart from God's righteousness, like a totalitarian state is strong. Or it can be "free," in some impoverished and mangy sense of that word, like a stray dog is free. But it won't be both.

Which brings me back to healthy churches. If there is hope for the nation, it's through the witness and work of churches. Our congregations have the opportunity to live transformed lives as a transformed culture through a transformed politics in their own fellowships right now—all for God's glory and our neighbors' good. And we will become such heavenly outposts when we focus first not on the public square, but on preaching the Word and making disciples. Together those disciples must grow up to maturity, into Christ, as each part does its work (Eph. 4:13–16). The resonant effects in the home, the marketplace, the public square, and the rest of life then follow.

God does not intend to display his own justice and righteousness and wisdom through the wise, noble, and powerful things of this world, but through the foolish, weak, and despised things. He means to magnify himself not primarily through the US Congress, the *New York Times* editorial page, or Ivy League philosophy departments, but through Brother Bob, Sister Sue, and Deacon Darnell down at Bumblestew Baptist.

Oh, nations of the earth, watch those three gathered in Jesus' name to see the way of God's justice and mercy. They are God's salt and light for you. Do you sense something distinct in them? See something bright? They are far from perfect, to be sure. But their King is perfect. And their lives together should offer you the first taste of his kingdom.

NOTES

Chapter 1: A Nation Raging, a Church Unchanging

1. Walt Whitman, "I Hear America Singing," 1966, accessed through the public domain.

2. Patricia Hill Collins, as quoted in Elizabeth C. Corey, "First Church of Intersectionality," *First Things*, August 2017, https://www .firstthings.com/article/2017/08/first-church-of-intersectionality.

3. Andy Kroll, "Meet the Megadonor Behind the LGBTQ Rights Movement," *Rolling Stone*, June 23, 2017, http://www.rollingstone .com/politics/features/meet-tim-gill-megadonor-behind-lgbtq -rights-movement-wins-w489213.

4. Mark Tushnet, "Abandoning Defensive Crouch Liberal Constitutionalism," *Balkinization* (blog), May 6, 2016, https://balkin .blogspot.com/2016/05/abandoning-defensive-crouch-liberal.html.

5. Jennifer Senior, "In Conversation: Antonin Scalia," *New York*, October 6, 2013, http://nymag.com/news/features /antonin-scalia-2013–10/.

6. "Political Polarization in the American Public," Pew Research Center, June 12, 2014, http://www.people-press.org/2014/06/12 /political-polarization-in-the-american-public/.

7. D. A. Carson, *Christ and Culture Revisited* (Grand Rapids: Eerdmans, 2008), 57.

Notes

8. Tip O'Neill with Gary Hymel, *All Politics Is Local, and Other Rules of the Game* (Minneapolis: B. Adams Publishing, 1995).

Chapter 2: Public Square: Not Neutral, but a Battleground of Gods

1. Ronald Dworkin, *Religion Without God* (Cambridge, MA: Harvard University Press, 2013), 1.

2. David Foster Wallace, *This Is Water: Some Thoughts, Delivered on a Significant Occasion, About Living a Compassionate Life* (New York: Little, Brown and Company, 2009), 98–101.

3. Dianne Feinstein, as quoted in Aaron Blake, "Did Dianne Feinstein Accuse a Judicial Nominee of Being Too Christian?" *Washington Post*, September 7, 2017, https://www.washingtonpost.com/news/the -fix/wp/2017/09/07/did-a-democratic-senator-just-accuse-a-judicial -nominee-of-being-too-christian/?utm_term=f211307afle9.

4. Michael J. Sandel, *Justice: What's the Right Thing to Do?* (New York: Farrar, Straus and Giroux, 2009), 251–54; see also *Democracy's Discontent* (Cambridge, MA: Harvard University Press, 1998), 100–108.

5. "*Socrates' Defense (Apology),*" translated by Hugh Tredennick, in Edith Hamilton and Huntington Cairns, eds., *The Collected Dialogues of Plato* (Princeton: Princeton University Press, 1961), 10.

6. See Tacitus, *Annals*, book XV, chapter 44. See also the comments of Porphyry in Robert Louis Wilken, *The Christians as the Romans Saw Them* (New Haven: Yale University Press, 1986, 2003), 156.

7. Quoted in Os Guinness, *A Free People's Suicide: Sustainable Freedom and the American Future* (Downers Grove, IL: InterVarsity Press, 2012), 128.

8. Southern Pacific Co. v. Jensen, 244 U.S. 205 (1917).

9. Note on Matthew 5:3, *Christian Standard Bible Study Bible* (Nashville, TN: Holman Bible Publishers), 1505.

10. John Locke, *Second Treatises of Government and a Letter Concerning Toleration* (Oxford: Oxford University Press, 2016), 218, 219.

11. Thomas Jefferson, *Notes on the State of Virginia*, ed. Frank Shuffelton (New York: Penguin Books, 1998), 165.

12. Quoted in Jon Meacham, *American Gospel: God, the Founding Fathers, and the Making of a Nation* (New York: Random House, 2006), 32.

13. John Villasenor, "Views Among College Students Regarding the First Amendment: Results from a New Survey," Brookings Institution, September 18, 2017, https://www.brookings.edu/blog /fixgov/2017/09/18/views-among-college-students-regarding-the -first-amendment-results-from-a-new-survey.

14. The Washington and Adams quotes taken from Guinness, *A Free People's Suicide*, 117–19.

15. John Dewey, *My Pedagogic Creed* (New York: E. L. Kellogg & Co., 1897), 16, 17.

16. Russell Dawn, "Why Public Schools Will Always Include Religious Indoctrination," *Federalist*, March 29, 2017, http://thefederalist .com/2017/03/29/public-schools-will-always-include-religious -indoctrination/.

17. Mary Eberstadt, *It's Dangerous to Believe: Religious Freedom and Its Enemies* (New York: Harper, 2016), 23–28.

Chapter 3: Heart: Not Self-Exalting, but Born Again and Justified

1. Alex Rosenberg, "The Making of a Non-Patriot," *New York Times*, July 3, 2017, https://www.nytimes.com/2017/07/03/opinion/the -making-of-a-non-patriot.html?mcubz=3&_r=0.

2. Anthony Doerr, *All the Light We Cannot See* (New York: Scribner, 2017), 11.

3. Arthur Brooks, "The Real Problem with American Politics," Harvard Kennedy School, Facebook, May 6, 2017, https://www.facebook .com/harvardkennedyschool/videos/10154251688431403/.

4. I discuss the idea of "two ages" in contrast to "two kingdoms" at length in *Political Church: The Local Assembly as Embassy of Christ's Rule* (Downers Grove, IL: IVP Academic, 2016), 274–78.

5. Mark Zuckerberg, "Bringing the World Closer Together," Facebook, June 22, 2017: https://www.facebook.com/notes/mark-zuckerberg /bringing-the-world-closer-together/10154944663901634/.

6. "Javert's Suicide," in *Les Miserables,* a musical by Alain Boublil and Claude-Michel Schönberg, lyrics by Herbert Kretzmer.

Chapter 4: Bible: Not Case Law, but a Constitution

1. The entire transcript of Kennedy's speech "Remarks of Senator John F. Kennedy on Church and State; Delivered to Greater Houston Ministerial Association, Houston, Texas, Sept. 12, 1960" is reprinted in Theodore H. White, *The Making of the President 1960* (New York: Harper Perennial, 1961), 391–93.

2. "How Kennedy Is Being Received—The Texas and California Tours—Reaction of Ministers," *New York Times,* September 14, 1960.

Chapter 5: Government: Not a Savior, but a Platform Builder

1. Philip Jenkins, "Is This the End for Mideast Christianity?" *Christianity Today,* November 4, 2014, http://www.christianitytoday .com/ct/2014/november/on-edge-of-extinction.html.

2. Samuel Hugh Moffett, *A History of Christianity in Asia, Vol. 1: Beginnings to 1500* (Maryknoll, NY: Orbis Books, 1998), 504.

3. John G. Roberts Jr., dissenting, in James Obergefell et al. v. Richard Hodges et al., 576 U. S. _____ (2015), 2.

4. Vern Poythress, "False Worship in the Modern State," in *The Shadow of Christ in the Law of Moses* (Phillipsburg, NJ: P&R Publishing, 1995), 296.

5. The only possible exception I'm aware of is Daniel 3:29, but one would be hard-pressed to demonstrate Nebuchadnezzar's words here are universally normative.

Chapter 6: Churches: Not Lobbying Organizations, but Embassies of Heaven

1. C. Kavin Rowe, "The Ecclesiology of Acts," *Interpretation: A Journal of Biblical Theology* 66, no. 3 (July 2012): 263.

2. Ibid., 267.

3. If you want to consider any of these matters further, I discussed them at greater length in a number of books like, *Understanding*

the Congregation's Authority, Understanding Church Membership, Understanding Church Discipline, and Don't Fire Your Church Members.

4. Samuel Hugh Moffett, A History of Christianity in Asia, Vol. 1: Beginnings to 1500 (Maryknoll, NY: Orbis Books, 1998), 509.

5. Jane Hyun, Breaking the Bamboo Ceiling (New York: HarperCollins, 2005).

6. Michael O. Emerson and Christian Smith, Divided by Faith: Evangelical Religion and the Problem of Race in America (New York: Oxford University Press, 2001).

7. Michael Horton, Covenant and Salvation: Union with Christ (Louisville: Westminster John Knox, 2007), 171.

8. John Piper, "Mission: Rescuing from Hell and Renewing the World," Desiring God (blog), January 13, 2014. https://www.desiringgod.org /articles/missions-rescuing-from-hell-and-renewing-the-world.

Chapter 7: Christians: Not Cultural Warriors, but Ambassadors

1. Research Institute on Christianity in South Africa, "Faith Communities and Apartheid: A Report Prepared for the Truth and Reconciliation Commission," March 1998.

2. Michael Gerson and Peter Wehner, City of Man: Religion and Politics in a New Era (Chicago, IL: Moody, 2010), especially pages 46–63 and 113–28.

3. Bill O'Reilly, Cultural Warrior (New York: Broadway Books, 2006), 1.

4. Oliver O'Donovan, The Desire of the Nations (New York: Cambridge University Press, 1996), 92–93.

5. "The Barmen Declaration," Encyclopedia of Protestantism, ed. by Hans J. Hillerbrand (London: Routledge, 2004), 327.

6. Leonore Siegele-Wenschkewitz, "Christians Against Nazis: The German Confessing Church," Christianity Today, accessed October 10, 2017, http://www.christianitytoday.com/history/issues/issue-9 /christians-against-nazis-german-confessing-church.html. Originally published in print in Christian History, issue 9, 1986.

7. Os Guinness, A Free People's Suicide: Sustainable Freedom and the American Future (Downers Grove, IL: InterVarsity Press, 2012), 17.

8. Tim Keller, *Generous Justice: How God's Grace Makes Us Just* (New York: Dutton, 2010), 158.

9. It might be better to call this the Madison approach. I don't think Luther was referring to his conscience as the ground of justice in the same way as the liberal tradition through figures like James Madison eventually would ("Conscience is the most sacred of all property.") Luther was treating his conscience in the role of judge for telling him what God would have him do. God was the ground of justice. Still, I am calling this the Luther approach because Luther elevated the role of conscience for everyone that followed.

10. "Letter from Birmingham Jail," in *Philosophical Problems in the Law*, edited by David M. Adams (Belmont, CA: Wadsworth Publishing Company, 1992), 60.

11. Institute for American Values: National Marriage Project, *Why Marriage Matters: Thirty Conclusions from the Social Sciences*, 3rd ed. (New York: Institute for American Values, 2011), 45.

12. Dan Graves, ed., "Polycarp's Martyrdom," Christian History Institute, accessed October 10, 2017, https://christianhistoryinstitute .org/study/module/polycarp/.

13. Nicholas Wolterstorff, *The Mighty and the Almighty: An Essay in Political Theology* (Cambridge: Cambridge University Press, 2012), 17.

14. John Rawls, *Political Liberalism* (New York: Columbia University Press, 2011), 150.

15. Russell Moore, *Onward: Engaging the Culture Without Losing the Gospel* (Nashville: B&H Publishing, 2015), 187.

16. Thanks to Nick Rodriguez who contributed to this section.

17. Philip Graham Ryken, Jeremiah and Lamentations: From Sorrow to Hope (Wheaton, IL: Crossway, 2012), 390–91.

18. Thanks again to Nick Rodriguez for help on this and the next paragraph.

Chapter 8: Justice: Not *Just* Rights, but Right

1. Michael Emerson and Christian Smith, *Divided by Faith: Evangelical Religion and the Problem of Race in America* (New York: Oxford University Press, 2000).

2. Jason Willick, "Terror in Charlottesville and American Decline," *The American Interest*, August 13, 2017, https://www.the-american -interest.com/2017/08/13/terror-charlottesville-american-decline/.

3. Nicholas Wolterstorff, *Justice: Rights and Wrongs* (Princeton: Princeton University Press, 2008), 393.

4. Chai Feldblum, "Moral Conflict and Liberty," *Brooklyn Law Review* 72, no. 1: 119.

5. Ibid.

6. Ibid., 115.

7. Planned Parenthood v. Casey, 505 US 833 (1992).

8. Jonathan Haidt, *The Righteous Mind: Why Good People Are Divided by Politics and Religion* (New York: Vintage Books, 2013), 150–79.

9. J. Paul Nyquist, *Is Justice Possible?: The Elusive Pursuit of What Is Right* (Chicago: Moody Publishers, 2017), 25.

10. Herman Bavinck, *Reformed Dogmatics, Volume 2: God and Creation*, trans. John Vriend (Grand Rapids: Baker Academic, 2004), 227.

11. This is one of the main arguments of Wolterstorff's book *Justice: Rights and Wrongs*.

12. Leon Morris, *The Biblical Doctrine of Judgment* (Eugene, OR: Wipf and Stock, 2006; orig. Inter-Varsity Press UK, 1960), 13.

13. Kevin DeYoung and Greg Gilbert, *What Is the Mission of the Church? Making Sense of Social Justice, Shalom, and the Great Commission* (Wheaton, IL: Crossway, 2011), 146.

14. Theodore Parker, quoted by Martin Luther King, Jr., "Out of the Long Night," Official Organ of the Church of the Brethren, February 8, 1958, p. 14. (Internet Archive archive.org full view)

15. Ta-Nahesi Coates, *Between the World and Me* (New York: Spiegel & Grau, 2015), 28.

16. John Perkins, *Dream with Me: Race, Love, and the Struggle We Must Win* (Grand Rapids: Baker Books, 2017), 129.

17. Andrew T. Walker, "Advice to Young Christian Politicos," *Andrew T. Walker* (blog), July 18, 2016, http://www.andrewtwalker.com/2016 /07/18/advice-to-young-christian-politicos/.

18. Nyquist, *Is Justice Possible?*, 79–80.

Notes

19. Ta-Nahesi Coates, "The Case for Reparations," *The Atlantic*, June 2014, https://www.theatlantic.com/magazine/archive/2014/06 /the-case-for-reparations/361631/.

20. Nyquist, *Is Justice Possible?*, 108–10, 112–18, 120–23.

21. See Peter J. Gentry and Stephen J. Wellum on this verse in *Kingdom Through Covenants: A Biblical-Theological Understanding of the Covenants* (Wheaton, IL: Crossway, 2012), 530.

22. Perkins, *Dream with Me*, 29, 30.

ACKNOWLEDGMENTS

For an in-depth version of the arguments in this book, see my *Political Church: The Local Assembly as Embassy of Christ's Rule* (IVP Academic, 2016).

Yet more than my academic work, this book grew out of my life at Capitol Hill Baptist Church in Washington, DC, where I first showed up in 1996. The pastoral posture toward politics that you will encounter throughout these pages has been learned from Mark Dever, Andy Johnson, Bill Behrens, and other elders. Yet it's the congregation as a whole that has taught me what it means to live out a redemptive politics. The body needs every part. How grateful I have been to serve as one of its elders or pastors (we use the words interchangeably) for some of that time.

Much of the material in this book was tested through teaching a Sunday School class on Christians and government several times at CHBC. Nick Rodriguez and Riley Barnes helped teach the material and contributed in conversation along the way. Jamie Dunlop gave me the opportunity to teach. Caleb Morrell, Kendrick Kuo, Garth Baer, Chesed Broggi, Steven Harris, Isaac Adams, and Thabiti Anyabwile also read either class lessons or chapters and offered good counsel. Thabiti especially helped me rethink a few key parts.

Acnowledgments

Thomas Kidd, John Wilsey, and Thomas Schreiner also reviewed some of the material and improved it. And I cannot begin to recount how many good conversations I have had with friends like David Wilezol, Hanz and Rebeccah Heinrichs, Paul Pelt, Matt Martens, Eugene Scott, and others. I know I'm forgetting some people, but thanks to all of these friends for their time and care.

Andrew Wolgemuth and Jessica Wong have both believed in and promoted the project through the publishing process. I'm very grateful for them.

Most of all I thank God for my wife and daughters. This book argues that politics begins in the church. Yet a case could also be made—as Aristotle did—that politics begins at home. Shannon, my wife, whom I love dearly, shapes who I am at home firstly and everywhere else secondly. My daughters, to whom I dedicate the book, certainly do the same. I love you each so much.

My prayer is that God would use this book to grant Christians and churches a more profound and biblical and beautiful vision of our lives together as embassies of his kingdom, so that we might better love each other and our neighbors, magnifying him.

ABOUT THE AUTHOR

Jonathan Leeman is the editorial director at 9Marks, a ministry that helps church leaders build healthy churches. He teaches theology at several seminaries and has written a number of books on the church. He is also a research fellow with the Ethics and Religious Liberty Commission. He has degrees in political science and English, a master of science in political theory, a master of divinity, and a doctorate in political theology. Jonathan served for years as an elder at Capitol Hill Baptist Church in Washington, DC, but has since left to plant a nearby church. He lives in the DC area with his wife and four daughters.